WESTMAR COLLEGE
VIA VERITAS VITA
Westmar College
Presented in Honor of
Dr. Clarence Attig
by
Alumni and Friends
Charles A. Mock Library

COLONIAL CAPTIVITIES, MARCHES AND JOURNEYS

The Prison in Quebec

COLONIAL CAPTIVITIES, MARCHES AND JOURNEYS

EDITED UNDER THE AUSPICES OF THE NATIONAL SOCIETY OF THE COLONIAL DAMES OF AMERICA

BY

ISABEL M. CALDER

KENNIKAT PRESS, INC./PORT WASHINGTON, N. Y.

Reissued in 1967 by Kennikat Press

Library of Congress Catalog Card No: 67-27581

Manufactured in the United States of America

PREFACE

For three quarters of a century the colonists of England and France struggled to possess the interior of North America. Throughout this period the nationals of one country spied on the movements of the other. English captives at Quebec peered through prison windows at the drilling of the militia and the shipping of the St. Lawrence, evaluating the strength of the French, and vainly hoping for the arrival of an expedition from New England. Indentured servants expected to finish their terms of servitude in warfare. A nurse jotted down the activities of the Indians on the frontier, aroused by the French against Braddock's expedition. Both English and French travelers in the valleys of the Ohio and Mississippi measured distances and were keenly aware of the presence of aliens. Their findings the observers jotted down in rude journals, surveys, and letters. Because of their contents rather than their style, these documents often found their way into the hands of colonial and home government officials. After the lapse of centuries some of them still survive in the Public Record Office and the British Museum in London, the Bibliothèque Nationale in Paris, and the Library of Congress at Washington.

To illustrate this seventy-five-year conflict, the National Society of the Colonial Dames of America publishes the following collection of heretofore unpublished journals, surveys, and letters. The selection has been made by Dr. J. F. Jameson, chief of the Division of Manuscripts in the Library of Congress. In preparing the documents for publication, superior letters indicating the omission of one or more letters in a word have been lowered, and the word has been represented as an abbreviation or a contraction. With this single exception, the spelling, capitalization, and punctuation of the original manuscripts have been carefully retained. The facilities of the Library of Congress have greatly simplified the task of annotating the documents.

I. M. C.

Wells College
November 29, 1934

CONTENTS

ILLUSTRATIONS

MILITARY CAPTIVITIES

A Fire Stove one of which
Was Put in Every Room
in the Prison, During
the Rigorous Season
See of November 26th

THE STOVE

THE JOURNAL OF A CAPTIVE, 1745–1748[1]

REMARKABLE Occurrences from the year 1745 to 1748, During the far greater part of which Time I was a Prisoner in the hands of the French and Spainards; Transcrib'd from my Private Notes in Rhode Island Anno 1748.

> Fates dark recesses we can never find,
> But fortune at Some hour, to all is kind.
> The Lucky have whole Days in which to choose,
> The Unlucky have but hours, and those they loose.
> —*Dryden.*[2]

Fri., December the 19th, 1745.[3] Ship'd on Board the Adventure of London Captn. Jno. Oldham Bound for Berbadoes.[4]

Tues., Feb'ry 25th. Sail'd from Gravesend was taken very Ill and Confined to my Cabin.

Sat., March the 1st. Put into Falmouth in the County of Cornwall Wind SW't, Hazey; Weather Caried on shore very Ill.

Sun., March the 30th. left Falmouth and came to sail wind

[1] Manuscript in the Library of Congress. Concerning himself the author of the journal gives us the following information. He apparently was a native of Weybread in Suffolk, a parish and village on the south side of the River Waveney, two miles south southwest of Harleston. His birthday fell upon March 8. On November 7, 1745, he left home, and on December 19, 1745, shipped on board the *Adventure* of London, a vessel sailing for Touchet and Company, London, West India merchants. On March 30, 1746, he left England.

[2] "Fate's dark recesses we can never find;
But fortune, at some hours, to all is kind:
The Lucky have whole days, which still they choose;
The unlucky have but hours, and those they lose."
—Dryden, *Tyrannic Love, or The Royal Martyr*, Act I, Scene I, lines 64–67.

[3] "*Fri.*, December the 19th, 1745" should read "*Thurs.*, December the 19th, 1745."

[4] Barbados.

at NNE in Comp with the Eliza. Captn. White for Boston New England; was now bravely recovered from my late Indisposition but Captn. Oldham in a Lingering State of health.

Wed., Aprill the 2d. Lost Company w'th the Eliza. in the Night She Steering more Westerly.

Fri. 4th. At 9 A M Saw a Sail to windward then Tack'd to avoid her and unfortunately fell in with 2. French men of war we Endeavoured to Stretch out a head of them and in So doeing caried away our Main Topmast, and e're we Could Clear it of the riging they brought us too in Lat'd 47° 00′ No and Meridian Distance from the Lizard 1°:26′ West They would not admit of any Ransom when offered them, but was going to burn her; but the men at the mast head on board the Largest Ship Saw and made a Signal of seeing 16. sail to Leeward of us which they then took To be an English Squadron; They then left our Ship with her Sails flying without takeing any thing out of her Hold; they Caried Captn. Oldham, Self, Dr. Coron and the Cook, on board the Smaller vessell; the rest of our people on board the Larger; then made Sail, The Largest of these 2. Ships was Call'd the Aurora. She mounted 50. Guns; the Smallest was Call'd the Castor, She mounted 28. Guns they came out of Brest on Thursday the 29th of March; but where bound we know not.[5]

Mon. The 7th. The Commodore on board the Aurora hoizted a Signal for Captn. Oldham and Self to goe on board, w'ch we did when after Some Examination with regard to the Capt'ns Papers etc. they Delivered them Up to him again and at our Earnest request Permitted us to goe on Board the Castor again.

[5] *L'Aurore* commanded by M. Duvignan and *Le Castor* commanded by M. de Saillies were frigates out of Brest, March 29/April 9, 1746. The *Adventure*, a brigantine commanded by John Oldham, sailed from London for Barbados, March 30, 1746. *New York Colonial Documents*, X., 50; excerpt from *The Boston Evening-Post*, March 9, 1746/7, printed in *New Jersey Archives*, XII., 338; *New-York Gazette revived in the Weekly Post-Boy*, March 16, 1746/7; *The Journal of Captain William Pote, Jr.*, edited by V. H. Paltsits (New York, 1896), hereafter cited as Pote, pp. 96–97.

Tues., Aprill the 15th. *Some* one of the French Soldiers plundered me of my Pocketbook.

Thurs., May the 1st. Chased and took the John Snow of Dartmouth in the County of Devon Captn. Robert David Roberts[6] for Lizborn with a Cargoe of Newfoundland fish; Lat'd 44° 00′ Longitude from Cape Broyl[7] 00° 14′ East.

Sat. the 3d. After Plundering the above Snow they Scuttled and Sunk Her.

Sun. the 11th. Buried a french man he was one of those which in boarding our vessell fell overboard and by that means Caught a Cold.

Mon. the 12th. Captn. Oldham and Self turn'd out of our Mess with Monsieur Furnier the Master by the Boatswain a Superstitious fool; but by applying to the Sieur Duvall was again restored and the boatswain turn'd out Captn. Oldham was now Confined by the Gout.

Tues., May the 13th. Saw sevorall Islands of Ice.

Wed. 14th. Chased a sail at night Lost her Lat'd 44° 14′ No. and Long't'd 47° 00′ from the Meridian of the Lizard West.[8]

Fri. 16th. Got ground on the Grand Bank of Newfoundland 35. Fathoms water Caught many Codfish Lat'd 44° 05′ No. we likewise Caught a female Dogfish with 18. young Whelps within her all in perfect Shape and ready to Cast which Whelps lived 48. hours in Salt water after they had been Seperated from the Dam; Some of which Whelps the french preserved in Spirits.

Sat. 17th. Buryed a 2d man; now Sickly.

Tues. 20th. Made Cape Race Newfoundland.

Sat. 24th. Early in the Morning the Commodore in the Aurora left us on bank Vert but where She is bound we Cannot as yet Learn; They are Sickly on Board.

Sun., June the 1st. Buried a 3d Man we are now Cruizing on Bancks Vert and Quero Caught many Fish on both.

Fri. 6th. This morn'g Dr. John Coron and Self fell to-

[6] On Captain Robert David Roberts, see Pote, p. 97.

[7] Cape Broyle, Newfoundland.

[8] Lizard Head, England.

gether by the Ears; At 10 A M Chased and Took the Sloop Squirell Zepheniah Pinkham from Nantuchet[9] Island bound on a whaling voyage in Company with the Sloop Raven which they Chased till Night but by Good fortune She got away and by that means if the Master have any Brains he may give a Good account of us in Newfoundland where he is bound.

Sat. 7th. Captn. Oldham and Self turnd out of our Mess again and Denied wine we Usually had because we refused to act when Desired in a manner highly Injurious to the Liberties and Properties of others and Scandallous to the Name of a Britain; the Case was thus. Yesterday in Chasing the above Sloop Squirell under English Colours and fireing their Bow Chase at her as She went away Large, her Concert the Raven Sloop Stood Close upon a Wind as the most prudent Method to get away which the french percieving; Monsieur Marine the 2d Captn. Came up to Captn. Oldham and Self and peremtorily Ordered us that So Soon as they had brought the Chase too we Should take the Trumpet and Haile the Sloop in English and order them to bring on board the Captn his papers; the mate and the greater part of the hands in their own Boate. This we foresaw was a Scheme of theirs to Catch the Sloop Raven which was all this while getting to windw'd we in submisive Terms told Monsieur that we could not in Justice doe as he required; and therefore beg'd he would not insist on it; yet if he would haul down the English Colours which Were then flying and hoise their French Colours we would to oblidge him, Haile them So Soon as She brought too; We Subjoyn'd likewise that we thought it was Contrary to the Law of Arms to burn Powder as they did under English Colours; Monsieur turn'd from us with a haughty Stride and Said he did not want to be Instructed in what he was to doe on Board his own Ship; we Seeing him in a *Chafe* about the affair we withdrew to our Lodgings betwixt Decks after Charging Dr. John Coron not to Hail the Sloop in English while English Colours was flying on Board the French man of war; This was the great affront for

[9] On Captain Zephaniah Pinkham of Nantucket, Massachusetts, see Pote, p. 98.

which we forfeitted our wine. This Day buried a 4th man an Officer.

Thurs., June the 12th. Took without Chasing the Sloop Dove, Dennis Field She had just come out of Placentia in Newfoundland and was bound for New York with a Cargoe of Fish; they took the Sloop in Tow and as is reported in order to Send away the English prisoners in her So Soon as the Ship can get an Oppertunity to wood and water. Buried this night a 5th man.

Mon. 16th. In going about the above Sloop Shot a head and Sunk under our Bows Buried a 6th man.

Tues. 17th. Got unto Bank Vert and Quero again buried a 7th man now very sickly.

Fri. 20th. Stood in for the Land and made the Northermost part of Placentia Bay, Saw a Large Ship under the Land to which they gave Chase under English Colours She Edged out to Sea after us with French Colours Flying; this gave the French Some Suspition She was an English man of war which afterward Proved to be his Majesties Ship Pembrooke of 60 Guns but unfortunate for us E're She had Stood towards us 2 Glasses a thick fogg came on under the cover of which the Castor bore away for the Cape Sable Coast and by that means got clear of Fire by G--d as the Boatswain Said.

Tues., The 24th of June. Midsummer Day; fell in with 3 Fishing Schooners 2. of which they took vizt. The Endeavour John Cox of Salem, The Tryall Joseph Dennen of Marblehead[10] the 3d got away, the Tryall was Sunk and the Endeavour was Taken in Tow.

Wed. 25th. Buried an 8th and 9th man; the French are now in great want both of wood and water; they are likewise very sickly on Board they have now 42. of their ablest and most active men down with a Malignant fever Therefore Captn. Charlee[11] of the Castor made this Proposal to the English Prisoners; that if any of them would undertake to Carry the Ship Castor into any Harbour where he could

[10] On Joseph Denen of Marblehead, Massachusetts, see Pote, p. 118.

[11] M. de Saillies.

safely wood and water he Should have as a reward the Endeavour Schooner which he had then reserved on purpose; and all the English Prisoners Should have the full Liberty to goe in the Said Schooner to any part of New England; This offer Captn. Zepheniah Pinkham Embraced,[12] and accordingly Mr. Bunkard his Mate was put on Board the Endeavour with some French men to take care of her, least the same Disaster Should befall her as the Sloop late Mentioned which was sunk in going about; they then Stood in for the Land of Cape Sable.

Thurs. 26th. Made the Land, about 9 Leagues to Leeward of Jebuctore, sent away Mr. Bunkard in the Scooner to make the Harbour; buried a 10th man.

Sat. 28th. Made the Harbour of Jebuctore[13] and Standing in for it fell in with and Took the Sloop Dove of New Norwich in the Collony of Conecticutt bound For Cape Briton with a Cargoe of life Stock vizt. Fat oxen, Cows and Calves, Sheep, Hoggs and all Sorts of Poultrey; this prize was a great relief to the French as they where now in a Missarable Condition they not having men Enough to keep the Deck; Mr. Samuell Story was master of this Sloop but She belonged to Mr. Hezekiah Huntington[14] who was on board as Supercargoe; at Evening got into Jebuctore Harbour and Anchored there at the Entrance of the NW't arm we see here nothing of Mr. Bunkard in the Scooner who parted with us the 26th to find the harbour.

Sun., June the 29th. Early in the morn came on board to our great Surprise the Master of our Late Commodore the Aurora which left us as Mentioned the 24th of May by whom we learned the Aurora had been here 28. Days and had on

[12] Pinkham was not permitted to depart for Nantucket *via* the West Indies until October 31, 1746. Pote, pp. 98, 99, 100; John Norton, *The Redeemed Captive*, annotated by S. G. Drake (Albany, 1870), hereafter cited as Norton, p. 37.

[13] Chebucto Bay, now Halifax Harbor.

[14] Hezekiah Huntington, Jr., of Norwich, Connecticut, was a graduate of Yale College in 1744. As soon as his father learned of his capture, he urged Governor Jonathan Law of Connecticut to procure his release. Pote, pp. 130–131; F. B. Dexter, *Biographical Sketches of Graduates of Yale College*, I., 762; "Law Papers," Connecticut Historial Society *Collections*, XV., *passim.*

her passage from Bank Vert to this Coast which was 6. Days Taken 4. Vessells Vizt.

26th May the Schooner Hopergrass Jno. Phillips[15] 7 men
29th. Sloop Endeavour Jonathan Salter[16] 21m: 5w: 3c
30th. Sloop Susanah Wm. Bagley.[17] 5 men
1st June Scooner Breeze James Jordan.[18] 6 men
all Except the first bound for Cape Briton on board of them was 39 men 5 Women and 3 Children.

Mon., The 30th of June. came on board again the Master of the Aurora then took up our Anchor and run round a small Island and came too an Anchor again within 2. Cables Length of the S'd Island which Intirely shut us of the Sea So that we Could no way be Seen by any vessells passing or repassing by the harbour, here on this Island they built an Hospital for their Sick; Buried a 11th man.

Tues., July the 1st. Sent on shore to their Hospital upwards of 60 persons with the Scurvy and an Inflamatory fever and wash'd and purified betwixt Decks.

Wed., July the 2d. Came in the Scooner with Mr. Bunkard who had ben Missing these 6 Days past.

Sat. 5th. The few they had on Board were Employ'd in getting their Hold ready for wooding and watering their Ship; at night buried a 12th man.

Sun. 6th. The French Officers went on Shore to see the Indians and Missionary at high Mass; they admired their singing.

Mon. 7th. The French Officers set to work to Draw a plan of the Harbour and began now to wood and water the Ship; Captn. Oldham went Onshore to the Hospital with the Scurvy Contracted as I aprehend by his Eating their Soop

[15] On Captain John Phillips of Marblehead, Massachusetts, see Pote, pp. 98, 99, 100.

[16] On the sloop *Endeavour*, Jonathan Salter, commander, bound from Philadelphia to Louisburg, see *ibid.*, p. 97.

[17] The sloop *Susannah*, William Bagley, master, was bound from Newbury, Massachusetts, to Cape Breton, *ibid.*, p. 105.

[18] The schooner *Breeze*, James Jordan, master, was bound from Rhode Island to Louisburg, *ibid.*, p. 116.

of Pork Liquor and his being for Some time before Confined by the Gout; his Leggs were now turned very black above his knees; buried a 13th man The Harbour of Jebuctore lies about 5 leagues to the Eastward of Cape Sambrea[19] on the Cape Sable coast it is one of the most Comodious Harbours I ever saw, the going in for Large Ships is by a small Island Call'd Trumpcap[20] which we leave to the Eastward; within that is a long Island which Stretches nearly East and West and by that means Covers the Harbour for at least one half of the Compass we keep the Western Shore on board where there is Water for Vessells of any Burthen; there is an arm which runs up about NW't at the mouth of which we first came to an anchor as Mentioned the 28th of June this arm is Navigable for Small Craft a good way up, and in Times of Peace our Fishermen from Marblehead, Salem, and Cape Ann usually come too for the Conveniency of putting to Sea again; About a League further up the harbour is a Small Island about a mile and 1/2 in Circumference in the Stream of which the Castor rode at Anchor; And on that Island was the Hospital for their sick built; from this Island about a League and half due No. Lies a narrow Streight which leads into a Spacious Bay Sufficient to Contain all the Royall Navy of England where they may lay land lock'd Secure from all the winds that blow; here rode the Aurora unpercieved by us. We found here an Indian Town whose Inhabitants are intirely in the French Interest for want of being better known to the English; here are vast Quantities of fine Timber and Conveniencies for Errecting water mills as Saw mills etc. A Natural Wharf to water all where the French laid the Sloop Dove of 60. Tons Longside the Wharffe and by a Leather Hoze fill'd the Casks in her hold; here is Likewise Vast quantities of Codfish Inasmuch as Cox and Dennen 2d Fishing Masters have told me they have Caught their whole fare of 50 Tons Each in the Bay or Upper harbour; The Indians freequently brought on board a great many fine Salmon

[19] Cape Sambro.

[20] Thrumcap Island in Halifax harbor.

and other fine fresh water fish Vast quantities of Strawberries, Rasberies, Goosberies, Currants etc. though thro. the wildness of nature they were Small yet it Shows the land is Capable of Cultivation They have actually Surveyed the Harbour and it is Concluded by all they have landed Cannon and Stores Since the Aurora was found To be lightned a full foot Round And therefore they Certainly intend to Settle and fortify it which may be done with a little trouble Since the Entrance into this bay is not Pistol Shot wide yet Depth of water for any first Rate Ship Should they be Suffered to settle it as they have now lost Cape Briton they will be able to annoy our Trade more then Ever they could doe out of Cape Briton since it Lies Directly in the Trade way of our Fishermen from Cape Cod Marblehead, Salem, Cape Ann And Even all the Trade from Great Britain, Ireland, Newfoundland and Cape Briton; to the Colonies on the main Continents and from those to them.[21]

Thurs., 10th of July. French very busie in wooding and watering their Ship and getting ready to put to Sea again;

Tues. 15th. The French had now wooded and watered their Ship and Captn. Chalee of the Castor had now given Zepheniah Pinkham the Scooner Endeavour, and had appointed Some of the Prisoners to assist in throwing out her fish which now Stank and Ballast her; Supplied her with wood and water, and all sorts of Stores for our Voyage to Boston, agreeable to his most Solemn promise; the sick was brought on board again from the Hospital amongst them was Captn. Oldham the Tents was pull'd Down and Everything made ready to put to Sea again.

Wed. 16th. Captn. Oldham and Self with 40. more of the Prisoners on board the Castor was sent up the Bay to the Commodore in the Sloop Dove and Schooner Endeavour when as soon as we came a Longside The Commodore he Sent his Longboate for Captn. Oldham Self our Cook and 5. of Captn. Roberts's People and Ordered us Imediately Down to the Castor Again for Old France as we belonged to Europe;

[21] After the return of Louisburg to the French in 1748, the English established the town of Halifax on Chebucto Bay.

but when we came on board the Castor again reflecting on our hard Missfortune Captn. Chalee Encouraged us and bid us not be Chagreen'd about the affair for he would Send his Lieutenant with a Letter to the Comodore in our favour and while he was writing the Letter he Ordered his Steward to bring us a Bottle of wine and some fresh provission to refresh our Selves with 'ere we went into the Boate again; Captn. Oldham and Self and the Lieutenant Set out again in a Whale Boate for the Aurora where we laid Longside till Midnight; when the Lieutenant came too us and told us the Commodore could not Comply with Captn. Chalee's Request but he must carry us on board the Castor again w'ch he Did at about 1. in the morning which we then Thought a greivance but happy for us had we Continued on board the Castor as in the Sequell will Appear.

Thurs., 17th of July. Weigh'd our Anchor and Warp'd Down little wind bound for Old France Captn. Oldham Complained to Captn. Chalee of his hard Usage Considering his Dangerous State of health and his being now Deprived of a Remedy which had he gone to Boston he could Easily have had; he likewise Subjoin'd in the Discourse that it had been much more Honourable in the Commodore to have set him on Shore amongst the Savages then to have ordered him to Old France where he was sure he Could not live out the passage; Captn. Chalee Said he was Sorry he could not have it in his Power to doe as he thought propper since he was here under the Commodore; Yet what was in his Power he would doe; which was to make life as Easy to him as possible; he then Ordered Captn. Oldham a Hammock to Lye in Likewise Ordered his Steward to give him fresh provissions Every Day from his own Table.

Sat., 19th July. came to Sea and Standing off from the Land Unfortunately fell in with His Majesties Sloop Albany[22] bound for Boston with a Paquett Commanded by Captn. Stephen Colby and Lieutenant Baker with 69 hands on Board; 10. Cariage and 12. Swievel Guns; they with Stood

[22] The *Albany*, commanded by William Lambert, was bound from Louisburg to Boston. Pote, p. 96.

the Castore 2. Glasses during which Time the Castor wounded the Bilinder's Fore Topmast and Mainmast Shattered her Sails and rigging and Hull'd her in 2. places vizt. abaft the Mainmast and in the Weake of the Fore Topmast backstay which Kill'd a man at the Oar while they were rowing to get away; they then Struck and were brought all Prisoners on Board the Castore.

Sun. 20th. Came into Jebuctore again with the Bilinder prize who had lost her fore Topmast in the Night past; The French Confined the Prisoners in the Hold with 2 Swiffle Guns at the Scuttle and Matches burning by them with 2 Centinals Day and night over them Except Captn. Oldham and Self And the Principle officers; buried a Man.

Tues., 22d July. Buried another man; NB there was more men buried from the Hospital then I could possible get an Account of, for the fever Raged very much amongst them and not any of the English which made the French often Say the Devil was in the English or protected them Since none of them Either Sickned or Died.

Wed. 23d. Came Down the Aurora with all the Prisoners which were Dispersed on board the prizes; the Billinders people was likewise Sent out of the Castor on board the Small Craft.

Thurs. 24th. Fell very Ill my Self with an Ague and fever for w'ch was Lett Blood 3. times in 30. hours; and reduced to a Low Condition.

Mon. 28th. Bravely recovered again heard we were all to goe for Boston Except Captn. Colby and the Principle officers, therefore gave Captn. Colby an account of our being Taken and Desired him to put us into the Gazette[23] at his arival in London; I Likewise gave Him an Account of the American Vessells being taken and plundered under English Colours by the French which we Saw.

Thurs. 31st. Sent us Prisoners to the N'r of about 150 to the uper part of the Harbour or Bay where the Aurora lately laid; with a strong Guard of Soldiers and Indians till

[23] *The Gazetteer and New Daily Advertizer* (London) was established about 1741.

the Ships Should saile; for the Comandore had promised and agreeable to that promise had given a Sloop to Captn. John Phillips and the rest of his Prisoners to Carry them to Boston as a reward for his Piloteing the Aurora into Jebuctore; and therefore we where Sent up here for a while that we might not (as they pretended) give any Account at Boston which way they went.

Fri., August the 1st. Unbent all our Sails and Carried them on Shore to make Tents on for the Soldiers and Indians; this looks w'th a bad face but we can't help it now Relapsed again into the Ague and fever we are now in General very Sickly; Captn. Oldham in a bad State of Health.

Sat., 2d August. Sail'd the 2 Ships vizt. the Aurora and Castor as per report of the Indians, for we are now so land-lock'd we can no way see them; this Day Died an English Indian of Captn. Pinkhams At night came down to us 200 Indians and Canadeans to be our Gaurd; Pox take them for their pains.

Mon. 4th. Threw out great part of our Ballast from the Sloop and Scooner and Haul'd them close to the Shore under a pretence of the sick Prisoners going the more readily on-shore but we were now able to put another Construction on it which was that our Boston voyage was now over.

Tues. 5th. A Blundering Fellow of a French man who pretended to be a Doctor came on Board and ordered all the Prisoners that were Ill Should goe on Shore and he would look after them; but my self and a few others rather Choose to trust to God and Nature on Board, then to goe on Shore with him who had not one Medicine to give them; but Medicine or none he Dragoon'd Us on Shore where we Lay languishing about 7 hours till we had taken about 2 hours of the Dew without any thing over or under us but the Heavens and the cold Earth; when he came and felt the Pulses of 2 of us, Shook his Empty Noddle and ordered us on board again; A Rare Reciept for a Malignant Fever.[24]

[24] In the margin opposite this paragraph is the note: "NB Edw'd Tew." Tew was a captive from Rhode Island.

S'r William Petty[25] in his Essay on Political Arithmetick is very much at a Loss to Guess the reason why the Northern Hive (as he Calls it) does not send out such swarms to Infest the Southern part's of Europe as they formally did; But had that great Author Considered that at that time there were no Doctors amongst the Inhabitants of Thor and Woden he would Easily have found a Sollution to his Quere; for we may lay it Down as a Maxim, that where a Country grows thick with Doctors, it grows thin of people.

Gibbons but Guesses and can Barely Save
But Morris Sweeps whole Parishes and Peoples Every Grave
Woulds't thou be Soon Dispatch'd and perish whole,
Trust Morris with thy Life, and Millbourn w'th thy Soul.[26]

Mon., 11th of August. was now Bravely recovered; we now Discovered though too Late to Remedy it, that we were to be march'd for Canada; for one Gootee[27] a Nuter Frenchman[28] but a D-n-d Rascall began now to pilfer the Materials out of the Vessells as he had one of the Sloops given him by the French The Missionary[29] had Captn. Jordan's Scooner given him; the rest were Disposed of to the Indians; This morning I heard great firing of small Arms, upon Enquirey I found it was on account of an Indian Wedding; I procured 2. of our people with a Frenchman for our Guard and made towards the place where we heard the firing, but when we Arrived the Cerimony was over and the Missionary gone; but here we found the Wedding Guest sitting round a Circle

[25] Sir William Petty, M. D., 1623–1687, the author of several *Essays in Political Arithmetic.*

[26] Guibbons but guesses, nor is sure to save;
But Maurus sweeps whole Parishes, and peoples ev'ry Grave;
And no more mercy to mankind will use,
Than when he robbed and murder'd Maro's muse.
Would'st thou be soon dispatched, and perish whole,
Trust Maurus with thy life, and Milbourne with thy soul.
—Dryden, *Epistle the Fifteenth*, lines 82–87.

[27] Possibly Joseph Gautez of Annapolis Royal, mentioned by Pote, pp. 28, 33.

[28] A neutral Frenchman, that is an inhabitant of Nova Scotia after its surrender to the English in 1713.

[29] Louis Joseph Le Loutre.

built up with Stone in the form of our Cock pits in the Centre of which Sat the Bride and Bride groom; At our Approach they rose and one Old Indian came towards us and in good English ordered us to Sit Down which we did amongst them; here I Observed the Dresses of the Wedding Guest; The Squaws (or women) where Covered with a Blanket and round their whrists, arms, Necks, and ankles where Severall Strings of Wampumpeg. Some of them had on their heads a Cap of coarse Cloath of wooll, others a sort of a Coronett of Party Coloured feathers; The Men and Boys where likewise Covered with a blanket without any Embelishments Except that Some of them had a hole in the thick or Lower part of their Ear big Enough for me to put my finger through, and in this hole was put Sundrey Strips of fine cloath of Severall Colours which cloath hung Down on their Shoulders like a Fore horses Top knot; Some of them had their pipe run through their Ear and hung by the Bole one Indian I observed had a hole bored thro the Bridge of his Nose and through it was put a Ring of Brass from which hung Pendant a Stone of a Pearl colour and about the Shape and Size of a Trushes Egg This Indian was of a Different Tribe from the rest; As for the Papposes or Small Children they where in Boxes made of Wood in the form of a Coffin without a Lid where they were hung upon the Limbs of Trees by the Head part; they were Laced into the Boxes with Leather Thongs very Pretily Diversified that they Look'd like Mummies in the Houses of the Egyptians;—After we had sat about half an hour the afforesaid old Indian led us without the Circle and sat us Down again upon Stones hard by when they began a Dance after their Manner; their Musick was an Empty flour Barrell on the head of which they beate with 2 Sticks; this set them all to Dancing round the Bride and Bridegroom but such odd unaccountable Gestures they had as I never before Saw; here was hooping, Hallowing, Howling, Yelling, Enough to Stun one's Ears, it brought into my mind Æneas's Journey to Hell by virtue of his Pasport the Golden Bough, and that these were all Fiends rather then Men; They then got to Screwing of their D——d Close Stool faces up that they look'd like so many Wrinkled Baboons Straining on a Hillock; Tired with this Sceen we withdrew to our Camp again.

Tues., 12th of August. The Commanding officer of the Soldiers Sent for the Captain and officers who was prisoners and Informed them that they and all the rest of the prisoners where to Travil to Canada and told them out of Complisance they might Choose when they would Set out, but as the Journey could not be Avoided they Choose to set out on the Morrow; here; French faith.

Wed. 13th. The French Draughted off about 40 of the Ablest Prisoners in Order to March them Towards Canada my Self was ordered for one, but I pleaded my Self off with the General officer in Consideration of Captain Oldhams Dangerous State of health who was now reduced to the Necessity of Transporting himself on his hands and Breech.

Thurs., 14th August. Draughted off about 80 more who Imediately Set forward on their Journey; Then the French Soldiers came on Board to Order all the Sick and Disabled on Shore; This was the most Mallencholy Sceene my Eyes ever Behield; In one part Lay many Languishing under a Malignant fever; In another lay as many with the Scurvy and flux and not able to help themselves; Some of which I Assisted in getting into the Boate w'th this proviso their friends Should assist me in getting Captain Oldham into the Boate, but like true Pumpkins So Soon as their own turn was Served they left me alone on board with Captain Oldham whom I Endeavoured to get out of his Cabin, but he was no sooner raised then he Imediately fell Down in a fit and so Continued for the Space of about 20. minutes, when he again recovered and the French coming on board we got him into the Boate and Caried him Onshore where they let him Lay in the boate till I went and Informed the officers who Presently Sent 2 men for him and brought him up in his Hammock to an Indian Wiggwam where they put him in.

Fri., 15th of August. At 5 A M found Captn. Oldham much better, he Slept well all Night, was now Entertaining Some hopes of going to Menis[30] by Water with one Gotee but

[30] Minas, a French village bordering on the Basin of Minas. Pote, p. 9 n.

those hopes were presently frustrated for at 7 the Guard came to our Wigwam and forced me from Captn. Oldham whom I was Oblidged to Leave in a helpless Condition in the Wigwam to the Mercy of A French Missionary[31] and Indians; In Company with John Greenleaf, his Unkle keeps the Kings arms in Piscatua; Zaceriah Hubart, his Unkle is Collonel Benjamin Pollard in Boston; Sam'll Horton of Marblehead; with one Johnathan Felt and three more whose Names I could not Learn, in all 8 Persons whom God preserve.

We Set out to the Number of 20 of us but very Ill the most of us were and Therefore Could Travil but Slowly; however we marched about 15 miles when we came to an Indian Encampment where we made bold with their Wigwams to Sleep in with a Large fire at our feet while we Slept, the Soldiers Guarded us all night.

Sat. 16th. Early on the Morn began our march again; Harness'd with 3. Days provissions at each of our Backs; when we had Traveled about an hour a voiolent Flux Siezed me which oblidged me to throw all my provissions away to keep up with the Company; for here was no Mincing the Matter, we must Either March or be left to perish in the Wild Desert or fall a prey to the more mercieless Savages; this Day we Travelled 9 miles e're we came to one Drop of water the weather very hot and Sultry however we came at last to a pond where many of Our Company laid themselves down on their Bellies near the Brink and Lap'd the water like So many Doggs; here those that had any victuals fell to Eate, for my part I dined with Duke Humphery,[32] nothing to Eate, I having thrown away all my provissions in the morn; This night we Lodged in the woods with a great fire at our feet.

[31] Le Loutre.

[32] "A promenade in St. Paul's Cathedral, much frequented by insolvent debtors and beggars in the sixteenth century, was popularly styled 'Duke Humphrey's Walk,' from a totally erroneous notion that a monument overlooking it was Duke Humphrey's tomb. 'To dine with Duke Humphrey,' i. e. to loiter about St. Paul's Cathedral dinnerless, or seeking an invitation to dinner, was long a popular proverb (*cf.* Shakespeare, *Richard III*, act IV, sc. IV, l. 176)." T. F. Tout, on Humphrey, Duke of Gloucester, 1391–1447, in the *Dictionary of National Biography*.

Sun. 17th. Early on the Morn Set out again, the Flux thanks to God had now left me; though the Traveling in these woods is very Perplexing; large Trees laying across the Rhode no biger then a Sheeps path the which we were under a Necessity of Climbing over, or Oblidged to goe round in the Bushes and thick underwoods; Besides the Fateague of Climbing high hills, the roots of the Trees Serving as so many Steps to keep our feet from Sliping Down again; then Decending into the vallies where we waded through Swamps or Morasses; however at Sun Set we Arived at the Skirts of the wood and got to the first house where I had the good fortune to prevail upon the Master to Kill us a Sheep, which we Cook'd and eat with the Soldiers, we could no way prevail with the Honest Farmer to let us lay in his barn but he provided us with some planks which we set up against a fence; Then the farmer Ordered his Servants to bring us some Straw on which we laid all Night.

Mon., 18th August. In the Morning we found 8 of our Company were So Ill they cound not Travil, however the Soldiers procured a Cart and Oxen to Carry them Down to the water Side in Order to Transport them by water in Petteaugers[33] or Small Boates Dugg out of a Tree; my Self and 12 more Traviled by Land; when about 4 P M we came to a River which we were Oblidged to ford up to our Middles for about 3/4 of a mile the Tide of Ebb runing very Swift, at night Lodged in a Barn.

Tues. 19th. This morning 9 of our Company were unable to Travil; however my Self and 3 more Set out under the Guard of 2 Soldiers and left them in the Barn to recover; now we began to live Tolorable well, for our Guard at our request would call at Every house we Saw, and we being but 4 in Number the people very readily relieved us with what they had in the house as Milk and Bread, apples etc, at 3 P M we Cross'd a Second time the river here the Tide run very Swift which Oblidged me to Suport my self with my Stuff otherwise I had ben Sweept away with the Tide.

By what I Could Observe of the then high water Mark, the

[33] A form of piragua or pirogue, a canoe.

Tide could not flow less then 30 Foot Perpendicular At night we arived at Menis were we found great part of our Company which Set out from Jebuctore 2 Days before us, here I meet with Captn. Rob't David Roberts and Mr. John Durant his Mate who Confirmed me in my Opinion of the French Intending to Settle and Fortifie the Harbour of Jebuctore; Our Prison here was a Barn where we lay on Straw it was Guarded without by Soldiers; our allowence was of bread 1 lb; of Beef 1/2 lb; or Pork 1/4 lb; at night 40 set forward on the Journey.

This Town of Meen or Meniss lies about 25 Leagues Distant from Anopoliss Royall atwart the Bay of Funda, it is Situated on the Skirt of a Large Plain which we have been these 2 Days Past in Travilling over; The Town Consist of about 50 Stragling Houses and near as many Barns or Cattle houses; here was about 700 Soldiers Encamp'd; the greater part of which was our Guard; Here the French gave us Shoes made of a red Leather Some were of Scal Skins but they had neither heels nor Soales which they and the Indians Call Mogazins; they then Ordered us to prepare for our March Tomorrow.

Wed., August 20th. This Day left behind us about 25 Sick in the Barn and March'd to the water Side where we Embarked on board a Small Sloop Triumph Captn. John White; to the Number of about 80 Prisoners and as many Soldiers here on board we was Oblidged to Stow in Bulk like Essex Calves in Rumford Wagons,[34] no Deck over head but a few planks laid at Random; The Hold wherin we lay was very Nasty with the Garbich of Cattle which had been on board; Whenever it rained as it did most part of the Night, it ran down upon us, Or if the Soldiers Above P'sd we were Sure to have it on our heads and Down our Necks; lice Innumerable and no water Except a Little which Stank; A hopefull voyage this in Crossing part of the Bay of Funda 2. nights and a Day Dist about 8 Leagues.

Fri., 22d August. At Day break we Landed in the rain, mede Several fires and by them Sat Down to breakfast on

[34] *I.e.*, of Romford in Essex, near London.

Some Carion beef and Stinking port but not one Morsell of Bread; we then began our March through woods again This morning the Gout Siezed me in Such a manner as Oblidged me to cut the upper Leathers of my Shoes e're I could get my feet into them; and as it rained very hard and Continued so till 4. P M I was hard Put too it to March thro' the Uneveness of the way the rain having made the Path very Slipery; I was now behind the rest of the Company Except Mr. John Pike[35] The Soldiers now observed we could not Travil so fast as the rest and in all Likelyhood we Should hinder them, they began now to Futere and Boogar us in French, and I as Often Curs'd them in Plain English; that at Length Monsieur began to push me forward with the Butt end of his Musquet which so Enraged me that I Stop'd and gave the Fellow to understand that I could not nor would not march any faster; this Did not Satisfie Monsieur but he Imediately Push'd me Down which being Observed by his officer who presently came up with us and Enquired of me the reason of the Soldiers pushing me Down; the which I gave him an account and Show'd him at the same time my ript Shoe; The officer Imediately ordered the Fellow to take up my Burthen and cary it for me and that he Should likewise see me and Mr. Pike forth coming at Night; this gave me Encouragment to march faster and made the fellow more ready to assist me when at Noon we came up with the rest of the People who had sat down to rest Themselves; my feet by this Time were grown warm and the Pangs very much abated; here's a remedy for the Gout tho' I Question much wether I Could have been prevailed upon to goe through with it had not I been Dragoon'd into it; I Traveled now pretty well till night when we fell to work with Hatchets to build us Tents to lye in with a Large fire at our feet, but not one Morsell to Eate.

Sat., 23d of August. At Day light the Soldier came to my Tent (by order of his officer I suppose) and took up my burthen again we then began our March the Gout was again

[35] John Pike of Rhode Island was freighter and owner of the schooner *Breeze*, James Jordan, master, taken by *L'Aurore*, June 1, 1746. Pote, p. 97.

very Troublesome to me; At 9. o' the Clock 2. Soldiers came to us Laden with Bread which was a great reliefe to us as we had Eat nothing for about 30 hours; we then Sat down to Breakfast after which we March'd about 3. hours which brought us through the Woods to a Small river where the French officers Chose out about 12 of the Ablest of us and gave us a piece of bread and a Dram and Escourted them by Land while my Self and the rest of the Company Satt Down by the Brink of the river or in Pettyaugers to wait for the Tide coming up which from the Time it began to flow till it was High water was not above 15. minutes we then went down with the Ebb with oars at the rate of 8. miles per hour which in 3 hours Time brought us within 2 miles of Boobazang or Seegenecture[36] which we walk'd; then we were put into a Barn where we lay all night with a Guard of Soldiers without.

Sun., 24th of August. here we rested all Day This Town of Seeganecture is much larger and more uniform then Meniss it has in it a Parochal Church and about 150 Dwelling houses; here we had very bad water which gave most of us the flux Our allowence here was of Bread 1 lb, of Pork 1/2 lb, per man per Diem.

Tues. 26th. Arived Sam'll Horton who was left with Captn. Oldham at Jebuctore sick by whom I had an Account of Captain Oldham Namely that he was plundered of his Pocket Book and papers etc. by the Indians or that Rascall Gootee; he Subjoined likewise that the French were Consulting to carry him in his Hammock between 2 mens Shoulders by soft and Easy Journeys which gives me hopes I may yet see him again.

Wed. 27th. Arived Dr. John Coron with 22 sick and Disabled left behind at Meniss heard by him that Captn. Oldham was arrived in Meniss with the Missionary; but this I take to be meerly Apocryphal I may believe it or not.

Thurs., 28th of August. At 9 A M Set out with 4 Carts to Carry the women, Children, and Disabled and our Raggs

[36] Beaubassin, at the head of Chicnegto Bay, at this time one of the three most populous places in Nova Scotia. Pote, p. 49 n.

which they had pleased to leave us: but the French Stop'd the Wife of Mr. Archibald Gutered[37] who was great with Child and ready to lye in; and oblidged the Husband to leave her in that Condition which in my Opinion was Barbarous; however on we march'd at a great rate till about 4. P M when we Encamp'd at the Skirt of a wood near to a small water Mill; we built our selves Tents to lye in; and the Carts some of them breaking Down we was Oblidged to goe to bed Supperless, but such a night of wind and rain as I believe the Oldest and most Experienced Seaman hardly Ever felt, our Tents all blew Down and not any Amongst us but what was wett thro all our Cloaths Notwithstanding we burnt before our Tent as much wood as a Waggon with 6 horses could Carry at Twice; About 7 sick men got into the Mill by Leave of the miller.

Fri., 29th of August. at Day break we saw come by us about 50 men women and Children upon horses and Mules who had been routed from the Island St. John's by Admiral Warren;[38] they came to our Tents and Cursed us on account of the aforesaid Brave Admiral who had drove them out of house and home; we asked them wether our Circumstances in their Opinion was not worse then theirs, Since they were amongst their friends and in a State of Freedom we were Prisoners and going to a Place where we had great reason to Expect never to return at; Least till the Conclusion of a Peace; this home trust Silenced them and away they march'd from us without giving us any Answer; about 7 A M the rain abated when the French drew out the ablest to the Number of 25 Prisoners and March'd them away for Bay Vert[39] Dist about 12 miles; In the afternoon my self march'd with the rest Except those left at the mill Sick; at the Close of Evening we got to Bay Vert or Green Bay when the French

[37] The name also occurs as Gutherage and Gartrage. Pote, p. 145; Norton, p. 50.

[38] Rear-Admiral Warren, governor of Louisburg, advocated the transportation of the inhabitants of the Island of St. Johns, the present Prince Edward Island, to France, but lack of transports prevented the execution of the plan. The group of Frenchmen were probably moving in anticipation of ejection. D. C. Harvey, *The French Régime in Prince Edward Island* (New Haven, 1926), pp. 109–120.

[39] The present Baie Verte.

men Drove their Cattle out of a Barn were 1/3 parts of the Roof was Blown off and ordered us in and set a Strong Guard over us; here was not a bit of Straw to lay on and the floor was Ankle Deep with water and the Garbich of Cattle so that we could no way set nor lye; but rouzed at this Indignity offered us we Issued out in a Body in Dispight of the Guard and gave them to understand we were not Beasts nor would we be Used as such and if they would not allow us better Lodging we would betake our selves to the woods again; this Resolution Startled the Monsieurs and the officers coming to see the Barn they gave us the Liberty to build our Selves Tents of the fences and remains of an Indian Encampment which Tents we Covered with the rindes of Trees or Fir Boughs; we kept Likewise a large fire at our feet while we Slept. This Bay Vert or Green bay is Situated in the Entrance of the Gulf of St. Laurance it Consists of 4 Dwelling Houses and 1 Barn, the Land very Poor and no Springs of water therefore not worth Notice.

Sat., 30 of August. last night Cornelious Mahanah (one of our Crew) and one John Tobin[40] made an attempt to get off and on that account had provided themselves with a Bottle of Brandy and a loaf of Bread they got into the woods and was in a fair way of getting clear off; but they sat them Selves down to the Bottle and Drank Success to their undertaking till they very fairly forgot what they were about and fell fast asleep in the Direct Path till this morning when they were found by the Soldiers and brought back again and put in Irons; our allowence here was of Bread 1 lb, of Pork 1/2 lb, per man per Diem; at night came into the Bay, 7 Sail of Small vessells and a 20 Gun Ship.

Mon., September the 1st. No bread to be got which caused great Murmering amongst us, Therefore the French officers drew up their men before us to the Number of 200; well armed in order as I suppose to terrifie us, but we grew still more Clamorous for Bread, or to put us on Board the vessells in the Bay, however they gave us 3/4 lb of fresh Carion Beef and about 1 1/2 lb of flower per man per Diem

[40] John Tobin finally deserted to the French. Pote, p. 152.

with which we fell to work and with water made it into a Cake which we baked on the Embers, instead of Bread; however we did amongst our mess purchase a Loaf of Bread for 10 Soluz[41] value 1:6d. the man protested to us that in Sparing it his Family must goe without; The Sick with Dr. John Coron just now arived from the watermill. Afternoon the french Held a Counsell amongst their Officers, and in Consequence of that they ordered us all out of our Tents and from amongst us Drew out 100 of us to goe on board the vessells in the Rhode; I then Enquired of the Commanding Officer after Captn. Jno. Oldham and was Informed by him of the Captains being at Meniss under the Care of a Doctor; at 6 P M 50 of us Embark'd on board fishing Shallops to be put on Board the vessells in the Bay but on the Tide of Ebb wee fell aground where we lay all night, much rain and in an Open boate.

Tues., 2d of September. At 4 in the Morning I got on Board the Sloop Sceal Captain Obar bound for Quebec; At Noon a very hard gale of wind at SSE. which Drove our Sloop Onshore with all the rest Soft Mud.

Wed. 3d. Got off the ground again, Saw them Embark the rest of the Prisoners on board the vessells in the Bay; Except about 40 which were reserved to goe to Quebec in small fishing Shallops.

Thurs. 4th. on board the Sloop Sceal, with Captn. Robert David Roberts, Mr. John Durant his Mate; with 9 others; here was as greate want of provisions as on Shore So that we fell according to the Homely English Proverb out of the Frying pan into the fire; however the French Captain did not want for good Nature, but Served us with the same Allowence he did his own people, and gave us for Supper Flower and water boyl'd up together *Al's Sadlers Glew.*

Fri. 5th. At 3 P M our Sloop Sceal, 2. Scooners and a Briganteen weigh'd and came to sail wind at East; at 4 D'o Came to an Anchor again by reason the 20 Gun Ship Turner could not Purchase their anchor out of the Ground.

[41] The French sou, plural sous, a coin worth one-twentieth of a livre—say a halfpenny.

Sat. 6th. At day light came to sail again and at 9 A M spoke with 3 Shallops who brought us an account but of what, Time only can Discover; they all Imediately wrought up the Bay again and came too an anchor again once more and Sent on Shore out of all the vessells 100 Soldiers, wether to save the provissions or on Some Expedition is at present a Profound Secret which only Time can Discover; At night Sup'd on *Sadlers Glew.*

Sun., 7th of September. At 7 A M Weigh'd our Anchor and came to sail again once more wind at SW't Sailing out of the Bay first ENE then NNE then NWW't at 9 D'o Saw an Island which I Judged to be St. Johns I was forbid to look on the Compass but I Judge by the Sun the Said Island to lay SSW't and NNE we sail'd between the Said Island and the main Land; our Course at Sun Set by his Amplitude I find to be NWBNo. Our allowence of bread was 1/4 of a small Biskit per man per Diem, In the morning a Dram of Brandy at Noon Soope made of Beef or Pork of which we had Each man 1/2 a pound; at night the old fare, *Sadlers Glew* but the best meal.

Mon. 8th. Came too an Anchor off an Island which I Judge to be Anti Costa[42] it lay North and South along.

Tues., September the 9th. At an Anchor off the above Island wind at NE it blew very hard and thick Hazey Weather.

Wed., September the 10th. At 2 A M weigh'd our Anchor and came to sail wind at SE Steering as I Judge about NEBNo. lost Sight of the 2 Scooners and Brigg here we caught many Codfish and at Night Sup'd on bare footted Fish that is with neither butter, oyl, vinigar, nor Salt; nor no more Bread then the aforesaid Allowence.

Thurs. 11th. Steering NBW't wind at SBE, much rain, at 6 P M made the Land NWBW Saw a sail to windward which we and all the French on board took to be an English man of war the Vigilent of 64 Guns She was to windward of us and in all probability never saw us; the worse luck for us or She'd have retaken us all.

[42] Anticosti Island.

Fri. 12th. At 2 A M we Entered the great river of St. Laurance Steering between the West and NW't; this river at its Entrance is about 18 Leagues Wide and 125. Leagues in Length up to the City of Quebeck.

Tues., 16th of September. Little wind from the SW't to the West; I was Observed by the Centinals over us that I often wrote in a Book which in truth was no more then these Notes from whence they had Concluded that I was Taking a Draught of the River on which account the French Captn. Ordered that we should all keep Down and that no one of us Should come upon Deck Except to Disburthen Nature.

Wed. 17th. Little wind at NE fair for us and therefore we were allowed Double allowence which verifies the Old Proverb vizt. large wind large allowence, but Scant wind Scanty messes at sea.

Thurs. 18th. At 3 P M came too an Anchor about 4. miles below an Island wind West.

Fri. 19th. At 10 A M weigh'd our Anchor and at 4 P M came to an Anchor again abrest of the aforesaid Island; now Scanty Messes at Sea.

Sun., September the 21st. At 1 A M weigh'd our Anchor and came to Sail wind Notherly at 3 D'o Came too an Anchor again wind at WSW't at 10 D'o weigh'd again and at 5 P M came too an Anchor once more; the Sloop would not nor they could not work her.

Wed. 24th. At 1 A M weigh'd Anchor wind at NE we are now about 55 miles NE from the City of Quebec.

Thurs. 25th. At 8 A M came too an anchor Calm at 10 D'o weigh'd again Little wind; out Oars and rowed at noon the wind freshned; at 4 P M came by a Notable Cascade the fall of which waters I judge could not be less then 400 Foot Perpendicular; at 8 P M came too an Anchor and Moored off the City or Town of Quebec after a fateagueing Passage of 25 Days from Green Bay during which time I laid on the bare planks with swarms of lice to keep me out of Idleness.

Fri., September the 26th. At 8 A M The Comissary[43]

[43] M. Guillemin.

came on board the Sloop and Demanded us of the Captain and after carying us before his Excellency the Marquis De Boharnoise[44] Governer who after a Short Examination he Ordered us to Prison where we found 127 Prisoners; the greater part of which were New England men; In the afternoon we had gave to us a Bed Stuff'd with Straw, a Blanket of Bethlem Broad Cloath; then left us with bread and water to our Private Meditations.[45]

Sat. 27th. Eate, Drank, and Loused our Selves Our allowence as now Setled was of Bread 1 lb; of Beef 3/4 lb; per man per Diem This Day the Gout Siezed me, which I Impute to my being So long Confined on Board the Sloop in the passage here; and through the Badness of my Shoes my feet got weet in coming up to the Prison from the Strand.

This City of Quebec Contains in it about 500 Dwelling houses; and have in it about (as I have ben Informed) 11 Churches but this I take to be meerly Apochryphal Since I never could see above 5, here are Colledges and Nuneries but how many of Each I know not; here is the residence of the Governer aforesaid of all Canada or New France; here are Lying in this Port 7 Sail of Vessells bound for Europe or the west Indies.

Sun., Mon., Tues. 30th. Nothing worthy of Note Except that the rest of the Prisoners which left Bay Vert with us and came in the 20 Gun Ship and other small Craft arived; Except those which were put on Board the Shallops; This day Took a list of the Prisoners by Order of His Excellency the Governer and found them to be in Number 259 Men, women, and Children.[46]

[44] Charles, Marquis de Beauharnois, governor of New France.

[45] On September 24 John Norton recorded the arrival of forty-three prisoners at Quebec, and on September 25 and 26, of about seventy-four more; on September 25 Captain William Pote, Jr., recorded the arrival of thirty-seven men, two women, and two children, and on September 26, of seventy-five men and two women; on September 26 Nehemiah How recorded the arrival of seventy-four men and two women. Norton, p. 36; Pote, pp. 96–97; *A Narrative of the Captivity of Nehemiah How in 1745–1747*, reprinted with introduction and notes by V. H. Paltsits (Cleveland, 1904), hereafter cited as How, p. 49.

[46] The number agrees with that given by Pote, pp. 97–98.

Wed., October the 1st. Came into Prison Mrs. Sarah Bryant Widdow taken by a Party of French and Indians at her House in Casco Bay in the Government of the Massachusetts Bay New England They Murdered her Husband and 3 of her Children before her face.[47]

Thurs. 2d. Came into Prison 2 Prisoners one of which was Johnathan Bradrick taken by the French and Indians in Anopoliss river he Continued with the Indians 17 months e're he made his Escape from them and arived here in a Tattered Condition.[48]

Sun. 5th. Came into Prison 12 Prisoners which where formally of our Company and Left Bay Vert with us and came up the river in Shallops; there was 14 of them but the other 2 Died in their passage thro hardships and want of Provissions Likewise came into prison one Mr. Stubbs late of Casco Bay New England.[49]

Wed. 8th. The French gave to those who wanted an Indian drest Deer Skin an ozinbridge Shirt and a Jacket but no Stockings nor Shoes; however they gave us Several Packs of Cards to pass away the time with: which hung heavy upon our hands.

Sat. 11th. French Abridged us of 1/3 part of our Beef on which account we petitioned his Excellency the Governer; Our allowence is now but 1/2 lb of Beef and 1 lb bread.

Sun. 12th. Severely cold; came into Prison 24 Prisoners from Bay Vert in 4 Shallops one Shallop Still remains behind; these Poor Wretches were very hard put to it they not having any bread for 30 Days but were Oblidged to live on Rock

[47] The journalists do not agree upon the date of arrival of Sarah Bryant. Norton enters the arrival of the "widow Briant" under date of September 25, 26. Pote says that "Sarah Bryant that was taken at Goramtown" entered prison September 30. Norton, p. 36; Pote, p. 97.

[48] Under date of October 2, Pote records the arrival of one Jonathan, and the editor of his journal erroneously supplies the name of Donham or Dunham although Dunham was already in prison. Under date of October 3, How records the arrival of one "Jonath. Batherick." Pote, p. 98; How, p. 49.

[49] This entry agrees with Pote, p. 98; Norton, p. 37; and How, pp. 49–50.

weed and Shell Fish;[50] this Day by the favour of Mr. Chalet[51] a Merchant in Town I wrote to Captn. John Oldham at Menis.

NB Our Prison house is a Large Stone Building, in Length 150 Foot; width 18 Foot on the Inside it is 2 Stories high the windows Sashed with Strong Iron Bars on the outside of them; in the Front is a yard or area Enclosed with Piquets about 30 foot Wide and the length of the Building; in which we are allowed to walk from 9. in the Morning till Noon, and from 3. P Noon till 5.

Thurs., 16th of October. no answer to our Petition Sent Last Saturday the 11th but to Day ordered 3/4 lb of Dry Fish 1 1/2 oz of oyl and 3 oz of vinegar per man for 3 Days provission NB this is Like making brick without Straw.

Sat. 18th. Petitioned his Excellency again but had no redress, nothing to Eate or Drink Except Bread and water; Severe Cold weather and much Snow I this Day Petitioned his Excellency to goe to Old France in some one of the Ships which was bound there.

Sun. 19th. Came into Prison 6 prisoners who left Bay Vert with us; in a Shallop but left her about 14 Days agoe to Travil by land over Mountains covered with Snow and Long Water'y Morasses where they were often up to the knees; one of which was Thos. Davis Aprentice to Captn. John Oldham NB no one of our Ships Company missing but him whom God preserve.[52]

[I.] *Mon.* 20th. Departed this Life Mr. Jacob Read an Inhabitant of Casco Bay lately; his son is here a prisoner and had been Taken and brought to prison about 6 months before the Father.[53]

Wed. 22d. This Day Saw the new man of war of 20 Guns hauld up in a small arm of the river for want of Rigging it

[50] Pote's entry is apparently a condensation of this entry. Both Norton and How record the arrival of the twenty-four prisoners. Pote, p. 99; Norton, p. 37; How, p. 50.

[51] Pote makes frequent reference to M. De Chalet, interpreter of the king. How calls him Mr. Shearly. Pote, *passim*; How, *passim*.

[52] The entry agrees with those of Pote and How. Pote, p. 99; How, p. 50.

[53] The entry agrees with those of Pote and How. Pote, p. 99; How, p. 50.

being burnt in the Magazine about 3 months past by some Axident; here is a new 70 Gun Ship on the Stocks ready to Launch but our men of war have Caught her Rigging etc. twice in coming from Old France.

Thurs., October 23d. Two Prisoners Vizt. Robert Dunbar and John Clootman late Inhabitants of Casco Bay made their Escape out of Prison; they were both very hardy men and well used to the woods through which they have to Travil upwards of 300 miles to their Habitation; they were furnished out with about 16 lb of Bread and Pork a hatchet, fire works, a pocket Compass and a Large Paquet of Letters for his Excellency Governer Shierly of Boston.[54]

Thurs.[55] 24th. Great noise and Bustle this morning amongst the French Officers who Treatned to send some of us to the Cashot or Dungeon for suffering the men to make their Escape very Pretty Begar: but the men who are gone knew better then to acquaint any with their Design but Such as they could trust, which Design Some months agoe had like to have Cost 3 men their Lives in an Attempt of the like Nature thro the Treachery of one MacClure a D——d Rascal. We have now 26 Ill of a Malignant Fever thro badness of water and want of Provissions.

Mon., October 27th. Wrote to Messrs. Touchet and Comp[56] per favour of Captn. Robt. David Roberts who have at length got Leave to goe to old France in one of the Ships now bound there.

Tues. 28th. Came into Prison an Indian Chief or Sacham and Demanded Mr. Stubbs who had ben taken by him as Mentioned the 5th past; he told Mr. Stubbs that he had wounded him in the Conflict but as he had now recovered he came to let him know he freely forgave him; he then

[54] The entry agrees with those of Norton and How. Pote enters the incident under date of October 24, the morning after its occurrence. Norton, p. 37; How, p. 50; Pote, pp. 99–100.

[55] An error for *Fri.*

[56] Samuel Touchet and Company, West India merchants, east side of the Mansion House, are listed among London merchants in *The Universal Director* (London, 1763).

Carried him out before the Governor and Assembley in the Court where the Discourse ran chiefly upon those 2. men who had made their Escape the 23d past; The French officers Said that as they took it Twas a Monstrous piece of Ingratitude in them or any Prisoners to make their Escape when they were so kindly used; Mr. Stubbs answered that it was no new thing for Prisoners Espically for those close Confined to make their Escape whenever an Oppertunity offered its Self, and that he knew of 4 French officers who were Prisoners in New England and had their Patrol of Honour allow'd them yet they ran away with a sloop out of the Harbour and the Prisoners which remain'd were not the worse Treated for it as we were Treatned; This Smart Rappatee Ended the Dispute and he was remanded back again to Prison.

Thurs., October the 30th. Much snow and likely to be a Severe Season; This Afternoon was talking with our Late Doctor John Coron when One John Bingham[57] Came Towards us and Saluted the Doct'r in this wise; what Devil have Set his Claws in your Haunches and brought you hither, if you don't know me I'll give you a Convincing mark which I am Oblidged to you for, he then Imediately Laid bare his Arm and Said to him this Poor Arm of mine you broke with you Cane when I was a Prisoner in Laguire at the Time I was Carying a great Stone and a Little one to Build a Fort in the Bay at the same Time you had a Captns Commission under the King of Spain and When Commadore Knowles[58] came against the place you then Comanded in a Fort of 6 Guns in a Rock and play'd against the English Shiping and did them prodigious Damage, this was an unexpected Salute for the Dr. nor could he with all his Low Cuning Evade the Least Tittle of what the fellow had Said to him but turn'd away from him in great Confusion.

Fri. 31st. This Day Captn. Zepheniah Pinkham and his

[57] On John Bingham of Philadelphia, who cooked and washed for the officers, see Pote, p. 102; Norton, p. 39.

[58] In 1743 Commander, afterward Admiral, Charles Knowles commanded a squadron sent to attack the Spanish settlements on the Carácas coast. On February 18, 1742/3, the squadron attacked La Guaira and was beaten off with a heavy loss.

Crew with Captain John Phillips and his Crew were taken out of Prison by the French as a reward for their Piloting the Aurora and Castor into Jebuctore; but to what part of the world they were Design'd is a Secret however I gave Captain Pinkham a Direction to find Captain Oldhams house in London in Case he should goe there; or if he Should goe to any other part of England I beg'd he would put us in the Publick Prints.[59]

Sat., November the 1st. this Day one John Pitman one of Captn. Phillips's Crew was brought back again into prison he being far gone with the Scurvy; A Scurvy Trick of the French; however the French took out of Prison at his Earnest request Dr. John Coron and one Joseph of French Extraction but Naturalized in England.[60]

Sun. 2d. Died John Read[61] the Son of the late Deceased; II.[62] allow'd 1 lb of Dry fish per man for 3 Days but neither oyl, vinigar, nor Butter; here is Living for you, I wonder they don't get a fasting Almanack printed on purpose for us.

> Wherein no Carnaval nor Christmass shall appear[63]
> But Lent and Ember Weeks shall fill the year.

But as to my own part I fared much better then any one in the prison of my rank by the favour of the following Gentlemen vizt. Captn. Wm. Chapman; Captn. James Sutherland Captn. Wm. Pote;[64] Captn. Robert David Roberts Captn. Johnathan Salter; The Reverend John Norton;[65] Mr. Wm. Lambert; Serjant Jno. Hawks Mr. John Boydle; Mr. John Pike and Sam'l Lingan; who had an apartment adjoyning To ours;

[59] This entry agrees with those of Pote and Norton. Pote, p. 100; Norton, p. 37.

[60] This entry agrees with that of Pote. Pote, p. 100.

[61] The other journalists give November 1, 1746, as the date of Read's death. Pote, p. 100; Norton, p. 39; How, p. 50.

[62] The Roman numbers in the margin represent the number of those who had died in the prison at Quebec since the arrival of the journalist.

[63] Unidentified.

[64] The author of *The Journal of Captain William Pote, Jr.*, edited by V. H. Paltsits (New York, 1896).

[65] The author of *The Redeemed Captive* (Boston, 1748), and republished with annotations by S. G. Drake (Albany, 1870).

and was allow'd by his Excellency 15 Soluz per man per Diem over and above the Common allowence; with this they lived Comfortabley and I allways shared with them Morn, Noon, and night; and as I Taught many of the forementioned Gentlemen Some Usefull Branches of the Mathemeticks we had in their Room a well regulated School; I had for some time past assign'd one hour per Day to read a Lession in French[66] but Could not make it break upon my Tongue nor can I See of what great use it can be to an Englishman Since our own is a much more Copious Language; I am far from Depretiating a Tongue of w'ch I know but very little of; but thus far I Can Say that Fountaine[67] one of their own Authors of Considerable Rank Speaking of their Language Says; it is the Scales of the Latin and the rust of other Tongues; but the Earl of Roscomon who undoubtedly understood the French Tongue as well as the English Says in his Essay on Poetry.

> But who did ever in French Authors See
> That Comprehensive English Energie
> The weighty Bulion of one Sterling Line
> Drawn to French wier will thro' whole Pages Shine
> I speak my private but Impartial Sense
> With Freedom and I hope without offence
> But I'll recant when France can show me wit
> As Strong as ours and as Succintly writ[68]

Again

> Can the whole world in Science match our soil
> Have they a Lock, A Newton, or a Boyl,
> Or Dare the greatest Geni of their Age
> With Shakspear or Immortal Ben Ingage
> Content with Natures bounty doe not crave
> The Little which to other Lands she gave

[66] The author of this journal was probably receiving instruction in the French language from Captain William Pote, Jr., "who Could Speak very good French," *post*, p. 93.

[67] Jean de la Fontaine, 1621–1695.

[68] Wentworth Dillon, Earl of Roscommon, "An Essay on Translated Verse," *Poetical Works* (Glasgow, 1749), pp. 19–20.

Nor like The Cock a Barly corn prefir
To all the Jewells which you owe to her
—*Epilogue to Pasquin—A Dramatic Satyr on the Times*[69]

Mon., November the 3d. Came into Prison 6 Prisoners who had ben Taken by the French and Indians on the Frontier of New York they had ben Prisoners at Mount Royal a City on this River Distant about 180 miles from which they Traveled here in 11 days.

Tues. 4th. Saild as per report 6. sail of vessells for Europe or the west Indies[70] Captn. Roberts is Left behind so no hopes of going away this fall nor of sending home any Accounts of us. The French this Day took out of the Prison 7 Free Indians belonging to Zepheniah Pinkham of Nantuchett and Delievered them up into the hands of the Canada Indians.

Wed. 5th. was this Day taken very Ill of a Flux Occationed as I suppose by my Drinking Vast Quantities of bad water.

Fri. 7th. This Day 12 months Left Weybread

Sun. 9th. This Day Died one Davis[71] a Soldier Late of Cape Briton taken at the Island Saint Johns by a Party of French and Indians we are now Ordered to have but 4 hours Liberty to walk in the yard.

III.

[69] More correctly:

"Can the whole world of science match our soil?
Have they a Locke, a Newton, or a Boyle?
Or dare the greatest genius of their stage,
With Shakespeare, or immortal Ben engage?
—Content with nature's bounty, do not crave
The little which to other lands she gave;
Nor like the cock a barleycorn prefer
To all the jewels which you owe to her."

—Henry Fielding, "Pasquin: A Dramatic Satire on the Times," *Works* (10 vols., London, 1871), III, 329.

[70] Pote records the sailing of the ships for France under date of November 5. Pote, p. 101.

[71] Pote and How record the death of John Davis, a soldier of the king's forces, at Louisburg, under date of November 9; Norton, under date of November 10. Pote, p. 102; How, p. 50; Norton, p. 39.

Wed., 12th November. This Day the French took Down the Centry Boxes which were on the outside the Piquets and Erected them within the Yard and Doubled the Guard upon us.

IV. *Thurs.* 13th. Died John Bingham[72] Late cook on board the Ownslow Captn. Wm. Chapman from Maryland for London Taken by a French Transport bound for Quebec ab't 160 Leagues Eastward of the Banks of Newfoundland.

Sun. 16th. Ordered by his Excellency the Governer that we be in or near our bed by 8 at Night and 6. in the morning in order to be Counted by the Officer of the Guard.[73]

V. *Mon.* 17th. Nathan Amis[74] a Soldier late of the Massachusetts Fort; we are now Guarded by the raw Melitia who are.

> Mouths without hands maintained at vast Expence.
> In peace a Charge in war a weak Defence.[75]

Tues. 18th. brought into Prison Robt. Adams late of Sheepsgut Taken by Indians.[76]

VI. *Wed.*, 19th of November. Died Andrew Hans late of New York; The Officers Ordered us this day out of our Room to make it an Infirmary but Countermanded at our request the Sick now Increase very fast thro' want of Provissions and badness of water.

VII. *Thurs.* 20th. This Day Died Jacob Grout[77] late of Albany

[72] The account of Bingham's death agrees with that of Pote and Norton. Pote, p. 102; Norton, p. 39.

[73] Pote records a similar order under date of November 13, Pote, pp. 102–103.

[74] The other journalists also record the death of Nathan Ames or Eames of Marlborough, Massachusetts. Pote, p. 103; Norton, p. 39; How, p. 50.

[75] "And raw in Fields the rude Militia swarms;
Mouths without Hands, maintain'd at vast Expence,
In Peace a Charge, in War a weak Defence;
Stout once a Month they march, a blust'ring Band,
And ever, but in times of Need, at hand."
—Dryden, *Cymon and Iphigenia*, lines 399–403.

[76] Pote records the arrival of Robert Adams of Sheepscot under date of November 18; How, under date of November 19; and Norton says, about November 20. Pote, p. 103; How, p. 50; Norton, p. 39.

[77] Pote records the death of Jacob Grout, a Dutchman taken at Saratoga; Norton, that of John Grote of Schenectady. Pote, p. 103; Norton, p. 39.

in the Province of New York At 4 P M was Maried in the prison one Leonard Liddle a Relation of Mr. James Smiter of Great Yarmouth to Mrs. Sarah Bryant Widdow brought in here by the French and Indians from her house in Casco Bay as mentioned the 1st of October past; Present at the Cerimony Monsieur Comissary and Monsieur Chalet performed by the Reverend John Norton Late Chaplin in the Massachusetts Fort.

The Capt'ns gave the new married pair their Supper afterwards we had a Dance when Monsieur Lorain his Wife and Daughter Joyn'd with us Allamode De France; but I cant see why a man who has his feet allready in the Stocks Should put fetters on his arms.[78]

Fri., November the 21st. Ordered 15 more men into our apartment to make Room for an Infirmary, and as the Devil put it into their heads they have allotted it in the Common Throughfare of the Prison which in General is very Sickly we have now 30 odd Ill of the Same Distemper which raged amongst the French in the Harbour of Jebuctore which is as Catching as the Small Pox; The rooms are now very much Crowded Espicially that which I am in which is but 34 Foot by 18 out of which is a Privy of 6 Foot Square and we are in Number 42 Came into prison John Macane[79] Late of Sheepsgut who brings an Account of 10 Sail of Frenchmen of war and 40. Transport being in Jebuctore.

Tues. 25th. Died John Bradshaw[80] late Steward of Captn. David Donahew; his Distemper was a Consumption he had been in the Infirmary adjoyning to the Nunery he died a Roman Catholick as 'tis said and on the Acc't was buried by the fellows of the Colledge. VIII.

Wed. 26th. Brought the Host to Prison in great Triumph to Administer it to those who were of that perswation or any

[78] Pote and How record the marriage, but Norton, strangely enough, makes no reference to it. Pote, pp. 103–104; How, p. 50.

[79] Pote records the arrival of John Macane, Maccaune, McNear, or McNeer under date of November 9; Norton says about November 20; and How, November 22. Pote, pp. 101–102; Norton, p. 39; and How, p. 51.

[80] The other journalists all record the death of John Bradshaw under date of November 24. Pote, p. 104; Norton, p. 40; How, p. 51.

others they could bring over for the Fathers were got to that pass that they Imposed upon many in their Last Moments by Endeavouring to Unhinge them. As the weather is now very Severe they this Day set up an Iron Stove of 2 1/2 Foot high and 2 Foot Square at Each End which being fill'd with Dry Cleaved wood and by the means of a Long Funell Defusses a great heat over the whole room; we have now one in Every Apartment.

IX. *Fri.* 28th. Died Johnathan Dunham Late of Cape Ann he belonged to Captn. Wm. Pote bound when taken for Anopoliss Royall.[81]

Sat. 29th. Some good Natured Gentlemen in the Town Sent us Prisoners about 6. Bushells of oynions to be Equally Divided amongst us They were a very Gratefull present to us and a great reliefe as we have Little to Subsist on but Poor Salt Beef.

X. *Sun.*, 30th of November. This morning Died Mr. Wm. Bagley[82] late master of the Susanah Sloop taken by the Aurora on the Cape Sable Coast; he have left behind him at Newberry nere Boston a Wife and Family; he died very much regretted by all.

XI. *Tues.*, December the 2d. Died Gratis Vanderwerick June'r[83] late of Saristoga on the Confines of New York his Father and mother and all the Family are here Prisoners.

XII. *Sat.* 6th. Died Pike Gordon late of Scarborough in the Province of the Massachusetts bay New England.[84] Enquired of Mr. Chalet after Captn. Oldham who Informed me that he was well at Meniss and that my Letter of the 12th of Oct'r Past was sent to him about 3 weeks agoe. Monsieur Chalet then gave me a pair of Stockings and a Parcle of Threed and Needles At night the Host was brought to Prison to Administer it to Guyant Brabon.
Memento MG

[81] Pote gives a detailed account of the disposal of the corpse. Pote, p. 105.

[82] Norton and How give November 29 as the date of Bagley's death; Pote, November 30. Norton, p. 40; How, p. 51; Pote, p. 105.

[83] Norton and How record the death of Gratis Vanderveriske or Geret Vanderverick under date of December 1; Pote, under date of December 2. Norton, p. 40; How, p. 51; Pote, p. 105.

[84] Pote, p. 106; Norton, p. 40; How, p. 51.

Sun., 7th December. Died Martha the Daughter of Jacob and Martha Quackinbush Aged about 10 years.[85] XIII.

Wed. 10th. Died Mariam the Wife of Moses Scot[86] now the Frost and Snow is very Severe however we are allow'd to keep a good fire in Each room besides the Stove and for our Amusement we have Cards. we Petioned the Lord Intendant for more victuals but got no redress. XIV.

Sat. 13th. A very Severe Season nay the Hard winter in the year 39 40 is no way to be Compared to the Rigor of this. we Complimented His Excellency and His Lordship the Intendant on the aproaching Season vizt. Christmass but we got nothing from Either of them.[87]

Sun. 14th. Christmass Day NS. A very Sharp Air and Little or nothing to Eate they no Doubt riot in the Town and had they let us have Teasted of their Bounty in this Rigorous Season it had been but Christian Charity Especially at this Time.

Mon., 15th of December. Died John Boon[88] belonging to the John Snow of Dartmouth in Compty of Devon Captn. Robert David Roberts The harships he went thro in Coming up the River St. Laurance in the Shallops in Some Measure hastned his End. XV.

Wed. 17th. Died Mary the Wife of Mr. David Woodall[89] She has left him here with 2 Small Children and a Daughter of about 19 years Old is now in the hands of the Indians. XVI.

Sun. 21st. New Year's Day NS. very severe Frost Monsieur Lorain our Keeper made a present to the Capt'ns Pris-

[85] How gives the age of the child as ten; Pote, as twelve. How, p. 51; Pote, p. 106; Norton, p. 41.

[86] The other journalists give December 11 as the date of Meriam Scott's death. Pote, p. 106; Norton, p. 41; How, p. 51.

[87] Pote and others in the officers' room wrote to the intendant to wish him a happy and merry Christmas, and received a keg containing three gallons of claret. Pote, pp. 106–107.

[88] Norton and How give December 15 as the date of Boon's death; Pote, December 16. Norton, p. 41; How, p. 51; Pote, p. 107.

[89] The other journalists all give December 18 as the date of the death of Mary Woodwell of New Hopkinton on the Merrimac River. Pote, p. 107; Norton, p. 41; How, p. 51.

oners a Large Dish of Pyes[90] of which according to Custom I took part Our allowence is now 1/4 lb of salt pork, 1/4 of a pint of Pease; per man per Diem or 1/2 lb of Salt Beef; per Diem; or 3 oz of fish 1 1/2 Spoonfull oyl and 3 Spoonfulls of vinigar per man per Diem with the usal allowence of 1 lb of very good bread; we have a Hogshead of Beer amongst about 35 of us brought to us Every Tuesday; we have a small Quantity of Tobacko per man the Begining of Every month; we are Likewise Shaved by a Barber sent to us Every Thursday.

XVII. *Tues.* 23d. Died Rebecka the Wife of Mr. Jno. Perry[91] we are now in great want of water the Intensity of the frost the Springs are Lock'd up and are oblidged to Boyl our Victuals in Snow water.

Thurs. 25th. Christmass Day OS; for Breakfast bread; for Diner 1/4 lb of Pork and 1/4 Pint of Pease at night the Capt'ns assigned over their Supper to the Prisoners in my appartment.[92]

XVIII. *Fri.* 26th. Died Wm. Daly,[93] Enquired of Monsieur Chalet after Captn. Oldham but had no just account that may be Depended upon heard the Prison Distemper is at Length got into Town; who pitys them not I.[94]

XIX. *Fri.*, January the 2d. Died Thomas Atkinson[95] a Native of Liverpool in Lancastershire he was Taken with Captn. James Swindle from Guinia for Jamaica; the Disceased was an able Sturdy Fellow and more Likely to Live then any one here.

[90] Pote records that M. Lorain sent the officers two bottles of brandy and some mutton pies. Pote, p. 107.

[91] All four journalists record the death of Rebecca Perry on December 23. Norton, who was captured with her, makes the most detailed entry. Pote, p. 107; Norton, p. 41; How, p. 52.

[92] The officers fared somewhat better, receiving several gallons of brandy from a gentleman in the town. Pote, p. 108.

[93] All four journalists record the death of Wiliam Daly or Daily or Dayly of New York under date of December 26. Pote, p. 108; Norton, p. 41; How, p. 52.

[94] "not I," seems to have been added by another hand.

[95] Pote and Norton also record his death under date of January 2. Pote, p. 108; Norton, p. 42.

Sat. 3d. Died Johnathan Hogardon[96] Late of Saristoga in the Province of New York. XX.

Sat., January 3d. Died of the Prison Distemper Joset Lorain Pereaux[97] the Eldest Daughter of Monsieur Lorain our Keeper aged about 15 years after Lingering 8 Days She was regretted by all or most of the Prisoners as being a faith-full friend to the English as far as was in her power; her Mother and Sister are now Dangerously Ill of the same Distemper; heard Father Chaveleze have ben given over by the Doctors in Town these 2 Days past he Caught the Prison Distemper by his frequent Visits to the Sick; we have now in the prison 27 Sick and 239 in pretty good health; 20 are allready Dead; 16 were Sent away in the fall of the year, and 2. run away in all 277.

Sun. 4th. was Buried the Daughter as above; the procession was headed by a personage w'ch I take to be a Lady Abbys Dressed in a Long black Gown, and before her and in her hands She Held a Crusifix on a Staff About 7 Foot Long; On the Left side of her went the Priest in his Gown. Next after him went 4 Youths in red Cowles by pairs, then 4 youths in white Cowles by pairs; After them followed the Corps in a white Coffin caried underhand by 6 Beares, then followed the People by pairs to the Number of 200.[98]

Mon. 5th. Died the Rever'd Father Chaveleze[99] he was a man of Great Learning and the Head of the Order of St. Francis and about 14 Days agoe brought his reasons in writing in Defence of the Roman Catholick Religeon prefirable to that of the Protestants; To the Rev'd John Norton; here we miss'd a paper war heard the prison Destemper rages in the Town by means of the Melitia who are our Guard by night.

Wed. 7th. Heard by Monsieur Chalet that Captn. Old-

[96] All four journalists record the death of Jonathan Harthan, Hogadon, or Hogadorn of Albany under date of January 3. Pote, pp. 108–109; Norton, p. 42; How, p. 52.

[97] Norton gives January 4 as the date of Joset Lorain's death. Norton, p. 42.

[98] Pote also records the burial of Joset Lorain, Pote, p. 109.

[99] Pote, p. 109.

ham was well at Meniss; at night the Room above the Captains took fier but timely Extinguished; the weather is now more Modurate the French are Employ'd in Throwing the Snow over the Piquets which is now 9 foot Deep.[100]

Mon., January the 12th. The French have ben this Week past in Rearing up an Hospital remote from the Prison and Town for the Sick;[101] for Since the Death of Monsieur Lorains Daughter and Father Chaveleze And a great many being Ill in the Town they have at Length bethought them selves the Distemper is Catching therefore they have this Day Carried out of the Prison all the Sick to the Number of 20 Amongst whom was William Galbreth our late Boatswain; I Dare Say there was Self preservation in this Otherwise it had not ben Done Notwithstanding all our former Remonstances.

XXI. *Tues.* 13th. Died Francis Andrews[102] Late of Cape Ann aged 50. years; he went to the Infirmary but yesterday.

XXII. *Thurs.* 15th. Died Jacob Bagley[103] Brother to Wm. Deceased vide Sun. 30th of November, he was Taken Ill but Yesterday morning and Caried to the Infirmary the Last Night.

XXIII. *Sat.* 17th. Died Guyant Brubbon[104] late Carpenter of Captn. Wm. Chapman he was an Inhabitant of Maryland he died as is Said a Roman Catholick and on that account was Decently Buried; three men were this Day Caried to the Infirmary vizt. Thos. Cragg; Michael Dogan, Nathaniel Hitchcock.

Mon., *Tues.*, *Wed.* Employ'd these 3 Days in white wash-

[100] The other journalists do not mention this incident.

[101] The other journalists also record the construction of a hospital and the removal of the sick. Pote, p. 109; Norton, p. 42; How, p. 52.

[102] According to Norton and How, Francis or Phineas Andrews of Cape Ann died on the night of January 12; according to Pote, on January 13. Only the author of this journal gives his age. Norton, p. 42; How, p. 52; Pote, p. 109.

[103] All four journalists record the death of Jacob Bagley on January 15. Pote, pp. 109–110; Norton, p. 42; How, p. 52.

[104] All four journalists record the death of Giat or Guy or Guyant or Guyart Braban or Braband or Brabbon or Brubbon of Maryland on January 17. Pote, p. 110; Norton, p. 42; How, p. 52.

ing Each room in the Prison and after that we burnt Vinigar and Rozin to Purifie the Rooms.[105]

Thurs. 22d. Died Samuel Lovet[106] a native of new England; we have now no water but what is brought to us in Casks and of that God knows we have but little. XXIIII.

Thurs. 29th. Hard gale of wind a ESE; at night Saw a house in the NW't End of the Town take fire.[107]

Tues., Feb'ry the 3d. Shrovetuesday NS a Great Holiday; gave to us about 1/8 of Rum per man; NB at night wett within our Walls.[108]

Wed., Feb'ry 4th. Ashwednessday NS. heads ach this morning Therefore great repentance for last nights work and in Consequence of that a Through Reformation resolved on by those whom I should be glad to see it in.[109]

Tues. 10th. Tolarable good weather over head and very hard Frost. Saw many Sledges Drawn by horses come over the NW't arm of the River with wood to burn This Day Died a Child of Moses Scot Aged 2 years;[110] its Mother Died the 10th of November past. XXV.

Wed. 11th. The Town Majore came to Visit us and upon Complaint made he Ordered 6 persons to be removed out of our Room he likewise Ordered us 6 hours Liberty in the yard vizt. 3 hours in the forenoon and 3 in the afternoon; heard just now that Wm. Gilbreth our Late Boatswain was Dead; he has left behind him a Wife in London great with Child, I doubt he had not fair play for his Life, but time may Discover it.[111] XXVI.

[105] Pote records the white-washing of the officers' quarters under date of January 21. Pote, p. 110.

[106] The other journalists record the death of Samuel Lovet under date of January 23. Pote, p. 110; Norton, p. 43; How, p. 52.

[107] This incident is not referred to in the other journals.

[108] Not referred to in the other journals.

[109] Not entered elsewhere.

[110] Pote and How record the death of Moses Scott, Jr., on February 10; Norton, on February 11. Pote, pp. 110–111; How, p. 52; Norton, p. 43.

[111] How gives February 10 as the date of the death of William Galbaoth or Garwass or Gilbreth; Norton and Pote, February 11. According to Pote, on his deathbed, he blamed another prisoner for his death. How, p. 52; Norton, p. 43; Pote, p. 111.

Thurs., 12th Feb'ry. A modurate Thaw; The French this Day caried into Town one Susan Phillips in Order for her Lying in there, She having by her Industery got her Belly up.[112]

Sun. 15th. Came into Prison from Mount Royall 7 men who had ben Taken on the Borders of New England last June, they gave us an Account that 2. Prisoners had made their Escape from Mount Royall last fall and was so Daring as to kill and scalp 2 Indian paposes; and that a party of our Indian Mohauks had taken Prisoners to the Number of 15 and burnt their houses in a French Villa near Crown point and got Clear off with their Booty.[113]

Tues. 17th. The French took out of prison a Young Child of Miss Ann Butchers al's Sheepheard al's Salter al's Mahanah etc. allso the French Caried into Town James Prince a Lad of about 14 Years Old to Continue with them.[114]

XXVII. *Wed.*, Feb'ry 18th. Died Richard Bennet;[115] The French took into Town to Nurse an Infant of John and Mary Smead the Mother being caried to the Infirmary 3 Days agoe; they took likewise a 2d Child of Miss Ann Butchers; this is Doing of business, for now She'l be at Leisure to get more.

XXVIII. *Wed.* 25th. Died Michael Dogan[116] he was Caried to the Infirmary Last night.

Fri., March the 6th. Severe Sharp air and Hail; came from the Infirmary Thos. Cragg the Nephew of Mr. Thos. Cragg a silk weaver near Catherine Wheel Ally Spittlefields; who, brought an ac't that Wm. Gilbreth Declared to him in his Last moments that the Bruises and hurts he rec'd from Jacob Nash and James Holms was the cause of his Death; the affair hapned the 1st of January OS; he kept his bed and

[112] The other journalists do not mention this incident.

[113] Pote, pp. 111–112; How, p. 53.

[114] Under this date Pote records that James Price, a lad taken at Saratoga, was taken from the prison to live with M. de Tonancour (Tonnancourt), the priest. Pote, p. 112.

[115] The other journalists record the death of Richard Bennet or Bennit under date of February 23. Pote, p. 112; Norton, p. 43; How, p. 53.

[116] Norton records the death of Michael Dogan or Dugan or Dugon, a sixty-year-old Irishman taken with Captain Salter, on February 24; Pote and How, on February 25. Norton, p. 43; Pote, p. 112; How, p. 53.

Lingered till the 12th when he was Sent to the Infirmary; the 11th of Feb'ry he Died; NB Holms and Nash lives in Shore Ditch London.[117]

Sun., March the 8th. My Natual Day Monsieur Chalet gave me a Bill of 6 Livers to buy a Cap with.

Wed. 11th. Came to visit us 2 French Gentle'n from whom we had an Account of an Affair at Meniss about 2 months past vizt. that about 550 men at arm within 2 vessells arived in Meniss Bason in Order to bring under the French there to a more just Observance of the Nutrality they brought with them Timber ready framed for a Block House but they never Erected it but were Suprised in the Night by about 500 French and Indians when 133 were Kill'd and 417 taken 367 of which were sent to Anopoliss with a Previso that Such a Number Should be returnd from Boston; 50 they kept as Pledges for the performance of the Above; they tell us in all this fray they Lost but 2. French men and 3 Indians; but I think this wants farther Confirmation.[118]

The French this Day took away our allowence of Fish and gave us in the Lieu of it very Ordinary Salt Beef; In this we fall according to the old English addage vizt. Out of the Frying pan into the fire; for the one gave us the Itch, and the other is likely to Create the Scurvy.

Sat., 14th March. Came to the Prison two Genteelmen and 2 Ladies and with them the Daughter of Mr. Jacob Quackingbush and Martha his wife which Girl they took out of this prison Some time agoe from her Parents; She's about 9 years Old and Drest Allamode De France they bring her at times to See her Parents, She talks very good French which her parents doe not understand nor will they Suffer her to Speake to them Either in English or Dutch.[119]

Mon. 16th. Mr. John Boydle was sent for out of Prison

[117] The other journalists do not mention this incident.

[118] Pote records the visit under date of March 10; Norton knew of the French expedition March 5. Pote, p. 113; Norton, pp. 43–44.

[119] This entry is evidently copied from that made by Pote under date of March 16. Pote, pp. 113–114.

by his Excellency the Governer; to the Counsell Chamber in Order to Read some Letters and papers which they had Seized at Meniss in that Action at Meniss as Mentioned the 11th Past; while the Officers were busie in Looking over the papers for Mr. Boydle to read he cast his Eye on some of His Majesties Orders and Instructions to the Governers of the American Collonies for raising men for the Intire reduction of all Canada the which being Observed by his Excellency he Said, you see young Gentleman your Countrymen are coming, the which Mr. Boydle answered in the affirmative; His Excellency returnd again in a Haughty Tone; Let them come when they will I am ready for 'em.[120]

XXVIIII. *Tues.* 17th. Wet within our walls in Honour of St. Patrick, and as usal went together by the Ears Concerning that Saints Wars with the Woolf Dogs;[121] This Day Died James Magraw;[122] we have now nothing to Eate but Salt Beef and Pease and of that god knows but very Little; A Modurate Thaw.

Thurs., 19th March. Vissited by Monsieur Morang an Officer who Says, the Prisoners left at Meniss Last fall were Sent away to Europe; I hope Captn. Oldham went with them; At Night came in here a man and a woman Prisoners; the Latter Disordered in her mind on Acc't as is Said of the Indians Siezing and Killing her Child.

Fri. 20th. Good Fryday, can now See the ground in many spots free of snow.

XXX. *Sat.* 21st. Died Mr. John Fort late of new York and XXXI. Samuel Goodman late of New England, Each Batcholars aged about 50 years.[123]

Wed. 25th. Our Ladys Day. fine weather, Saw the water

[120] Boydle was taken with the *Albany*. The other journalists do not mention this incident.

[121] Pote records that the Irish received brandy from the intendant with which to celebrate the feast of St. Patrick. Pote, p. 114.

[122] Norton and How record the death of James or Thomas Magra, Magraw, Megraw, or Margra, an Irishman taken in the *Albany*, under date of March 18; Pote, under date of March 20. Norton, p. 44; How, p. 53; Pote, p. 166.

[123] Norton records the death of John Fort and Samuel Goodman under date of March 21; Pote and How, under date of March 22. Norton, p. 44; Pote, pp. 114–115; How, p. 53.

above the Ice in the NW't arm of the River, the Snow now goes away a great pace; Monsieur Comissary sent me this Day a Quire of writing paper and some Threed According to promise.

Sun., 29th March. Died Mary the wife of Mr. John Smead late of the Massachusetts Fort, She has Left him here with 4 Small Children;[124] Came into prison once more Miss Susan Bolosin[125] who had ben Caried out October last very Ill and have ben in Town in Quality of a Servant e're since now fornication will goe on again. [XXXII.]

Mon. 30th. This Day Twelvemonth left England, but when am like to see it again God Only knows; tho' the Town Major gave us some Encouragement but he is So much of a Scoundrell we Can't Depend on him.

Sat., Aprill the 4th. This Day Twelvemonths was unfortunately Taken by the Aurora and Castor; the Ice in the River broke in many places.

Mon. 6th. The Snow is gone for the far greater part and the River Intirely Open Fine weather; now the French begin to Expect the Arival of Ships from France.

Tues., 7th Aprill. The Sickness begins to Rage again People going dayly to the Infirmary the far greater part are now Taken with a Slow Nerverous Fever Amongst which is Leonard Liddle who Maried here as mentioned the 20th of November past; he could by no means Prevail on the Governer to suffer his Wife to attend him at the Infirmary Nor will his Excellency Suffer anyone to vissit the Sick in the Infirmary not so much as to let them into their affairs at home nor to make a will tho Earnestly Petitioned.

Wed., Aprill the 8th. Died John the Son of John and the Late Mary Smead[126] Likewise Phillip Coffling[127] both of the Massachusets bay New England. XXXIII. XXXIIII.

[124] How records the death of Mary Smead or Smeed under date of March 28; Pote and Norton, under date of March 29. How, p. 53; Pote, p. 115; Norton, p. 44.

[125] Pote records the return of Susan or Susanah Boilison or Bolosin under date of March 30. Pote, p. 115.

[126] Norton records the death of John Smead or Smeed, Jr., under date of April 7, 1747; Pote and How, under date of April 8. Norton, p. 44; Pote, p. 116; How, p. 53.

[127] How records the death of Philip Scaffield of Pennsylvania under date of

XXXV. *Fri.* 10th. This Day Died Antonia a native of Portugal,
XXXVI. Likewise Mr. James Jordan Late Master of the Breze Schooner.[128] Came into Prison again Susan Phillips[129] who went into Town to Lye in as Mentioned the 12th of February past She brought in with her a Female Child 3 weeks Old whom the French Soldiers by Order of the Serjant forc'd from its mother and gave it to a French woman who had waited for it by Order of the Governer as is Supposed The Frenchwoman Caried it into Town and left the Mother here in the Prison Raving and Distracted; but I am very much Misstaken if She does not soon forget it in Endeavouring to get Another. Thos. Davis Aprentice to Captn. Oldham was Sent to the Infirmary very Ill; there are now 27 gone to the Infirmary.

XXXVII. *Mon.* 13th. Died Amis Prat[130] late of the Massachusetts Fort New England Mrs. Sarah Liddle has at Length Prevailed on the Governer to attend her Husband now he is in a fare way of Recovering but She is very Ill her Self and must have gone to the Infirmary had not her Husband ben there.[131]

XXXVIII. *Tues.*, Aprill the 14th. Died this Day Mr. Timothy Cummins[132] taken by the Indians on the Frontier of New England and brought into Canada by them to an Indian Town; when the Christian Preist Saw him he made Signs

---

April 7; Norton and Pote, under date of April 8. How, p. 53; Norton, p. 44; Pote, p. 116.

[128] How records the death of Captain James Jordan of the schooner *Breeze* and his man, Antonio, a Portuguese, under date of April 9; Pote and Norton, under date of April 10. How, p. 53; Pote, p. 116; Norton, p. 44.

[129] Pote also chronicles the return of Susan or Susanah Phillips. Pote, pp. 116–117.

[130] Norton and How chronicle the death of Amos Pratt of Shrewsbury, Massachusetts, under date of April 12; Pote, under date of April 13. Norton, p. 44; How, p. 53; Pote, p. 117.

[131] Pote wrote the petition of Mrs. Sarah Liddle to the governor, April 12. Pote, p. 117.

[132] Norton and Pote record the death of Timothy Commins or Cummings under date of April 13; How, under date of April 14. Norton, p. 45; Pote, p. 117; How, p. 53.

to him to hide himself under the Communion Table which he did and by that means got Clear of the Indians; As soon as he Saw the Indians were gone and the Coast Clear he got from under the Table and began to Examine the Contents above and finding amongst other things Some Consicreated Brass Meddles he made bold to Seize them Imagining them to be Gold; he brought them to Prison with him and was in great perplexity of mind what to doe with them till the affair was blown.

Thurs. 16th. Saw Jno. Coron our Late Doctor in the Adventeure he was walking in the Garden belonging to the Jesuits oposite our Prison The French very busie in making Facine Baskets; No Ships as yet arrived from Old France they are now Aprehensive The English will pay them a visit hauld the new 20 Gun Ship off the Ground and are Got to work upon her but they make no Scruple to let us know they have no rigging for her the English having Siezed it 3 Times in coming from Old France.[133]

Fri. 17th. Died Mr. John Dill[134] late of Nantaskett near Boston; Samuell Vahghan[135] late of Plymouth New England Joseph Dennen[136] late Master of the Tryall Scooner and Samuell Evens[137] Late of the Massachusetts Fort; all of them under a Strong Suspition of Pyson by a Draught given them and 13 more for the Itch. who the Devil but this Blundering Deaths Harbinger would have prescrib'd an Internal Medicine (Except Sulpher) for this Distemper;

XXXIX.
XL.
XLI.
XLII.

[133] Under date of April 14 Pote records that the hull of a man-of-war, twenty guns, was hauled out of a creek. Pote, p. 117.

[134] Norton records the death of John Dill of Nantasket or Hull under date of April 16; Pote and How, under date of April 17. Norton, p. 45; Pote, p. 117; How, p. 53.

[135] The other journalists record the death of Samuel Vahghan, Vaughn, Vaughan, or Venhon of Plymouth under date of April 18. Norton, p. 45; Pote, p. 118; How, p. 54.

[136] Pote records the death of Joseph Denen, Denning, or Denox of Cape Ann, master of the schooner *Trial*, under date of April 26; Norton and How, under date of April 27. Pote, p. 118; Norton, p. 45; How, p. 54.

[137] Norton records the death of Samuel Evans or Evens of Newbury, Massachusetts, under date of April 17; Pote, under date of April 27; and How, under date of April 28. Norton, p. 45; Pote, p. 122; How, p. 54.

well may our Laws Exclude Doctors from Serving as Juries in Cases of Life and Death when they Dally in this manner with the Lives of their fellow Creatures.

On Doctor Breaux who Murdered 4 Persons with a Doze for the Itch, and basely Neglected my worthy Friend Captn. Wm. Chapman.

Base Sordid Monster, Mercanary Slave,
Thou Church yard Pimpe, thou pander to the Grave,
Deaths Busie Factor, Son of Desolation,
Thy Country's Curse, and grevience of a Nation.
How Shall I Trace the, or how Shall I begin,
To Lash a villain Crusted o're with Sin,
Sure in Some Powder mill, that hotbrained Sot,
Thy Father, in the Dog Days the begot,
And Some She Bear in Horid woods alone,
Suckled the young, and Nursed the for her own;
Hence thy Souer Brutal Temper first began,
The Beast was thinly Platted by the man.
Oh had'st thou Lived in that Curst Tyrants reign,
By whose Command the Inocents were Slain,
Herod might then have Spared his men the Pains,
At Bethlem to beate out the Childrens brains,
Thy Draughts alone the Fatal work had done,
And soon Dispatched them Every mothers Son.
Why with good Laws vain volumss doe we fill,
When such as thou has't Previlidge to Kill;
Mean Lousy Fellons for Less Crimes by far
Have oft recieved the sentence at the Bar
In the Face of Day thou Robs't us of our health
And yet art never Questioned for the Stealth
But Lawyers, Hangmen, Midwifes, Doctors Bill
All by a Licenced way of Murder Kill
May none Seek help from thy D—d remedies
But Senseless Fools that health and fame Dispise
And sots on whom each Canting fool Imposes
And Carted Bawds and Strumpets without Noses
Be the most Scorned Jack pudding of the Pack
And Turn Toad Eater to Some other Quack
But if thou Needs must pick up Nasty pence
Turn Farrier in thy own Defence
Cure Hoggs of Measels vissit Labouring Swine
And order Dozes for thy Neighbors Kine
Reign Over beasts from Bersheba to Dan
But never Never Meddle more with man

May Pox and Gout and all the attending Ills
Which thou so Oft have Treatned in thy Bills
Light fast on the and make the Smart
And own thy Self a Blockhead in thy Art
Then may you Stupid and relentless Die
And Heaven its Self forgive no more then I
And so be D—d of mere Necessity.[138]

Sun., 19th Aprill. Rain all Day Wind ENE no Ships as yet arived from old France The French begin now to look about 'em as fearing now of being Invested on both Sides by a Fleet and army. Came into Prison again Miss Ann Butcher without her Children the French having taken them away from her to keep within the Town now fornication is like to be Caried on again as usul.

Sun. 26th. The week past fine weather; Came back from the Hospital Thos. Davis Aprentice to Captn. Oldham; Jno. Martin one of our Crew Sent away to the Hospital This Day came into prison 3 men taken at Saristogua allso Mr. Williamson[139] Taken at his house at Sheepsgut on the Frontier of New England by a Party of Indians the 14 ult who bring us Sundrey accounts.

1st. That Admiral Waren[140] went to Europe last fall and in Consiquence of that he Dispatch'd two Paquets one to the Governer of New York, the other to the Governer of Boston which paquects arived 14 Days before he was Taken from whence we Learned Admiral waren had Desired the Land forces might be in readiness for that he was Coming with 18 Sail of the Line and Expected to arive in America Some time in May in Order for the Intire reduction of all Canada.

2dly. That the Pretender[141] who made Such noize and

[138] Unidentified. Possibly the author of the journal is improvising.

[139] On Jonathan Williamson of Sheepscot, see Pote, pp. 118–119; D. Q. Cushman, *The History of Ancient Sheepscot and Newcastle* (Bath, 1882), p. 130; W. D. Williamson, *The History of the State of Maine* (Hallowell, 1839), pp. 245, 252; *New York Colonial Documents*, X., 95, 96.

[140] Admiral Peter Warren, who commanded the fleet that took Louisburg.

[141] Charles Edward, the Young Pretender, who was defeated at Culloden Moor, near Inverness, Scotland, April 16, 1746.

Bustle in Scotland Disappear'd like will of the Whisp or the Ignus Fatuus.[142]

3dly. That our Affairs on the Continent of Europe went on with Tolorable Success and that Admiral Martin[143] had drove all before him on the Coast of Old France in Bombarding Some places and Taking others; this in Some Measure Confirms what we had from 2 Gentlemen of France some time agoe Namely that our fources had taken the Town of St. Martins on the Isle De Roy[144] in the Bay of Biscay.

4thly. That a very large fleet of the line with Store Ships etc. arived in Jebuctore from Old France late in the fall of the year under the Command of a General Officer, he thinks it was the Marquis De Avilla he had Possitive orders to take Anopoliss Royall and then to reduce all New England; A very Pretty Errand but a grevious Sickness raged amongst the Fleet while in Jebuctore wether Caught at Sea or Contracted in that wild Uncultivated Desart is Uncertain however it raged to that degree that with the Small Pox and an Inflamatory Fever it Sweept off upwards of 3000 of them and by that means Intirely frusterated their Designs the General Officer wether Disordered in his head by the Small Pox or Dispairing of Carrying his point fell upon his own Sword and left them in the Lurch The next under him took upon him the Command but he took a Doze and Genteely Slip'd asside and bad them all good Night and the next morn he was gathered to his brethren The 3d Succeeded in the Command and hearing by an English Sloop which they had then taken, that a Powerfull Fleet was coming to pay him a Visit he in great Hurry and Confusion took up his Anchors and run out to Sea Design'd as is Said for the west Indies but a Voiolent Storm oretook him on the American Coast and its Generally concluded the greater part went to the bottom however our Cruizers pick'd up two of them, one

[142] *Ignis fatuus.*

[143] Admiral William Martin.

[144] St. Martin de Ré.

they caried into Boston the other into Cape Briton[145] I cannot Conclude this affair without making this remark vizt. that this Jebuctore is the very place where the French So Basely betray'd their faith and honour to us last August when Instead of Sending us to Boston agreeable to their most Solemn promise Delivered us over to worse then Savages an Army of Canadans wether we are come where when he Tempted Christ the Devil put his Thumb.

5thly and lastly. That the affair at Meniss as mentioned the 11th of March past[146] was in truth this, that about 550 men under the Command of Collonel Noble[147] and Capt'ns Gorem,[148] Noble[149] and How;[150] that for the better bringing under the French there to a more just Observance of the Nutrallity granted them the Above Officers and men billeted them Selves at the Houses of these Nuter French when those Rascals betray'd them to an Army of Canadians and Indians[151] who came upon them in the night and basely Murdered them in their beds to the Number of 73; amongst whom was the Brave Collonel Noble This is the great Exploit

[145] Planning to retake Louisburg and Nova Scotia and to attack Boston, in the summer of 1746 the French government sent a squadron of ninety-seven sail commanded by Nicolas de la Rochefoucauld, Duc d'Anville, to America. Misfortune dogged the footsteps of the enterprise. Meeting with contrary winds, the Duc d'Anville arrived at Chebucto with only slightly more than half of the fleet, September 13–15. On September 20 the leader died of apoplexy. On October 1, while ill, Vice-Admiral d'Estournel committed suicide. On October 12, Jacques Pierre de Taffanel, Marquis de la Jonquière, third in command, sailed out of the harbor and abandoned the undertaking. R. Rolt, *An Impartial Representation of the Conduct of the Several Powers of Europe Engaged in the Late General War* (4 vols., London, 1749–50), IV., 346–352; "Law Papers," Connecticut Historical Society *Collections*, XIII., 301–302; J. B. Brebner, *New England's Outpost* (New York, 1927), pp. 115–116.

[146] *Ante*, p. 45.

[147] Lieutenant-Colonel Arthur Noble.

[148] Captain John Gorham.

[149] Probably Francis Noble.

[150] Probably Edward Howe.

[151] Under the command of Jean Baptiste Nicholas Roch de Ramezay. Pote, p. 121.

the French have Magnified so much and so much Exulted in.[152]

> But Rogues Mistaking Scandal to be fame
> Deem that their Honour others think their Shame[153]

Tues., Aprill the 28th. About 7. in the Morn a fire broke out in our prison house,[154] how or by what means is Uncertain; it was first Discovered on the very ridge of the Roof, which was of Chingles, they being very Dry and the wind blowing fresh it Soon Spread its Self over the whole Roof, and put those who were in the upper Rooms in great Danger of their lives; Some of them Staid so long in the Garrets to save their beding etc., that the fire broke in upon them e're they left their appartments. The Old France Soldiers who before had been Our guard unlocked our Rooms and let us into the Area; I am willing to believe it was by Order of their Officer. The Area or yard was piquetted round, its width was about 30 foot, its length was Equal to the length of the House, here we remained to the Number of 207 Prisoners men, women, and Children, while our Prison House was all on Flames This with the Drums beating to Arms, and the Alarum bell Soon raised the Town,

> And raw in Arms,
> The rude Melitia Swarms.[155]

There was a great many officers and Gentlemen came not to assist at the fire but to keep us within bounds as Appeared by their Drawn Rapiers There was likewise Some Fryers from A Neighbouring Convent with whom and the forementioned

[152] At this point Pote and the author of this journal were undoubtedly exchanging notes. Pote's entry was probably copied from that in this journal, for both writers refer to a previous entry of March 11, although Pote had entered the report of the Minas affair under date of March 10! For a French account of this expedition, see *New York Colonial Documents*, X., 91–92.

[153] Unidentified.

[154] Norton, Pote, and How mention the fire. Pote is obviously following this journal. Norton, pp. 45–46; Pote, pp. 122–125; How, p. 54.

[155] *Ante*, note 75.

Gentlemen was a Contest for Some time Concerning us as wether we Should remain in the prison Yard while the flames were Spreading and the Stones of the walls of the prison House so soon as they grew hot would burst and doe us Incrediable Damage but one good Natured preist at the head of the Order of St. Francis who Disdained to Contend with men void of Humanity took up a hatchet and soon made Locks, bolts, and Staples fly and Imediately Set open the Great gates And with an Audiable voice Cry'd March Englishmen which we did with our beds, blankets, and Egyptian Cattle at our backs through the Melitia who Conducted us into an Open Court before the Governers Palace where we Continued with our beds, Blankets etc. till his Lordship had Consulted with his Officers what to doe with us, the result of which was that for the Present we Should be Lodged in the Primative Houses of Canada Al's Tents in the form but not half so good as Our English Bulk heeds which they Imediately Set to work to build for us against Night Here we remaind in the Governers yard from About 9 in the morning till night During which time we heard many Pretty turns of Canada Railery, Some though but very few pitied us; others and the far greater part Said that when the fire broke out why did not the Officers Confine us in our respective Rooms and Fry us in the fire of our Kindling; A very Christian like thought this; but what Else can be Expected of the Canadians, when

Hither from all parts of France they come
The Spew and Vomit of their Jayls at home.[156]

Add to this His Majesty of France allows About 10£ Sterling to any one who will Marry with the Indians, this no Doubt produces a hopefull Issue unknown to Dampier,[157] Mourdant[158] or any of their Antient Travelers but 'twas our Missfortune to find them. At noon they regaled us with a

[156] Unidentified.

[157] Probably William Dampier, 1652–1715, freebooter, explorer, and author, who published numerous accounts of his travels.

[158] Probably Robert Morden, author of *Geography Rectified* (various editions).

piece of bread per man and Adams Ale; Indeed about 10 Capt'ns had a Dish sent us from the palace of Horse beans Boyled but as black they were as a Negroes Arse, they had likewise Some butter or rather Sour Cream; a Thousand times better I have Smear'd Top masts with. About 4 P M we being very Cold we had Each man a Dram of Good Brandy gave us when we was Ordered to give way for the Melitia To be Drawn up before us; but Such a Sight of Tatterdemolians my Eyes never beheld; And when they came to Exercise the Farce Still grows more Stronger for they Stood

> Considering wether the right or left Shoulder
> Was the most proper to Cary the Arms of a Souldier
> And after an hour was Spent and near
> To Learn right from Left and the front from the rear
> And often Questioning how and which way
> They were drawn up at last into battle array[159]

and off they march'd in order to Conduct us to our Rendezvous, which was about 1/4 mile out of the Town under an Old wall where we had 2 Long Tents built up for us and in they Drove us alltogether without any Distinction of Age, Sex or Condition; Those who were so fortunate as to save their Beds, Blankets etc. laid down upon them So, So; those who had neither was Oblidged to Pigg in heads and Tails like Smithfield Cattle in their Penns, but every one Superless.

Wed., Aprill the 29th.[160] Morning fair but Night past Severely Cold, our water within our Tents covered with Ice; and as before we had ben Used to Stove Rooms Our Present Situation did not sit easy upon us and as if the Devil rode Post hast upon Our Misfortunes nothing to eate or Drink but bread and water however in the Afternoon they brought in beds and blankets in Lieu of those that were burnt Yesterday they set to work to Piquet the Camp round and Erected 2 Centry Boxes on 2. Eminences which

[159] Unidentified.

[160] Under this date Pote makes an almost identical entry. Pote, p. 125.

Overloock'd our Camp; we have now larger Liberty, I believe our Camp Contain 1/4. of an Acre of Ground in which we have Liberty to walk from Morn till Night; they likewise began to build a Guard house without the Camp, the frame of which was taken from an Hill about 1/4 mile from us Our Guard now Consists of 50 men And Officers who Day and night are upon Duty; they this Day took away the Old France Souldiers who had all along ben Our Guard, which causes amongst us some Matter of Speculation.

Thurs., 30th April. Fine weather; Delivered out more Beds and blankets and gave us Salt Beef as usal but such stuff I never Saw Indeed the fresh Beef we before was Served with was better because not So Liable to Create the Scurvy amongst us but it look'd very much like Horse flesh I Cannot Say it was really such, but I verily believe we have Eaten the Same Ox who the Day before brought us in wood to burn in our Prison house.

How did the Toiling Ox his death Deserve
A downright Simple Drudge and born to Serve
O Tyrant with what Justice canst thou hope
The promise of the year a Plentious Crop
When thou Destroyest thy Labouring Sire who Till'd
And Plow'd w'th Pains thy Else Ungratefull field
From his yet Reeking neck to beare the Yoke
That neck with which the Surly clods he broke
And to the Hatchet yield thy Husbandman
Who finished Autum and the Spring began
—*vide Ovids Metamophosis Lib'm 16th*[161]

[161] More correctly:

"How did the toiling ox his death deserve,
A downright simple drudge, and born to serve?
O tyrant! with what justice canst thou hope
The promise of the year, a plenteous crop;
When thou destroy'st thy lab'ring steer, who till'd,
And plough'd with pains, thy else ungrateful field?
From his yet reeking neck, to draw the yoke,
That neck, with which the surly clods he broke;
And to the hatchet yield thy husbandman,
Who finish'd autumn, and the spring began!"
—Dryden, *Ovid's Metamorphoses*, 15th Book, lines 176–185.

In the afternoon a great many people came to see us in our new Encampment which they were not permitted to doe while we remain'd in the prison House but they were not Suffered to come nigh the Piquets, there was Indeed Some Ladies who came within Our Camp with their Husbands or relations who were Officers[162] but I could not Discover not even in those of the Femanine Gender any thing that look'd like Comisaration or Pity but the Contrary.

> O Mortals blind to fate, you little know
> To bear high fortune or Endure the Low
> The Time may be your Own when you'l repent too Late
> You Ever Trifled with another fate
>
> —*Virgil*[163]

Fri., May the 1st. The French this Day dug between the Buttresses of the walls and over the Trenches they had made they Erected Privy Houses they likewise began to build a Tent Seperate from ours for the Captains Prisoners of which there were 11 in Number, but the Tent when finished was not Wide Enough to swing a Cat by the tail without Danger of Dashing her brains out against one side or the Other The Captains then petitioned his Excellency and his Lordship the Intendant for better Accomadations.[164]

XLIII. *Sat.* 2d. Died this Day Jane Carter an Infant Made out of Susan Phillips and Cornelious Mahanah one of Our Crew.[165]

Sun. 3d. Finished a Magazine for Monsieur Lorain our Officer; The Town Majore Came this afternoon and told the Capt'ns that in Consiquence of their late Petition His

[162] Pote records the visit of the townspeople and women under date of May 1. Pote, p. 126.

[163] "O mortals, blind in fate, who never know
To bear high fortune, or endure the low!
The time shall come, when Turnus, but in vain,
Shall wish untouch'd the trophies of the slain;"
—Dryden, *Æneïs*, Book X., lines 698–701.

[164] Pote makes an almost identical entry. Pote, pp. 125–126.

[165] Pote also records the death of the child of Susan or Susanah Phillips. Pote, p. 126.

Excellency and Lord Intendant had provided for them a house in Town. But that they were not to Stir beyond the bounds prescribed them on pain of their highest Displeasure.[166]

Mon., 4th May. much rain the night past and I believe not any amongst us but what were wett more or Less; however in the Afternoon it cleared up Just time Enough To Dry our Bedding. Monsieur Portrove[167] Came and Countermanded the Orders gave by the Majore yesterday, for that his Excellency and Lordship the Intendant had Considered of it again and found so many Inconveniencies attended the Captains being in Town that they were resolved to build them a Comodious House in their Camp. At night Daniel Lary was Sent to the Cashot or Dungeon for presuming to Ask Monsieur Lorain a Modest Question when he the Said Lorain had at that Time at least 2 bottles of Courage in his head.

Tues., 5th of May. fresh Gale of wind Easterly and very cold; Monsieur Morange Jun'r[168] gave us an Account that the prisoners left behind Sick at Menis were Exchanged by a flag of Truce from Anopoliss Royall Amongst which was Captn. Oldham though we have heard many times they were Sent to Old France and lately they were Coming up the River in Shallops from Bay Vert or green bay but I have Learned to place no great Confidence in any thing they tell us.

Wed. 6th. Fair weather the Guard is relieved Every Day, though I Observe the same persons here Every 48 hours, this shows they have not many men to Spare; So much the better, am hartily glad to see them put thus to Inconveniencies as well as Extraordinary Expences; for I have ben Informed by a good hand that since the fire they have laid out the Sum of 2200 Livers for Bedding; Skins for Shoes, and Shirts; the latter have not yet Ben given Out to us but are hourly Expected. Another thing I

166 Pote makes a similar but more detailed entry. Pote, p. 126.

167 Joseph Portois. Pote, pp. 126–127, an almost identical entry.

168 M. Marin, jr. Pote, p. 127, an almost identical entry.

observed this morning was that one of the Soldiers who before had ben our guard and when the House was burnt down his Coate was burnt with it; He came into our Camp with only a weastcoate on and being Asked the Question why he had not got Another Coate, he frankly told as they had not any Cloaths in the Town nor have not had for these 2. years past. This puts me in mind of King James IIds army he left behind him in Limrick in Ireland in the month of June.[169]

> Whose pay was Brass and Cloaths was bare
> And Courage out of Tune.[170]

This Day Collin Campbell[171] our late cooke went to the Hospital Ill with the Scurvy he was one of those who Survived that fatal Expedition to Porto Bello under the Command of Admiral Hosier;[172] he has often told me that the while the Fleet lay at the Bastimentoes he kept a Tally of upwards of 470 which he for his own Part Sew'd up in their Hammocks in the Time he Served on board 3. Ships; And now himself is far gone in the Same Distemper.

Thurs., 7th May. Wind Easterly Cold Sleate, no Ships as yet Arived French very much Chagreen'd; The Country Farmers and their Sons are now our Guard who Informed us His Excellency had siezd 500 head of their Cattle and had orderd 50 of them Every Day upon Duty to the great Neglect of their Business at this Season which has Caused great Murmering amongst 'em They have now Call'd in all their regular Troops from all parts.[173]

[169] After James II left Ireland in 1690, his supporters in the city of Limerick were twice besieged. The surrender and evacuation of the city, October 3, 1691, marked the end of the struggle between England and the exiled Stuarts. R. H. Murray, *Revolutionary Ireland and Its Settlement* (London, 1911).

[170] Unidentified.

[171] Regarding Campbell, Pote makes an almost identical entry. Pote, pp. 127–128.

[172] Early in 1726 Vice-Admiral Francis Hosier commanded an English squadron sent to the West Indies to prevent the sailing of Spanish treasure ships. While the ships blockaded Porto Bello, a virulent fever caused the death of many of the crew and finally of the Vice-Admiral himself.

[173] Pote makes a similar entry. Pote, p. 128.

Fri. 8th. Cold wind at ENE; at night much rain and Thunder and Lightening; this Day Died Sarah the wife of Leonard Liddle who was Maried in the prison as mentioned the 20th of November past.[174] XLIV.

Sat., May 9th. This Day fair weather and warm; at about 10 A.M. Saw a young Girl without the Piquets which proved to be the Daughter of Mr. David Woodall as Mentioned the 18th of December past; She was in Company with an Indian his Squaw and 2. of his paposes; the Girl was Dressed after the Manner of the Indians with a great Quantity of Wampumpeg which the Indians Call Extraordinary Embelishments; her Father and two of her Brothers got leave to goe without the Gate to Speak with her for about 15. minutes when the Indian and his Squaw etc. march'd off and took the Girl Away with him again; About 2 hours after Came in one of the Rever'd Fathers of the Church whom Mr. Woodall would have Interested in his favour to recover the Girl out of the hands of the Indians; but the Rever'd Father's advise was—that 't were more Safe for the Girl to remain with the Indians then to be Taken from them and brought into Town amongst the French Officers where he might be very well assured She would be ruined by them The more Shame to them who profess Christianity that a wild Barbarian Should out doe them in this point of Honour with regard to a Female Captive whose virtue they ought to protect.[175]

In the Dark race of vice when once begun
We Start on Mischiefs we most wish to Shun
Push'd by the fate of guilt and thence Accurst
New crimes grow Needfull to Support the first
Till from Dishonour we to ruin fall

[174] How records the death of Sarah Liddle under date of May 7; Norton, under date of May 9. Pote's entry is identical with that of this journal. How, p. 54; Norton, p. 47; Pote, p. 128.

[175] At this point the author of this journal is apparently copying from Pote, for although both writers refer to an entry of the previous December 18, the author of this journal entered the information referred to under date of December 17, and Pote, under date of December 18.

And one Disjoynted virtue Loosens all
Therefore be Obstinately Just
Indulge no passion nor Decieve no Trust
Let never man be bold Enough to Say
Hence and no farther Shall my passion stray
The first crime past Compells us into more
And guilt grows fatal which was but Choice before[176]

Mon., 11th May. very hot till 4. P.M. when we had much rain with Thunder and Lightning; People goe Daily to the Hospital very Ill, and many that are there now are Taken with a Fever which in 48. hours make them raving mad; This Day was Daniel Lary Sent to the Hospital from the Cashot or Dungeon where he had Contracted a Numbness in his Limbs in Laying in the Dungeon 7. Days and Nights with nothing to Eate but bread and water, and no Day Light but what Enters in at 3 holes in a small Iron plate of 4. Inches Square; NB he is the 3d Person who has been Sent to the Cashot or Dungeon on frevolous Occations.[177]

Tues., 12th of May. night Past much rain and hard gales of wind at NE; it Raind all Day and I believe not one of us but were wett in our Tents.[178]

Wed. 13th. Night past much rain and hard Gale of wind, at noon it Cleared up, but in the afternoon Squally; The Evening more Moderate; This Day died Daniel the Son of John and the late Mary Smead Lately of New England.[179]

XLV.

Thurs. 14th. Morning fair, came into our Campe a Prisoner John Larmond taken at Sheepsgutt on the frontier of New England by 11. Indians who Kill'd his Wife, his Son, and Daughter in Law and brought away their Scalps with them. At 4 P M came into our Campe his Lordship

[176] Unidentified.

[177] Pote makes an almost identical entry. Pote, p. 129.

[178] Under this date Pote gives additional information. Pote, p. 129.

[179] All four journalists record the death of Daniel Smead or Smeed. Pote's entry is almost identical with that of this journal. Norton, p. 47; Pote, p. 129; How, p. 54.

the Bishop of Queebec, he took a turn or two round our Camp and made but very little Stay.[180]

Fri., 15th May. This Day died Christian Vader late of Saristogua on the frontier of New York; and Joseph Gray late of Maryland one of the Crew of Captain Wm. Chapman; Likewise Mr. Hezekiah Huntington[181] Late of New Norwich in the Collony of Conecticutt he was Taken by the Frigate Castor in a Sloop of his Father's as Mentioned the 28th of June past bound for Cape Britton. he had but Just left the University and was as far as I Could Observe a promising young man; and no Doubt but he will be a great Loss to his Parents. I believe the Oldest of these 3 persons did not Exceed 23 years and 14 Days agoe was as likely to live as any one here; came from the Hospital tho' lame Daniel Lary who was sent to the Dungeon the 4th brought in the frame of an house for the Captains it is about 20. foot square. XLVIII. [XLIX.]

Sun., 17th May. Rain for this 48 hours past[182] in the Afternoon Monsieur Chalett gave us Shirts and Stockings to those who wanted amongst them I had a Shirt and a pr. of Stockings gave me of w'ch I stood in great Need.

Mon. 18th. Rain for the far greater part of this Day and likely to be a wett Season This Day Died Lamuel Martin late of new Norwich in the Collony of Conecticutt a Jolly Young Man not Exceeding 23 years Likewise the Daughter of John and the late Mary Smead Aged 10. months. She was born in the woods the 3d Day after her Father and Mother was taken Prisoners and on that Account the Child was Baptized by the Name of Captivity.[183] Came into our [L.]

[180] Both Norton and Pote record the arrival of John Larmon, Larmond, or Lermond, and Pote, the visit of Henri Marie du Breil de Pontbriant, Bishop of Quebec. Norton, p. 47; Pote, pp. 128–130.

[181] How records the deaths of Christian Fether, Tedder, or Vader and Hezekiah Huntington, Jr., under date of May 14; Norton and Pote, under date of May 15. How, p. 54; Norton, p. 47; Pote, pp. 130–131.

[182] Pote says that the morning was fair; the afternoon, rainy and cloudy. Pote, p. 131.

[183] Norton records the deaths of Captivity Smead or Smeed on May 17, and of Samuel Martin of Lebanon, Connecticut, on May 18. Pote undoubtedly copied his entry from this journal. Norton, pp. 47–48; Pote, pp. 131–133.

Camp 9. Prisoners vizt. 4 belonging to the Sloop Tortola Captn. George Morris from Philidelphia for Antigua; Taken by Monsieur Simane in a Small Scooner from Martinico bound here; he took the forementioned Sloop in Lat'd 24°00'; the Captn. and 4 more of the Crew were sent away in the prize to Martinico. 2. prisoners taken at Saristogua and 2 others at Sawco; one of the Latter brings an account that he was at the House of Mr. Cloutman about 5. weeks agoe and he is not got home; therefore 'tis generally concluded he perished in the Woods, or the Indians Kill'd him Since he made his Escape the 23d of Oct'r past Allso George Savaloni a native of the City of Corinth in Greece, late Mate of a Sloop in Meniss Bason Taken in that Unfortunate affair as mentioned the 11th of March past, who Confirms what we had heard from Mr. Williams the 26th of Aprill past with this Addititon Concerning the Jebuctore fleet; that they burnt 2 of their line of Battle Ships in the Said Harbour for want of Men to Man them; and that 1500 Troops they had on board for Canada they were Obliged to cary them out to Sea with them to man there Scattered remains of a fleet for Europe instead of the west Indies. He likewise Informed me that Zacheriah Hubart whom I left in Company with Captn. Oldham in the Indian Wighwam at Jebuctore Came up in the same Shallop with him but that a Gentleman in Town had taken him to his House. Monsieur Portrive brought into Campe Several letters for the prisoners here who belonged to New England by which we learn that Pinkham and his Crew got home who were sent away from hence the 31st of October past. At night came in Zacheriah Hubart; but too late for me to talk with him.

Tues., 19th of May. ND/MG. This Morning Zacheriah Hubart gave me the following account of Captn. Oldham; that after I had left him in the Indian Wigwam at Jebuctore he remained there in a weak Condition 24 Days vizt. from the 15th of August, to the 9th of September on no other Subsistance then bread and water; when at length the French Soldiers Caried him in his Hammock thro' the woods to Meniss where so soon as he got vegitables to Eate he Recovered from the Scurvy; The French then March'd him away for Segenecture or Bobazang where he and 9. more were so fortunate as to be sent away in a prize Snow for Old France in or about the Month of November in Good health. Thanks to God. 'Tis well my friend; Let man but view the Dangers he has allready past, and none will feare what yet are still to come; That Providence which hath preserved your life in Sickness and from the worst of Savages, make you Still his Care, while you are Just. This Day Died Mr. Samuel Burbank and Mr. Abraham Fort both aged 60 years and both of them Lately Inhabitants of Albany in the Province of New York.[184] LII.

Thurs., 21st of May. fine Weather Came into our Camp Captn. Le Crox who had been a Prisoner at Cape Briton and Boston these 2. years past and lately relieved he brings us a great Deal of News but it must be Understood in the same Manner as the Hebrews Read; that is Backward. Collin Campbel our Late Cook came from the Hospital somewhat better; he brings an Account of the Death of Robert Williams[185] one of our Crew late of Chichester near Portsmouth he was Poisoned last night by that Blundering Death's Harbinger Doctor Breaux who gave him a Liquid to wash his Gums as a remedy against the Scurvy and the fellow Died 4 hours after. Came likewise from the Hospital a young Lad taken with those at Sawco as Mentioned the 18th he had been wounded in the Shoulder but is now in a fair way to recover, he is about 12 Years old and after he was wounded he Discharged his piece twice upon the Indians e're he would ask for Quarter.

Fri., 22d May. fine Weather Peter Peraine one of our Crew Cut his finger allmost off with a hatchet on which account he was sent to the Hospital; This Day Died Na- LIIII.

[184] Norton and Pote also record the deaths of Samuel Burbank and Abraham Fort; How, that of Fort. This is the last entry in How's journal. Taken ill about the middle of the month, he was sent to the hospital, where he died, May 25, 1747. Norton, p. 48; Pote, p. 133; How, pp. 55-56.

[185] Norton and Pote record the death of Robert Williams. Pote's entry resembles that in this journal. Norton, p. 48; Pote, p. 134.

thaniel Hitchcock[186] late of the Massachusetts Fort New England. Heard that a Party of our Indians under the Command of Captn. Johnson have ben lately on Chambalee River and Taken and kill'd many Families; this is the 3d Time he has been upon that River on the French Settlements vizt. in the fall of the year he Caried off 30 Prisoners; in the Spring he Caried off 40 and now 100 Prisoners besides what they have Kill'd These Indians are of 3 Nations and are Call'd Mohauks they are a Crewell and Mercyless Enemy if not restrain'd by their Leader; this Day the Capt'ns House is finished[187] for them to go into it but Captn. Robert David Roberts and Captn. William Chapman are both Dangerously Ill with a Fever.

LV. *Mon.*, 25th May. Severely Cold; Died Mr. Neamiah How late of the Massachusets Bay, he was the first Prisoner brought in here this war.[188]

Tues. 26th. Morning fair but the greater part of the Day very Cold wind at East and much rain. Died Mr. Jacob

LVII. Quackinbush late of New York Collony he was the Father of the Young Girl taken into Town and kept as Mentioned the 14th of March past. About half an hour after died Isack[189] his Son aged about 20. years his Mother is at the point of Death and knows nothing of the fate of her Husband and Son Her Father and Mother, Gratiss, and Martha Vanderwerick, are very old and are here Prisoners with us, and in Queen Anns Wars Old Grattiss was here a Prisoner. This old Couple its very likely will See here the End of their Race; what man would Covet length of Days when it is Attended with Such Inumerable Ills such as themselves and their Hopes Carried into Captivity, there to undergoe Inumerable

[186] Norton and Pote record the death of Nathaniel Hitchcock. Norton, p. 48; Pote, p. 134.

[187] Pote records the completion of the captains' house under date of May 23. Pote, p. 134.

[188] Both Norton and Pote record the death of Nehemiah How. Norton, p. 49; Pote, p. 135.

[189] Both Norton and Pote record the deaths of Jacob and Isaac Quacinbush, Quackinbush or Quaquinbush, Pote undoubtedly basing his entry upon that in this journal. Norton, p. 49; Pote, p. 135.

Hardships without having it in their Power to assist, or being assisted by them; and at length to see their Tender Ofspring even to the 3d generation Cut off before them, and Drawn on Sledges to be thrown into a pitt or left on the Strand a prey to birds and Beasts or to be cut up and Mangled at pleasure by the more Merciless Savages; and all these Ills befalling them when thro' the Infirmity of Age they are less able to Support them Selves under them.

> Mistaken Blessing, which Old Age we call,
> 'Tis a long Darksome, Nasty, Hospital.
> A Ropey Chain of Rhumes a Visage Rough
> Deformed Unfeatured and a Skin of Buff
> A Stichfallen cheek which hangs below the Jaw
> Such Wrinkles as a Skillfull hand would draw
> For an old Grandam Ape when with a Grace
> She Sits a Squat and Scrubs her Leathern face
> —*vide Juvenal.*[190]

Wed., 27th of May. Very hot; Thus it is, one Day we freeze, the other Fry; Good Lord; what a Pitifull Poor Country this is; It were no small Punishment to be Banished Hither[191]

> Had Cain been Canadian, God would have chang'd his Doom
> Not forc'd him to Ramble, but Confin'd him home[192]

Thurs. 28th. Nothing worthy of Note Except that 3 D—d Whores Quarelled and fought about their Honesty, when they made it appear to Each other that the 1st was

[190] More correctly:

> "Mistaken blessing, which old age they call!
> 'Tis a long, nasty, darksome hospital:
> A ropy chain of rheums; a visage rough,
> Deformed, unfeatured, and a skin of buff;
> A stitch-fallen cheek, that hangs below the jaw;
> Such wrinkles as a skilful hand would draw
> For an old grandame ape, when, with a grace,
> She sits at squat, and scrubs her leathern face."
> —Dryden, *The Tenth Satire of Juvenal*, lines 305–312.

[191] At this point Pote's entry is quite different. Pote, p. 135.

[192] Unidentified.

whiped at Philidelphia for Stealing Linnen; the 2d Was Whip'd for being found in Conjunction with a Negroe fellow and the 3d was Drum'd out of the Company in which She had been Sometime for Scowering her Musquet too often.[193]

LVIII. *Sat.* 30th. This Day Died Jacob Sheepherd[194] late of the Massachusetts Fort; The Rev'd John Norton; Captn. Roberts, Captn. Wm. Chapman are all very Dangerously Ill.

Tues., June the 2d. This Day very hot so that one may Strip and Committ Murder on his own flesh and blood without Danger of Catching an Ague.

LIX. *Wed.*, 3d June. much rain the Night past; the morning fair weather; About 9 A M Died my worthy friend Captain Robert David Roberts[195] of Dartmouth in County of Devon Taken as Mentioned the 1st of May 1746 by the Aurora and Castor; he was taken Ill on Saturday the 16th of May past; Mr. John Durant his mate got leave to make him a Coffin at his own Expence into which he was put and Caried away to be buried NB he is the only prisoner who had the Priviledge of a Coffin Except those who had recanted their Errours as they Term'd it, and Died Good Catholicks.

Fri. 5th. This Day the Town Majore came and Informed us that we were all to be sent away to Boston in a few Days and upon that account Ordered a List to be drawn up of all the Prisoners and find them to Ammount to 233 Men, Women and Children; Since the 19th of October last there has Died 59. vide margin; at Menis 1 at Green Bay 2., Coming up the River 2, and before I came into Prison 2, in all 66; 15 were sent away in the fall and 2 runaway Total 316 besides 7. Indians Delivered up to the Canadians and a Vast Number of Children now in the hands of the Indians and some in the Town of Quebec At Evening came in 2 prisoners taken at Peniquid; 12 of their Company were Kill'd, one run

[193] Pote's entry for May 28 is again quite different. He enters the quarrel of the women under date of May 30. Pote, pp. 135–136.

[194] Norton records the death of Jacob Sheperd, Shepherd, or Sheepherd under date of May 30; Pote, under date of May 31. Norton, p. 49; Pote, p. 136.

[195] Both Norton and Pote record the death of Captain Robert David Roberts. Norton, p. 49; Pote, p. 136.

away and 2. brought here by a Party of Indians who Surprised them.

Mon. 8th. Came into our Camp 11. Prisoners from bay Vert or Green Bay;[196] this Day Katherine the Wife of Thomas Maclockland was sent into the Town in order for her Lying in, She being great with Child.

Tues. 9th. Died John Pitman[197] Late of Marble head, he should have gone away with his Master John Phillips in the fall, but The Scurvy he then had prevented him.

Wed., June the 10th. Longest Day fair weather Great noize and bustle amongst us when any one comes into our Campe in Enquiring after News; as Wether we are to goe away and when for our Barometer of Hopes and fears rise and fall according to the Current of News; for Time we look upon here as a thing of Nought and wear it out like an Old Shirt, the faster the better, In the Morn we wish for night to approach in the Night we as Earnestly wish for the Day, One time we are told we goe away in 10. Days; in another 3. weeks; then again we are told we goe not away till the fall of the year; this has been the Constant round e're Since the 5th past.

Fri. 12th. Died Abraham De Graves late of Albany; Came into our Camp 5. Gentle'n Prisoners vizt. Captn. Elisha Done; Captn. James Crocker, his Son, Lieutenant George Gerrick; Ensign Wm. Jerman taken at Meniss January the 31st as mentioned the 11th of March and 3 more from Bay Vert vizt. old Drumer and 2 others.[198]

Sun., 14th June. Was Informed by the Gent'n who came in here the 12th that the Pretender[199] and his party were Intirely routed by the Conduct and Vigilence of His Royall Highness Wm. Duke of Cumberland.

[196] Pote records the arrival of the prisoners from Baie Verte under date of June 7. Pote, p. 137.

[197] Norton and Pote both record the death of John Pitman or Pitmann of Marblehead, Massachusetts, under date of June 10. Norton, p. 49; Pote, p. 138.

[198] Norton and Pote also record the death of Abraham De Grave or De Graves of Albany or Schenectady under date of June 12. Pote records the arrival of the prisoners from Baie Verte under date of June 12 and 13. His account is more detailed than that in this journal. Norton, p. 49; Pote, pp. 138–139.

[199] *Ante*, note 141.

Unhappy youth, how is thy greatness crost,
And all thy Gaudy Dreams of Empire Lost,
Which proudly Sat thee on a fancied Throne,
And made Imaginary Realms thy own;
At Length Surrounded with allarms,
Thou hopes't Assistance from the Galick Arms,
The Galick arms in Safety Shall Advance
And Crowd thy Standard with the Power of France.
While to Exalt thy Doom, the Aspiring Gaul
Shares thy Destruction, and adornes thy fall
—*Addisons Campaign*[200]

One would have thought the remembrance of the year 15. Should have Detirred his Friends in Scotland and Elsewhere from the like attempt, but bouy'd up by the ambitious views and Destructive Scheems of themselves and others, they fell Victims to the Policy of Rome

O Charles tho', bred at Rome,
The Polititians School,
To Scotland thou must Roam,
To Learn their art but prov'd their Tool;
Besides, hast thou not read,
The Scots will Sell a King,
As well as Corn, or bread,
Or any other thing;[201]

By the best Accounts I Could gather, the Pretender Saved himself by flight; but about 16. of his friends were taken

[200] "Deluded prince! how is thy greatness crost,
And all the gaudy dream of empire lost,
That proudly set thee on a fancied throne,
And made imaginary realms thy own!
Thy troops that now behind the Danube join,
Shall shortly seek for shelter from the Rhine,
Nor find it there: surrounded with alarms,
Thou hopest the assistance of the Gallic arms;
The Gallic arms in safety shall advance,
And crowd thy standards with the power of France,
While to exalt thy doom, the aspiring Gaul
Shares thy destruction, and adorns thy fall."
—Addison, *The Campaign*, lines, 207–218.

[201] Unidentified.

and brought to the Block; and many others Died of the Quinze in the most Airy part of the Town; vizt. Tyborn

> When by Just Judgment Impious
> Mortals Perish; the Gods behold their
> Punishment with pleasure, and lay
> the uplifted Thunderbolt asside;
> —*Addisons Cato*[202]

Mon., 15th June. Heard this Day that a Woman and 4. of her Children were brought into Town Prisoners there to remain, At night Arived a Sloop with 21. prisoners from Bay Vert 4; of which were formerlly of our Company vizt. Jean the Wife of Serjant Archibald Geutered and 2. of her Children and Johnathan Felt whom I left in Company with Captn. Oldham at Jebuctore by whom I had the Agreeable News Confirm'd of Captn. Oldham's releasment by way of Old France; 12. more were brought in here and 6. were sent to the Hospital very weak, besides 3. who died in the Passage here, hear'd Just now that our Boston voyage like that at Jebuctore is over or laid asside, for a Gentleman whose varasity we never Questioned came here some Time agoe and assured us on his Honour we should Certainly goe away in a Short Time, and that Nothing but some Extraordinary Axident or Some Unforeseen Event could hinder it; Now he Came again to let us know that we could not be Sent Away for that a Woman with her 4 Children were lately taken and brought in here and had given an Account to His Excellency the Governer and Counsell that 2. Flags of Truce were Coming from Boston vizt.; the Lesser for Arcadia the Greater for Quebec; here's an Unforeseen Event who the Devil Could have Imagined that a Gossops Tale told in New England could have gain'd so much Credit in Canada. But I dare boldly aver that unless the French will send us away our Good Natured Saints in New England will never

[202] "When by just vengeance guilty mortals perish,
The Gods behold their punishment with pleasure,
And lay the uplifted thunderbolt aside."
—Addison, *Cato*: *A Tragedy*, Act III, Scene V, lines 70–72.

think it worth their while to come for us; for this plain reason, that here is neither Sugar, Rum, Cotton, Ginger, Mollasses, nor Indigo, to Truck for Provissions; and therefore 'Tis not worth the Saints While to fit out a flag of Truce to release a Parcell of lousy Ragged Rascalls who the farr greater part were Taken fighting in the Defence of the Collonies.[203]

Wed., 17th June. fair weather; this Day 2. Years the Town and fortifications of Louisburgh Surrended to his Britanick Majesties arms, on which account we wore in our hatts and Caps a Twig of Green Spruce which was highly resented by Monsieur Lorain our Keeper and as it was fine weather a great many Gentlemen officers with their wifes and Relations came to see us in our Camp who Enquired of Lorain the reason for it but he did not Care to make him any Direct answer an Impudent fellow Step'd up to the Gentlemen and in Good French told them as above; on which account Lorain offered to Strike the Fellow, but the Gentlemen Ordered him to Desist and Concluded his Discourse about it, with this Motto; Tandem Triumphans; a Dog will have his Day; the French Gentlemen were very Merry upon it and at their going away left the Captains Prisoners money to Drink their healths of which as usual I took part with them. Though the Taking this Important place of Louisburgh does not Sit easy on them nor I cant See how it can When Mr. Chalet who was allways at the head of affairs in Arcadia as well as in Canada assured us once that in the year 1742. it had Cost his most Christian Majesty 45000000 French Livers besides what it had cost Since. This Day 4. Dutchmen of Albany were brought into Town and 12. Indians all in Indians Dresses and on that account were put into the Common prison.

Thurs., 18th of June. Fine Weather; Came in here 2. Prisoners they were taken on the Frontier in Aprill Last and

LXII. have been at Mount Royall ever Since to get cured of their

[203] In the main this agrees with Pote's entries of June 15 and 16, but the accounts are quite different. Pote, pp. 139–140.

wounds This Day Died Samuel Stacie[204] one of those who arrived in the Town the 15th ult.

Fri. 19th. Fair Weather Errected a 3d Tent or rather Cattle Penn for those Prisoners who came in last it is about 40. foot Long.

Sat. 20th. This Morning one Denis Donahew[205] a Deserter from Anopolis Royall was taken out of our Camp at his request to serve the French Died William Mason[206] the 2d of that Company who came to Town the 15th past. NB Puzell Case His Most Christ'n Majesties Attorney General is this Day Captain of the Guard over us.

LXIII.

Tues., June the 23d. This Day Mrs. Anne Butchers 2. Children were brought into the Camp to her and are as is said to remain with her; at Evening arived 4 Sail of Ships as per report from Old France one of them is a man of war of 26. Guns and have on board 200 Soldiers for this place: They are the remains or foreruner of a Fleet.[207]

Wed. 24th. Midsummer Day; heard that the Man of War and 3 Sail which Came up Yesterday were the remains of a Squadron it seems there are 7. Sail more Expected up here Every Day; They Came out of Old France the Latter End of March OS; the Squadron Consisted of 55 merchant Ships and Three East India Ships outward bound under the Convey of 10 men of war from 70 to 40 Guns, who the 5th Day after they came out of Port fell in with a fleet of English men of War Consisting of 18 Sail of the Line who attack'd the Convey while these Ships by a Signal from their Admiral made the best of their way and left them Ingaged How the Fortune of the Day turn'd Time only can Discover; but by the Appearence of the French on the arival of these Ships, 'Tis Generally Concluded they were worsted; and that most if not all were Either taken or Sunk.

[204] Norton records the death of Samuel Stacie or Stacy under date of June 17; Pote, under date of June 19. Norton, p. 49; Pote, p. 140.

[205] Pote also records the desertion of Denis Donahew. Pote, p. 141.

[206] Norton and Pote also record the death of William Mason or Nason of Casco Bay. Norton, p. 49; Pote, pp. 140–141.

[207] Pote also records the arrival of the ships. Pote, p. 141.

For this Old Ocean pleased our Ships recieves
For this Stern Bornois Royall Master Greives
For this Proud Monsieurs are fore doom'd to feel
The Scourge of Heaven in Britains Spurning Heel[208]

we hear there was a new Governer for Canada and 1200. Soldiers for this place on board the Squadron.[209]

Thurs. 25th. Heard yesterdays News Confirm'd with These Additions First that the Fleet or Squadron Came out of Brest and that the English Fleet that fell in with them had Great Numbers of Men on board more then their Complements and that they had not one Merchant man or Transport with them but were the far greater part tall Stout Ships; from Which 'Tis Concluded it was Admiral Martins Fleet and not Admiral Warens as was first Suspected. 2dly that the States of Holland have at length Declared War Against France and her Adherants which we hope is True. 3dly that the English have Taken a Frenchman of war of 70 Guns in the Chanell last Winter.[210] NB very hot Weather Petitioned His Excellency the Governor for redress, we having Stinking Salt Beef Served us at this Season; when His Excl'y was pleased to Order us one half of our usual allowence in Salt Beef; the other Moity Fresh Beef.

Fri., 26th June. Fair Weather but very hot, heard from the French officers they have taken lately 106 Prisoners at Saristogua who are Expected here very Shortly; there has Certainly been an Action but hope the French have not Taken So many Prisoners as 106 They are Cuning Enough in addition.[211]

Sat., 27th June. Rain for the far greater part of the Day; Came up to Town 3 Sail part of those 7. Expected up the river, one of them 'Tis said is the Black Prince Privateer late of Bristol.[212]

[208] Unidentified.

[209] Pote's entry for June 24 is almost identical with that in this journal. Pote, pp. 141–142.

[210] Pote enters the preceding information under date of June 25 and 26. In both accounts are to be found details not in the other. Pote, pp. 142–143.

[211] Pote includes similar information in his entry for June 26. Pote, p. 143.

[212] Pote's entries for this and the three succeeding days are similar to the entries in this journal. Pote, pp. 143–144.

Sun. 28th. Fair Weather; This Day Peter Peraine one of our Crew came from the Hospital who brings me an account that the Frenchman of war of 70 Guns Taken as Mentioned the 25th ult was the La Mars She was Taken by Admiral Waren in the Chester and Vigilent in Comp'y going home last fall of the year; NB This La Mars is the Ship which took His Majesties Ship Northumberland. The Ships which Came up Lately have brought a Sickness with them and great Numbers of the Crews are now in the Infirmary on which account Doctor Breaux, or rather Gripeum Vomitum Gutsout have Declared he Cannot attend the Sick in our Hospital as usual.

Mon., 29th June. Fair but some Showers of Rain, At night came into our Camp a Prisoner Taken at Saristogua Fort about 12. Days agoe, he brings a Poor Account without any Conection; There was it Seems a Lieutennant taken with him who is Expected here very Shortly; hope to have a more Adiquate account from him.

Tues. 30th. Fair Weather with Some Smally Showers of Rain; This Day a party of Swiss which Came over with the Ships last arived are now our Guard; but

Coates they have on,
Little better then none,
Confoundedly tore at the Elbows;
That they look as Absurd,
As a Seaman on Board,
That has lain half a year in the Billbows.
Hatts they have on
Which so Greasy are grown
Remarkable are by their Shining
One Side is Stick'd up
Stead of Button and Loop
But the Devil abit of a Lineing[213]

Wed., July 1st. Much rain the Night past, This Day came into Prison Mr. Jos. Chew Lieutenant and 6. of his Company there was 42 of them taken at Saristogua by a Party of Indians and French Instead of 106. mentioned the 26th past but this is not the first time the French Lie for we

[213] Unidentified.

have now one for Every Day of the Week. This Day died Mathew Lorin, he was one of those left at Jebuctore last fall.[214]

LXV. *Thurs.* 2d. This Day Died a young Girl of Serjant Archbald Geuterade born at Meniss aged about 4 Months She Caught the Fever of her Mother.[215]

Fri., 3d July. Fair weather; This Day died John Pringle late of the Massachusetts Bay New England; Came in an-
LXVI. other Prisoner Taken at Saristogua. Saw the Roof of the Cazans our late prison House raised up and boarded fit to Chingle.[216]

Sun. 5th. Fair weather; Hear there is a flag of Truce in the River St. Laurance but this we may set down as the lie for the Day.[217]

Mon. 6th. Fair the former part of the Day; the Latter part rain; Came into our Camp another Prisoner Taken at Saristogua which is the 10th There are 32. still remain behind; we have now 296. Prisoners, Men, Women, and Children hear there are now 7. Sail of French Ships in the River which are look'd for up here Every hour; no more talk of the Flag of Truce.

Tues., 7th July. Fair Weather; This Day Came into our Camp a young Girl about 14 years of Age; the Daughter of Widdow Quackingbush, She made her Escape from the Indians in whose Keeping she hath ben these 20. months past, by getting a Canoe and Crossing the River at a place Call'd the 5. Rivers about mid way between Mount Royall and Quebec; from whence She hath been Traveling these 4 Days,

[214] Pote again makes a very similar entry. Pote, p. 144.

[215] Norton records the death of Archibald Gartrage, the young son of Charles Gartrage; Pote, of the four-month-old daughter of Archebald Gutherage. Norton, p. 50; Pote, p. 145.

[216] Pote records the death of John Pringle under date of July 3; Norton, that of William Prindle under date of July 4. Pote's entry again resembles that in this journal. Pote, p. 145; Norton, p. 50.

[217] Pote's entries of July 5–10 are similar to the entries in this journal. He gives the age of the daughter of the Widow Quackingbush as sixteen, however, and the name of the settlement between Quebec and Montreal as "3 Rivers." Pote, pp. 145–146.

the French pezants assisting her till She arived in Town where She was Conducted to the House of a Gentleman who took her in and Cloathed her and brought her to Prison to see her Mother but she is to remain in the Town.

Wed. 8th. Came into our Camp another of the Saristogua Prisoners he made his Escape out of the Hands of the Indians The manner very Extraordinary our Number is now 298 as per margin. 298.

Thurs., 9th July. Fair weather; About 4 P M 2. D—d Whores Quarelled and fought about their honesty and had like to have Involved some of the men in the Fray; we have now 298 Prisoners of all ranks and Degrees—as—

Knights without Honours, Esquires without Estates
Quakers, Capt'ns, Cully's, Beaux, and Cheats;
Citts, Fidlers, Porters Coblers, Grooms and Carmen
Whiggs, Tories, New Lights, and Such kind of Vermin
Nay more then these we have the Females too
As though other Plagues, there were yet but a few
For Punks, and Jilts, Flux'd Bauds, and Pox, the Whores
You'd Swaer that Hell had Drain'd its Common Shores
And that Grim Pluto had resumed his riot
And here Confined these Enemies to Quiet
Their Ever moving Clacks no Charm can bind
Artists might here Perpetual Motion find
No Truce is hield with their Eternal Brawles
Battles and Confusion Dwell within our walls
Thus wishing you and all our friends their health
See here a View of Limbo's Common Wealth
—*To Mes'r Thos. Sayer Norffolk*[218]

Fri., 10th July. Fair weather; Monsieur Chalet gave us a Parcell of Damaged Tobacko; French very busie in blowing up Rocks for these 3. Days past and Carying the Rubish to the walls Came in 4 Prisoners of those Taken at Saristogua remain behind 27.

Sat. 11th. This Morning Died Corporal Daniel Norwood[219] he Served his Aprenticeship in a Baking office near

[218] Unidentified.

[219] Norton records the death of Corporal William Norwood; Pote, that of Corporal Daniel Norwood. Norton, p. 50; Pote, p. 146.

Gun Dock Wapping London, he belonged to one of those Regiments lately Sent from Gibralter to Louisburgh he was taken by the Indians on the Island St. Johns the 10th of July 1746; Heard His Excellency Governer Boharnoise have lately rec'd a letter from Governor Knowles[220] at Louisburgh as well as one from Governer *Shirley*[221] at Boston Concerning an Exchange of Prisoners But this I take to be the lie for to Day, we shall have it Contradicted To Morrow.

Sun., 12 July. This Day was Maried (a kind of as it were) John Simpson and Miss Susan Bolinson who was Drumd out of the Company as mentioned the 28th of May past. Am Informed This Nuptial Cerimony of Taking Each others word will be binding in America, if so he is bound 'Tis True, 'Tis Pity, Pity, 'Tis 'Tis True. This Day Captn. Spafford and Ensign Joseph Stockman was Ordered to take His Excelency Governer Boharnois Bounty and for the future to Mess with the Gentlemen; I Should, had it been my Case, have thank'd His Excellency for nothing, Since 'Tis plain this Step of his was only to serve his own Ends and therefore I should have let him know I Could Subsist on the Begarly Support one month more as well as he had made me doe it for these 20. months past.[222]

Mon., 13th July. Great Cavelcade on Acc't of the Late Wedding fair Weather Monsieurs Chalet and Portrove came into the Camp and assured us there was 2. Ships fitting up for Flags of Truce and would be ready in a Week to Carry us to Boston and Cape Briton; They Then took a List of the Prisoners those who belonged lately to His Majesties Service was Set Down in the List for Cape Briton to the Number of 93, and 183 were Set Down in the List for Boston there are likewise 26. now Sick in the Hospital and am affraid they will not be well Enough to goe with us As to those whose Children are in the hands of the Indians when they Demanded them they were Told they must make Themselves

[220] At this time Charles Knowles was governor of Louisburg.

[221] William Shirley, 1694–1771, governor of Massachusetts from 1741 to 1757, who proposed the capture of Louisburg by the English.

[222] Pote records this information under date of July 11 and 12. Pote, p. 147.

Easy about that affair for that they could not be taken away from the Indians till the Conclusion of a Peace.[223]

Wed., 15th July. Fair Weather, Monsieur Chalet came to let us know that the Oldest or first Prisoners Should be sent away first for fear there Should not be room Enough for all on Board the Vessells, he hinted that those Prisoners who were Taken at Meniss about 6. months agoe with those lately taken at Saristogua would be Detained. Peter Perain one of our Crew is now Sick at the Hospital; This Day I cut off my hair which I had let grow ever Since I Left England. I not having a hatt since I was Taken, and the Weather is Excessive hot.[224]

Thurs., 16th. Some Showers of Rain; Died this Day James Dayle the old Drumer lately come from Meniss and when Taken by the Aurora was bound for Cape Briton.[225] 301. LXVII.

Fri., 17th July. Fair Weather; Came into our Camp Monsieur Comissary to view us, and Amongst other things Assured us the Ship was ready to carry us to Boston, I hope Sunday will be the Day; And he further assured us that During the Time of our Imprisonment we had Cost them the Sum of 150000 Livers value about 6250£ Sterling. This Day died Phenias Forbush lat of the Massachusets Fort Several People came from the Infirmary who are so far recovered as to be Able to goe with us hear there are Lately Arived in Town 400 French Mohawks they are Painted and Dress'd up for war; they are Quartered in Town, 3 or 4 in a House Poor Peeter Perain one of our Crew is now very Ill in the Hospital; fear he will not be Able to goe with us. Captn. Wm. Chapman I fear will be Left.[226]

Sat. 18th. Heard this Day from a good Author that this

[223] Pote records the visit of M. De Chalet and M. Portois under date of July 14. Pote, pp. 147–148.

[224] Pote's entry for July 15 is almost identical with that of this journal. Pote, p. 148.

[225] Both Norton and Pote record the death of James Dayle, Doile, or Doyl. Norton, p. 50; Pote, p. 148.

[226] Norton records the death of Phinehas or Phinihas Forbush or Fourbush under date of July 16; Pote, under date of July 17. Norton, p. 50; Pote, p. 148.

Sending us away was in Complience with Positive orders from France; Therefore Conclude a Complaint has ben Made that no regard have here ben paid to the Carteel Subsisting between the Crowns of Great Britain and France. We likewise hear the New Governer[227] for this place is Taken and Caryed into Boston, if so; he may be Glad to claim the Benifit of the Carteel as Marchall Bell Isle Lately did, and no Doubt but it will be Granted him. we have Petitioned for the Benifit of the Carteel but could get no Answer.

> Thus Petty Rogues Submit to fate,
> That Great ones may Enjoy their State.
> —*Garths Dispensitory*.[228]

In the Afternoon came in a young Girl the Daughter of Widdow Quackinbush[229] who was Taken from the Indians and have ben with the French these 20 mo. Past, and at Times was permitted to see her Mother, Grandfather and Grandmother as Mentioned the 14th of March past her mother would have Detain'd her here as we are now in hopes of going away very Shortly but the French gave her to Understand that the Moneys which they paid for her Redemption out of the hands of the Indians must and Should first be paid to them again On which Account Captn. Elisha Done and Lieutenant Jos. Chew offered their Bond for the Payment of it; but they would not Admit of it, and Imediately a Soldier Forc'd the Child out of the Mothers Arms and push'd the Poor Old Grandfather Down and ran away with the Child out of our Camp. This Poor Woman is very unfortunate for her Husband her Father and Mother 3 Daughters and a hopefull Son, were Taken Prisoners with her. On the 7th of December Past Died her Daughter Martha, Aged About

[227] Jacques Pierre de Taffanel, Marquis de la Jonquière, succeeded Beauharnois as governor of New France.

[228] "Where little Villains must submit to Fate,
That great Ones may enjoy the World in State;"
—Samuel Garth, *The Dispensary* (London, 1726), Canto I, lines 9–10.

[229] Pote also tells of the visit of the Widow Quackinbush's daughter. Pote, p. 149.

10 years; On the 26th of May past Died her Husband and Son and the 7th of this month her Other Daughter made her Escape from out of the hands of the Indians, nor will the French release her any more then the former.

Sun., 19th July. Fair Weather, Saw the Melitia of the Town march the Back of the Walls in Order to be Drawn up for Exercise as they have done Every Sunday past; But to Day they were much more in Number then Ever we Saw Before; for as they March'd along 'Twas Easy to Count their Number Since there was 4 in Each file and 175 files Total 700 men under arms Including Officers; The Prisoners got on the Top of the Tents to view them as they pass'd along but was not ordered by the Centinals to keep Down as usualy they were; Conclude from thence that the French have some Political view in marching so many men in our Sight. His Lordship the Intendant of Quebec after the Review was Over Came into our Camp to take his Leave of us as he was pleased to Express himself and Seem'd Highly pleased to see us so healthy but as for those who lately came from the Hospital and look'd very poorly he told them that it was not for the Wellfare of the rest that they should goe with us.[230] At Eve Came in the Eldest Daughter of Widdow Quackinbush who lately Escaped from the Indians This was done by his Lordship the Intendant to whom we Addressed our Selves in behalf of the Widdow; and great Interest is now making for the Same Previlidge for the yongest Daughter to goe home with her Mother.

Mon. 20th. Fair weather, brought us Meat for 2 Days Conclude by that we Embarque To morrow afternoon NB Lieutenant Jos. Chew and Monsieur Celorin the Town Majore had some Words on a Punctillo not much to the Credit of the Lattor [231]

Tues., 21st July. Rain for the far greater part of the Day; no Talk of our going away To morrow; Thos. Davis Aprentice to Captn. Oldham is now very lame he has Complain'd

[230] Down to this point Pote's entry for July 19 is similar. Pote, p. 150.

[231] Pote's entries for July 20 to 25 are quite different from the entries in this journal. Pote, pp. 150–152.

of a Rhumatick Pang in his Leg; but yesterday Contrary to my Express Orders he got a Blundering Fellow to Bleed him in the Foot and now he's much worse then Ever, and am affraid I must leave him behind me This Day Katherine the 302. Wife of Thomas Maclockland was Delivered of a Daughter in the Town.

Wed. 22d. Rain the Night past and the far greater part of the Day; Died Jonathan Bridgman[232] late of the Massachusetts Fort New England. Came in 2 Prisoners Lately 303. taken at Saristogua remain behind 25. and if they don't come Shortly we are like to give them the Slip We are this Day Served 2 Days allowence.

Thurs., 23d July. Rain the night past but Morning fair; was this Day Informed by His Excellency's Secretary we should Embarque the 25th; This Afternoon the French brought in the Child of Mr. Jno. Smead which had been in Town to Board.

Fri. 24th. Monsieur Chalett and Gripeum Vomitum Guttsout; Came into prison and Examined the Prisoners; those who were not well was Dash'd out of the List and not to goe with us which if it be fair Weather we Embarque tomorrow. Unexpectedly this Evening the following persons went out of our Camp with a French officer in Order as 'Tis Said to take up Arms

John Macclure	his Wife
Thos. Macglockland	and Wife
Daniel Lary	George Wainwright
John Tobin	Thos. Anderson
John MacDonnell	Peeter MacMillion
Wm. Mullally	David Berry in
James Middleburgh	all 12 men and
Robert Willson	2 Women.

Sat., 25th July. We are in high Spirits as being very well Assured of our being Embarque'd this afternoon for Boston. At 4 P M Monsieur Chalet with an officer and Some few Guards Came into our Camp and Draughted us off and Ime-

[232] Norton records the death of Jonathan Brigman or Bridgman of Sunderland under date of July 21; Pote, under date of July 22. Norton, p. 50; Pote, p. 166.

diately march'd us to the Warfe where we Embarqued on board the Ship Grace a Flag of Truce for Boston.[233]

At Length the Time is Come w'n Heaven was pleas'd to Show
His Care and Conduct of the World below
Men who their Long Captivity bemoan'd
And Sighs of Widdows which in Excile groan'd
Are now relieved
With Joy Fraternal abounds my kindred Soul
That Slaves no more Shall Britans sons Controul
Thy Sons O Freedom to thine Arms return'd
With their Tender ofspring w'ch in Excile Mourn'd
Oh Liberty thou Goddess Heavenly bright
Profuse of Bliss and Pregnant with Delight
Secure of the the Pezant Joyfull Sing
And tunes his Voice Exulting in the Spring
'Tis Liberty that Crowns Britanies Isle
And makes her Bleak Rocks and Barren Mountains Smile[234]

Sun., 26th July. Lying off the City of Quebec Wind at NE right up the River; we have now on board 172 Prisoners, men Women and Children; The French sent us off a pair of Mogazins per Every one of us which is the only thing we are like to Expect from them. This Day a New Moon, and by what I observed be the Ships Tending down I find it flows here in this Harbour SEBS and NWBN or 9 ho:45 min on the full and Change Days. This City of Quebec is Situated on an Island in the Great River St. Laurance and lies in Lat'd

[233] At this point the author of this journal and Captain William Pote, jr., part company, the former embarking for Boston on the afternoon of July 25; the latter, for Louisburg on the morning of July 29.

[234] "The day was come when heaven designed to show
His care and conduct of the world below."
—Addison, *The Campaign*, lines 257–258.

"States that their new captivity bemoaned,
Armies of martyrs that in exile groaned,"
—*Ibid.*, lines 251–252.

"O Liberty, thou goddess heavenly bright,
Profuse of bliss, and pregnant with delight!"
—Addison, *A letter from Italy*, lines 119–120.

"'Tis liberty that crowns Britannia's isle,
And makes her barren rocks and her bleak mountains smile."
—*Ibid.*, lines 139–140.

47°10′ No. and Longitude of 69°55′ West; The Difference of Time between here and London is 4 ho. 35 minutes later. The City as I said is on an Island but the Istmuss as the NW't part of The Island as I have been Informed is Fordable at High water and firm and Dry at Low water. The Island Orlance[235] lyes about 4 Lgs. below the City, between which is a fine Bay were Ships of any Burthen may Ride Secure Especially Towards the SW't part of the City where I Observe the Men of war Usually Ride. At the Front of the City, the Bay branches into 2. Arms or Distinct Rivers, the one runing by the So. Side of the City the other by the NW't Side of the City; the former of which is Navigable for small vessells up to the Town of Mount Royall; I never could hear of any vessells of Greater burthen then 80 Tons ever Arived there; That Arm which runs by the NW't Side of the City Inclines So far toward the West as to form the Istmus forementioned; here their Ships are built, one of 70 Guns is now on the Stocks but Cannot be Launch'd for want of Materials for her; here they lay up their Ships in the winter as a 20 Gun Ship was laid up in our Sight for want of Rigging as mentioned the 22d October.

As to the Strength of this City, it is from what I Could observe no way Capable to make any Stand Against a much Less force then what was lately Employ'd in Reducing Porto Bello.[236] As I lay on board the Flag of Truce right off the City from the 25th to the 27th of July I had the Oppertunity to Observe their Strength in that part of the City which faces the Bay; of which as follows. At the South part of the Town is a Battery of 12. Guns; it is close to the water Side and have been lately Built. About 1/4 mile from the aforesaid Battery and to the Northward on the Summit of the Hill is a small Fort in which are 10 Guns. On a large Opening to the Southward of the Governers Pallace, is a Platform on which are 30. Cannon; most of them Appear to be small Field Pieces. To the Northward of the Pallace, at the

[235] Isle of Orleans.

[236] Vice-Admiral Edward Vernon took the Spanish town of Porto Bello on the Isthmus of Panama in November, 1739.

Common Landing or fish Market by the water Side; is a Regular Bastion of 16 pieces. On a Hill at the Northermost part of the City is a large Platform which as the Point of land tends towards the west it lyes in the form of a half Moon or Cresent on which are 32 pieces but Neither this nor the platform fore mentioned have any thing to Screen them, not so much as Faciens, but are Exposed in the same Manner as the Guns on Tower Warff London. Besides which they have Fire Stages on Some of their Eminances Loaded with Tar Barrells; Barrells of Turpintine and other Combustibles which are laid ready for Launching on Bulghways on the Aproach of a Fleet of Ships. On all the Forementioned places are 100 Guns but of what Size Cannot Say any otherwise then by the Shot I Observed in the Court before the Governers Palace were we were put the 28th of Aprill past when our Prison House was burnt Down This was their Magazine of Shot and I have great reason to believe it is the Only one they have. These Shot were Disposed of in Regular Pyramids by which means 'Tis very Easy to Discover the Number In Each of them; Since their Areas as they rise one Above Another are in Arithmetical progression wherein the Number that Crowns the Top is the first Term; the Number at the Base the Last Term; and the Number of Areas or rows, the Number of Terms. The Largest of these Shot are 18 pounders and are Disposed of in one Pyramid, their Number are thus found

First $10 \times 7 = 70$ Area at the Base

2dly $4 \times 1 = 4 + 70 = 74 \times 3.5 = 259$ the Number of Shot of 18 pounds Each; by the Same rule I find the N'r of shot of 12 pound

to be	396
Of 9 Pounders	427
Of 6 Pounders	512
Of 3 Pounders	1040
Shells of 9 Inches	27
Mortars	2
Cross Bar Shot Ab't	500
Hand Granaders Ab't	300

Besides 2 pieces of Brass Canon before the Governers Door; A Privilidge belonging to the Marshalls of France. Thus for its Strength towards the Water Side fronting the Bay; but with regard to its Strength on the Backside of the City Little can be Said; There is Indeed a Wall built with Slate the 2 Ends of which is now pretty Strong because lately built but as to the Middle under which we were Lately Encamp'd it is so rotten that I have Seen the Prisoners beate Down with Stones a Loade or 2. at a Time; There is a Battery and Bomb Proof the backside of the Prison House which was Lately burnt down and now repaired again; but they have not one Gun for it. There is Likewise a Battery at the NE End of the wall aforementioned at which the French have wrought these Two years past in filling it up with Mould; but this like the former has no Guns nor have they any for them; but if an Army Should Attack 'em by Land 'Tis probably they would remove the forementioned pieces from the Platform and place them there.

The Governers Pallace is the most remarkable Building in the City of Quebec, it is Situated on a very high Rock and that part of it which Fronts the Bay is a very Dangerous Precipiece. The City Consists of 2. parts vizt. the upper and the Lower, the Latter is Easily Demolished for at Top of High water it may be burnt by Small vessells propperly Disposed Since their Roofs are of Chingles and their Sides are of Clap board. The Upper Town lyes more Difficult (tho they Join Together) but bombs may and would doe them great Damage Espicially if the Bomb Vessell be laid to pass So as to Bring the Steeple of the New Church Open with the Governers Pallace about a handspike Length to the Northward, for Shells or Carcasses thrown with that Direction will fall in the very Center of the Town. Another Bomb Vessell to lay at the Entrance of the NW't Arm will doe them great Damage but She must not goe far up Least She Take the Ground at half Tide.

The Inhabitants of this City are under Continual Apprehensions of the English paying them a Vissit both by Land and Sea; which if they Should the Inhabitants are Consious to them selves they cannot Stand Against 'em. The Country is not So Numerous as may be Expected from its long Settlement; and for want of proper Encouragement there are very few Handycrafts amongst them. The Soil is indeed Inviting as being very fertle but their winters are very Seveere.

The Canadians tells us Somtimes they are able in Case of Need to bring 30000 men into the Field this I take to be Meerly Apocryphal I may believe it or I may not men I know are not made with a Puff any more then with a Goose quill. If they Can bring half that Number to bare Arms 'Tis the Opinion of good Judges as much as they can doe in Case of an Attack; it is pretty thick Settled Above Quebec to Mount Royall; but below Quebec their Settlements are very thin with regard to Inhabitants, for where you see one Mansion house there are at Least 2 Barns and 4 Cattle Houses, these run for a good many leags along the bank of the River St. Laurance but a 60. Gun Ship with her Lower Tier will Rake the back of their Settlements even to the very Skirts of the woods.

The Farmers are in great fear of the Countrys being reduced as they have no Interest in old France they have made no Scruple to tell us they would Imediately Turn to the English to Save their Estates; nor are their Indians to be Depended upon Except one Tribe Call'd the Herons; Nay the Old France Soldiers who had been all along our Guard wish for nothing more then an English Fleet and Army as having no other hopes of getting to Europe again but by the Reduction of Canada which may it be Soon Affected is the Harty wish of all English men and Should claim the Attention of those their Neighbours on the Continent of America.

Mon., 27th of July. At 5 A M unmoored and at 7 D'o came to Sail wind at SW't Direct Trade, Hazey weather; At 1 P M Captn. Martin Loree[237] desired that all Persons without any Distinction Should goe off the Deck in Complience with the Governers Orders, for we were now come to the Place call'd Dangerous which is a Narrow passage be-

[237] Captain Larregni. *New York Colonial Documents*, X., 118.

tween the Island Orlance and the Main on the North Side; here is a Reef of Rocks which runs from the NE point of Orlance and therefore the Passage is Narrow and the Tide Runs very Swift. NB This Passage hath 2 Battery's one on the NE point of the Island Orlance, the Other on the main Land Nearly Opposite but the Strength of Either can give no Account not further then this; that as Ships must allways take the Tide of flood and a Leading wind they will in few Minutes be Shot so far through as would be Impossible to bring one Gun to bear upon Shiping as they pass by.

At 1 P M as I said we were Ordered Down; at 2 Do. we was Call'd up again and as the Flood had then made up Strong against which we run with a fresh Gale till 6 Do. when we got Sight of 2 Islands where as we was told is a Dangerous place and as the Sun was then growing Low The Pilote would not Venture through but brought the Ship to an Anchor In About 10 Fathams water about 2 miles below the Said Island off a Church and Some few Houses which are as I Aprehend the Residence of Pilotes Since there is no Cultivated Land though we are not now above 14 Leagues or 42 miles Distant from the City of Quebec.

Tues., July 28th. At 7 A M weigh'd and came to saile wind at WSW't at 8 Do. Captn. Loree desired we would all goe down again which we Imediately complied with for we was now come to the 2d Dangerous which is between the Isle La Coudree[238] and the main on the No. Side the River St. Laurance where there are Reefs of Rocks; and as this Passage like the former is very Narow The Tide runs with great Rapidity Likewise here is a Large Indraught from the River St. Paul[239] which Makes a Counter Tide; and without great Care Ships will in their Passage through be Hurried over to the Reefs which should She once Touch She would Imediately oversett and no Hopes of Saving Life Even in a Calm. This the French are very Apprehensive of and are in great Agitation of mind when e're they pass through for I could hear the Pilote with great Emotion Cry out take care of

[238] Isle aux Coudres.

[239] St. Paul's Bay lies directly to the north of the Isle aux Coudres.

your Helm!, Mind your Helm!, least She Should Cast for then there is no Hopes of Recovering her again; nor doe they Ever pass through here without going to prayers which as-soon as Ended we were Call'd up again when we found our Pilote had Taken his Canoe and gone Onshore; we then set Studing Sails and made our Course between the No. and NE at Noon Dist. from Quebec 20. Leags or 60. miles.

Wed., 29th July. Fresh Gale at SSW't and an Ebb Tide our Course till 6 P M between the NNE and ENE Edging over to the Southern Shore Pass'd by Several Islands with Reefs of Rocks about them; Saw Great Numbers of white Porpasess: At 6 P M brought too about a mile above a Large Island where we Took in our Boate and Sent a Lieutenant and 11 Soldiers Onshore in a Boate of their Own who had Attended us Down the River by Order of the Governer to see that his Orders were Strictly Complied with at the Fore-mentioned Dangerous Places. here I had the Opertunity to Observe the Strength of the Tide in this part of the River St. Laurance which is now at Least 10. Leagues Wide; where from the Time we brought too till we made Sail again which was not an hour we had Drove as appeared by the Island above 4. Miles. Assoon as we made Sail again we Saw a Sail with whom we spoke with and found her to be a Brigenteen a Flag of Truce from Louisburgh at 6 A M Saw a Sail Standing to the Northward which did not Speake with us; Conclude from thence she is no Cruizer of ours but a French Merchant man of About 200 Tons Now Steering about ENE Wind at SWBW; At Noon Cape La Chat[240] bore ESE Dist: 12 Leagues; we are now 60. Leags from Quebec Can see no sign of Inhabitants nor any Cultivated Land.

Thurs., 30th July. At 4 P M Cape La Chat bore SEBS Dist: two Leagues; at 8 Do. abrest of Cape La Chat and therefore Distance from Quebec 72. Leagues From 8 P M to 10 A M fresh Gales of wind at WNB Steering between the East and SEBS; At Noon Cape Rosea[241] bore SBE Dist:

[240] Cape Chat.
[241] Cape Rosier.

per judgm't 5. Leagues; are now 120. Leags or 360 Miles. Distant from Quebec.

Fri., 31 July. At 4 P M Cape Rosea bore NNW't Distant 3. or 4. Leagues; and the Island Bon Vent[242] SW Dist. 2. Leag; Little wind, brought too and Caught Some Fish 80 Fathams water At 8 P M the Island Bon Vent or the High Land of Gaspa [243] bore SWBW't Dist 4. Leagues Steering SE wind NW; At Noon the High Land of Gaspa bore NWBNo. Dist. 69 miles or 23 Leagues.

Sat., 1st of August. At 6 P M the Isle Lazore bore So. La Margretta[244] SBE and Breo[245] SBW't; Saw Great Numbers of Manattees or Sea Cows; Sounded 85 Fathams Rocky Ground. At Noon the Island St. Paul[246] bore SEBS and the North Cape on the Isle De Gaspa or Cape Briton[247] Bore SSW Dist per Judgment 5. Leagues.

Sun., 2d August. The former part of this 24 hours light Airs of wind at SW Hazey Weather; Turning between the Island St. Paul and Cape Britton; A Noon Cape Britton bore NWBNo. Dist: per judgment 10. Leagues. we see here none of our Cruizers out of Cape Britton though I hope there will be a Good many in the Gulph and River St. Laurance in the fall of the year; For when we left Quebec there was 17 Sail of Topsail vessells vizt. One man of war of 28. Guns, 12 Sail of Merchantmen from 150. to 300. Tons with 18 and 20 Guns Each There are Likewise 2. Brigenteens and 2 Snows; all or the far greater part of which are bound in the Fall of the year for Europe or the west Indies and may be Good Prizes should our Cruizers be so fortunate as to fall in with them NB they must Cruize Late for the above vessells will not leave Quebec till the Begining of November.

[242] Bonaventure Island.

[243] Cape Gaspé.

[244] Probably Magdalen Islands.

[245] Probably Byron Island.

[246] St. Paul Island.

[247] Cape North, Cape Breton Island. Norton also records the passing of Cape Breton Island. Norton, p. 50.

From *Sun.* the 2d to *Thurs.* the 13th of August. Nothing worthy of Note; we have had the wind for the far greater part between the West and SW't; and when we had light airs of wind and on Fishing Ground we Used to lay too and Fish, a while; but when any of the English Prisoners Caught any Fish, Monsieur as if he still Owed us the old Grudge used to Order his Officers to take it away from them; As Mr. Cox of Salem Caught 4 fine Fish and Desired one of them for his Mess but it would not be granted; Mons'r Loree Likewise Put one of his own People in Irons for no other Reason then giving one of the English Prisoners a Cod hook; These were Pitifull Actions and no way becoming a Gentleman of so Polite a Nation as France, we had Certainly never Tamely Submitted to these things and Several Others but for 2. Reasons First, as he was Capt'n of a Flag of Truce and the first that e're was sent from Quebec and on that account were not willing to give him Any Umbrage; The next reason was that we did not know but such an Action might Disoblidge His Excell'y Wm. Shirley Esq'r to Whom he was sent Or otherwise we should Certainly have Oblidged Monsieur to have been more Bountifull with that which Heaven had put in Our Power for a Reliefe as many of us had ben Prisoners 2. years and in Eating Salt Provissions were Far gone with the Scurvy. We have not Seen the Land Since *Sun.* the 2d of August but Judge we are now off the Harbour of Jebuctore which I left this Day 12 months in order for Our March to Canada; Buried one Nicholass Bert late of Dartmouth in the County of Devon.[248]

Fri., 14th August. Early in the Morn made Pidgeon Hill or Cape Ann; Caught many Mackrell and Cod.

Sun., 16th August. At 4. in the Morning made Boston Light House, at 6 Fier'd a Gun for a Pilote; at 7 Do. took a Pilote on Board; at 11 Came to an Anchor off the Long Warff Boston; and at About 1. in the Afternoon Landed at Boston. GLORIA DEO. NB Saw Mr. Robt. Ball a Na-

[248] Norton records the death of Nicholas Bert or Burt under date of August 11. Norton, p. 50.

tive of Great Yarmouth; he by good Fortune for me was our Pilote.[249]

Mon., the 17th of August. At my Lodgings Mr. John Williams in King Street Boston I this Day wrote to Messrs. Touchit and Compa. To Captn. John Oldham London likewise to Weybread via London by a Brigenteen.[250]

Wed. 19th. Drew up a Declaration in Order to Protest with regard to the Adventure The French having refused to give a Coppy of her Condemnation.

Fri. 21st. Saw to my great Surprise Captn. John Oldham which prevented my Protesting. Rec'd of Justice Hubart[251] by Order of the Honourable Committee 5 old Tenor value Sterling Ten Shillings which procured me a pair of shoes and Stockings of which I was never in Greater Need.

Sat., 22d August. I this Day fell in Company with one of the Honourable Comittee who Amongst other things Assured me he had Seen his Exell'y Governer Boharnois's Letter to His Excellency Wm. Shirley Esq'r Governer of Boston[252] wherin amongst Other things he Assured His Excellency Governer Shirley of his great Tenderness and Clemency to the English Prisoners Notwithstanding their Refractory Humers nay Somtimes they were Incorigable to a very High Degree as in Setting fire to the Prison House and burning it Down as Mentioned the 28th of Aprill last past. But under Favour his Excellency hath forgot Himself in that respect: for when the Prison was burnt Down We were Conducted into a Court before the Governers Pallace when About an

[249] Norton also records the arrival at Boston, August 16, 1747. Norton, pp. 50–51. *The Boston Gazette or Weekly Journal* of Tuesday, August 18, 1747, prints a list received from Norton of the arrivals in the *Verd de Grace*. Among those listed must be the author of this journal. The *New-York Gazette Revived in the Weekly Post-Boy* of August 24, 1747, also tells of the arrival of a flag of truce with one hundred and seventy-one prisoners from Quebec at Boston, August 16, 1747.

[250] *Ante*, notes 1 and 56. A James Williams lived in King Street in 1744. Record Commissioners of the City of Boston, *Selectmen's Minutes from 1742/3 to 1753* (Boston, 1887), p. 79.

[251] Nathaniel Hubbard, justice of the Superior Court of Judicature.

[252] For the letter of Beauharnois to Shirley, see *Collection de Manuscrits . . . relatifs à la Nouvelle-France* (4 vols., Quebec, 1883–1885), III, 371–377.

hour before we March'd for our Rendezvous His Excellency; His Lordship the Intendant, Monsieur Comissary, and the rest of the Hon'ble Assembly in the Palace Sent for Captn. Wm. Pote (a fellow Prisoner with us) who Could Speak very good French and in His Excellency's Propper Ear and before the Whole Assembly then Sitting His Lordship the Intendant rose up and told Captn. Pote that they had Enquired into the Cause of the Prison taking fire and had found Sufficient reasons for Honourably Acquitting Every Prisoner of setting fire to the House as was as first Suggested.[253] He further Subjoin'd his reasons as appeared upon Examination of the Officer and guard which were these

First, that the fire broke out at 7 o'th Clock in the Morning when Every Prisoner was Lock'd up in his or their Respective Rooms.

Secondly, that there was no fire in any of the rooms belonging to the Prisoners all the night past.

Thirdly; that the Prisoners could not Either by Day or night get at the Place where the fire broke out and was first Discovered which was on the very Ridge of the Roof on the Outside and at the Center of the House over the Room in which the Guard Lay, in which Room was a Large fire all night and since at the Joining of the Roof to the Chimney was the place the fire first broke out, it Appeared very plain before His Lordship and Counsell That the Sparks of fire which blew out of the Chimney (which was not 4. Foot above the Roof) lit upon the Chingles they being Dry and the wind blowing fresh fired the House and not any of the Prisoners.

Nay the French in Rebuilding the House have to remedy the like Inconvenience Set the roof the Same height it before were but raised the Chimneys full 4. foot higher then they were.

And as His Excellency Boharnois Mentioned his Great Tenderness and Clemency to the Prisoners, I shall Instance a few Cases well known to Every Gentleman who was Prisoner with me which Cases will in the Opinion of any Impar-

[253] This agrees with Pote's entry of April 28, 1747. Pote, pp. 123–124.

tial Person Appear to be the Reverse of what His Excellency has so Largly Insisted on. As the 2 Prisoners who Died first were Strip'd and their Bodies thrown Out upon the Strand in the NW't Arm of the River Opposite the Prison and the Savages Suffered to Mangle their Bodies at Pleasure in Sight of the Prisoners in the House. This was very Pathetically Complain'd of in a Letter to His Excellency by Captn. Wm. Chapman of Patuxent River Maryland; and on that Account no one Ever knew rightly what became of the bodies of those who Died Afterwards.

That on the 11th of October 1746. His Excellency Abbridg'd us of 1/3 part of our former Allowence and Continued it till our releasment which was on the 25th of July 1747

That thro' the Scarsity and badness of the Provissions an Epidemical Disease raged amongst us which Sweept off a Great many; and he having Allotted a Room at the Common Throughfare of the House for an Infirmary many were Daily falling Ill of which we Often Complain'd to His Excellency but Could get no redress; At length the Eldest Daughter of Monsieur Lorain our Keeper Caught the Distemper and Died of it, at the Same time his Wife and Second Daughter lay Ill of it and was given Over by the Doctors as past recovery It in the same Week Caried off The Rever'd Father Chaveleze who used to vissit us and by his means got into the Town as mentioned the 4th and 5th of January; however at The Earnest request of Monsieur Lorain our Keeper his Excellency Did Order an Infirmary to be fitted up for the Sick about 1/4. mile out of Town after the Distemper had Caried off a Great many Prisoners.

That after this new Infirmary was fitted up and any was sent there and found Themselves Declining, His Excellency (tho Earnestly Petitioned) would not permit any one to goe to them in Order to be let into his or their private Affairs or to make a Will. Children were Debar'd from seeing their Parants in their last Moments; Wifes were not permitted to attend on their Husbands in their Sickness tho' as I said before Earnestly Petitioned.

That on Tuesday the 4th of November 1746 His Excellency Delivered up 7. free Christian Indians lately belonging to Captn. Zepheniah Pinkham of Nantuckett Isle into the hands of the Barbarian Canada Indians.

That His Excellency Debar'd us of Every Advantage which we might have reap'd from the Charity and well Disposed Persons in Town who would very readily have Suply'd us with vegitables at their own Expence by Treatning us with the Cashot or Dungeon if we Dar'd to speak with any one thro the Piquets Nay So very Rigorous was he in this respect that Mr. Gratis Vanderwerick a Native of Albany in the Government of New York Aged 68 years was Kept in the Cashot 7 Days and Nights at bread and water for no Other reason then beging a Pipe of Tobacko of a Frenchman who was on the Outside the Piquets.

That His Excellency gave an Unlimited Power to his Officer Monsieur Lorain our Keeper who most Scandalously abused us in many Articles and whenever we Appealed to his Excellency for redress as we frequently did by Petition those Petitions must goe through Lorains hand and as they Chiefly Concern'd him Lorain took Care never to let his Excellency see them; by which means he Gull'd us out of our Properties and Laught at us into the Bargin. These were Agravating Circumstances of which we Often Complain'd to the Gentlemen who vissited us but they allways told us it was not in their Power to redress them, nay they dare not cary a Petition to his Excellency. We then got the Clergy in our favour to Convey our Petitions which then our Greviances were redress'd for about a Week and after that Lorain went on in the Same Course as before and Continued till we Came Away When the Rascall had the Impudence to Ask of the Gentlemen Prisoners a Letter in his favour to the English Officers and Gentlemen in Case the Town and Country Should hereafter be Invested by them.

That on Wednessday the 17th of June The French brought into Quebec 4 Gentleman Volantiers belonging to Albany in the Province of New York who were Taken Prisoners near mount Royall with 12 Indians; These Gentlemen Were not brought to our Camp but Put into the Common Prison with Fellons and the Indians taken with them We aske'd Some Gentlemen Officers who frequently vissitted us the reason for So Extraordinary a President; when they Inform'd us it was His Excellency's Pleasure that as those Gentlemen had ben Taken in Comp'y with the Indians they Should share the same fate Notwithstanding they were Gentlemen of Good Families and Fortunes and bore Commissions under Governer Clinton of New York Now it is Notorious that the French Themselves not only Soldiers but Officers During the Present War when they Come upon the British Settlements with Indians (as they too frequently doe) they Dress and Paint in the same Manner as the Indians doe Nay the Rev'd John Norton Assured me that When he was beset and Taken att Fort Massachusetts he Could not Distinguish the one from the other but the French Appear'd in all respects like the Indians not only in their Dress but in their Gesture and Hellish Din the Indians make at an Assault; the Same I have heard often Confirm'd by the Prisoners in our Camp who were Taken at Albany.

Lastly His Excellency keeping the young Children from their Parants under The Pretence of the Money's for their Redemption from Out of the hands of the Savages not being paid; see one Instance at large on the 18th of July last; His Letting the Children to the Number of 30 remain in the hands of the Savages whose Parants we left in Quebec nor will they admit of a releasment without their Children All which Considered with the foregoing as they are Facts Cannot be Taken as marks of his great Tenderness and Clemency. To Conclude; I think with respect to the great place his Excellency fills; A little more truth as well as Common Sense had Certainly done his Letter no harm.

* * *

Remarks On the Town of Boston the Principle Town in New England. This Town is Situated on a Peninsula of about 2 miles in Length and one in Breadth at the bottom of the Massachusetts Bay which makes a Noble Harbour for

Shiping as there are many Islands lye in this Bay Tho' our Men of War Usually ride in Nantasket Roade which is a small Bay to the SW't; The Town is Defended by a Fine Fort on an Island Directly in the Trade Way, and has in it . . . Guns[254] from . . . pounders to . . . Pounders here are likewise Several Battery's at the Town near the Water side. Here are a Great many Warffs, Steaths, and Keys, for the greater Conveniency of Landing and taking on Board all Sorts of Merchantdize Tho' the most remarkable is the Long Warff on which is a fine Crane; it has Likewise a Battery at the very Head of 11 Pieces of Cannon Erected at the Time the French Grand Fleet Laid in Jebuctore. This Town makes a very Pretty Prospect from an Eminance on The back side of it Call'd Bacon or Beacon Hill; it is much Larger then the Town of Great Yarmouth in the County of Norff but I very much Question Wether there are more Inhabitants then in Yarmouth The Town is very Conveniently laid into Streets which are paved with Stone and Kept Tolerably Clean. Here are a Great many very Sightly Houses built of Brick but to the Honour and Glory of the Lord; their Churches are of Clap board and Chingles. Their Religion is Chiefly Presbetry but in that they Differ very much Even in the most assential Articles of Faith this Creates Annamosities and Heats amongst them Inasmuch as that Pastor who Drew all the Congregations to Himself in the Spring of the Year yet in the Fall he may Preach to Empty Pews 'till he has thought of somthing New which will Certainly bring them all back again; In short they are of the same Stamp with Hudibrass whose Religion the Facetious Butler have so Ingeniously Describ'd when he Says

His Religion it was fit
To Match his Learning and his Wit
'Twas Presbiterian true Blew
For he was of that Stubborn Crew
Or Errant Saints whom all men grant
To be the True Church Militant

[254] The author of the journal apparently intended to fill in this and the following blanks later, but failed to do so.

Such as Doe build their faith upon
The Holy Text of Pike and Gun
Decide all Controverssies by
Infallable Artillery
And Prove their Doctrine Orthordox
From Apostolick blows and Knocks
Call Fire and Sword and Desolation
A Godly Thrower Reformation
Which Allways must be Caried on
And Still in Doeing never Done
As though Religion was Intended
For nothing Else but to be Mended
Still So perverse and Oposite
As though they Worshiped God thro' Spight
One thing they one way will Abhor
Another Long Another for
As though Religion it had Catch'd
The Itch on Purpose to be Scratch'd
A Sect whose whole Devotion lies
In odd perverse Antipathies
In falling out with that or this
And finding Somewhat Still Amiss
More Pevish Cross and Spleenatick
Then Dog Distract or Monkey Sick
That with more hast keep Holiday
The Wrong then others the right way
Compound for Sins they are Inclin'd too
By Damning those they have no mind too
For Saints may doe the Same thing by
The Spirit in Sincerrity
Which Other men are Tempted too
And at the Devils Instance doe
And yet the Action be Contrary
Just as the Saints and wicked vary
For as on Land there is no Beast
But what at Sea's in Fish Exprest
So of the wicked there's no vice
But what the Saints will have a Spice
They'l prove they to the Devil may goe
If they have Motives thereunto
For as there is a War Between
The Devil and them it is no Sin
If they by Subtill Stratagem
Make use of him as he does them
Is it not Rediculous and Nonsence

A Saint Should be a Slave to Consience
That ought to be above Such Fancies
As far as above Ordinances
—*vide Butler's Hudibrass*[255]

But what has Greatly Increased their Desentions amongst them was the Coming over of thier Dearly Beloved in the Lord George Whitfield[256] that Montabank in Divinity whose Tenets hath Set the Father against the Son and Mother and Daughter at varience; The Son leaves his Trade and Occupation and Commence Teacher who with a Parcle of Tatterdemolians at his Arse runs about the Country with their Exhortations and Preaching of Repentance to a Sinfull People; The Daughters Leave the Mothers House and joyns with another Party wherin there is neither Brother nor any Relation Except that of Brother and Sister in the Lord and whatever is done and Caried on in this way is Righteous and Pure tho' it is to be Questioned very much whether the flesh does not get the better of the Spirit Sometimes. Besides these Exhorters there are your Seven Day Gentry[257] your New Lights[258] your Levelers[259] etc. etc. These have a Good many followers But they are Chiefly Lazy Rogues who live upon the Credelity of others Here are other Parties which meet in Private Houses and hold forth their Doctrines to the People in Such a manner as is hardly to be Credited Their Dealing about Large Quantities of Brimstone and fier, Hell, and Damnation; and his Laying about him with Such Vehemence one would take him to be a Freeholder in Bethleham Moore Fields;[260] Thus when he has wrought his Audience to a Pitch that many of both Sexes have fall'n into a

[255] Samuel Butler, *Hudibras*, Part I., Canto I., lines 189–206, 217–220, 165–166, 207–216; Part II., Canto II., lines 235–250; with slight variations.

[256] George Whitefield, 1714–1770, leader of the Calvinistic Methodists, at this time on his third visit to America and preaching in and around Boston.

[257] The Seventh-Day Baptists had founded a church at Newport, Rhode Island, in 1671.

[258] The followers of George Whitefield.

[259] At the time of the English civil wars, the term designated the republicans.

[260] Bethlehem Hospital for the insane, commonly known as Bedlam, at this time located in Moorfields.

fit and others have ben Assisting them, he has had the Impudence to Call to them Aloud to let them alone for that the Holy Spirit was then Actuating them and that the Lord Jesus was Showing his Power in making of them Converts through his means; He would then lay bare His Bosom and with Great Emmotion Cry out Come in Sweet Jesus come in! repeating the same many times over till the Congregation has ben wrapt'd up in wonder and Amazement At another time this Gentleman was Preaching against the Pomp and vanities of the World and from thence took Occation to handle that of Dressing in Perticular wherin he Insisted that a Garment of Sackcloth was most propper for a Deciple of the Lord Jesus and in Order to Inforce his Doctrine on his Audience he Imediately pull'd off his Velvet Bretches and threw them into the fier which was seconded by many of His Congregation who threw in their Velvet Scarfs, hoods, Aprons, Handkerchiefs, and other Loose Attire; They then fell to burning Books some of which was the English Common Prayer but as this Gentleman has at Length Made a Publick Recantation of all his Errours he shall be Name less.

With this Gentleman Several Others have likewise recanted and return'd to their Lawfull vocations and it must now be Said that this Spirit of Anthusism is of Late very much Diminished. When Mr. Whitfield first came over the Clergy of all Sects allow'd him the free use of their Pulpits but he at length got to the same Height as he did in and about London when the Clergy for the Same Reason Refused him their Pulpits he then betook himself to the Fields and High ways where I see him with his Congregation about him Thus

With Native Squint See Whitfield Stands
Tuneing his voice and Ballancing his hands
How fluent Nonsence Trickles from his Tongue
How Sweets the Periods Neither said nor Sung
For him the Shuttles left by Lazy Weavers
And Butchers Drop their Marrow bones and Clevers
And whilst the Weavers Wife forsakes her Loom

Susan Leaves half unmop'd the Dining Room
These are the Dreggs the Rubish of Mankind
Sight less themselves and Guided by the Blind
Strangers to virtue as unknown to Schools
As Every like is like Fools Cherish Fools[261]

But to proceed; with regard to keeping the Lords Day I believe it is no where more Strictly Observed then in the Governments of the Massachusetts Bay, New Hampshier and Conecticutt wherin they are very Strickt as not Suffering any Person to ride Except for a Midwife or Doctor which by the by is allways the Pretence when they are stop'd So here's a D—d lye told to Compound for a little Recreation; nor will they suffer Any one to walk Abroad tho' after Divine Service is over for that Day which have Induced many to play at Cards in their Rooms and so goe to the Devil purely out of Spight; I my self went out of Curiosity To see a Large Vessell Launch'd which had fall'n out of her Cradles the Saturday before the Tide serving about 6 in the Afternoon but I was Escourted to my Lodgings by 3 Constables at my Arse Nay so very Strickt are they in this regard both to man and beast that I have ben Crediabley Informed that in one of the forementioned Governments they made the owner of a Stalion Transport his beast to the west Indies or otherwise they would have Kill'd him for Horsing a mare on the Lords Day.

There was an Elder in Conectucutt who Considering he was Oblidged to present any Inormaties he knew of upon Oath would not let his Neighbor and fellow Elder rest till he had presented him for Conubiall rites with his Wife on the Lords Day and he paid his fine Accordingly.

A Deacon in the Massachusetts Government Hung his Cat on the Moonday Morning for that it was proved against her she had Caught a mouse on the Lords Day While he was at Meeting, these 2 Last mentioned persons are now alive.[262]

[261] Unidentified.

[262] With such stories as these current in New England, the exaggerations of Rev. Samuel Andrew Peters in his *General History of Connecticut* are more easily understood.

As to their Laws they are for the most part the same as in Old England yet they put Iniquity to't with a vengance Lip Lechery they will by no means Admit of As a Master of a vessell who had ben a Long voyage and Coming home on the Lords Day and meeting with his Wife in the Street he Salluted her for which he was Oblidged to pay the fine to save his back from the Whiping post. Though the Pretty Girls will by no means Loose their Teeming Time which is Generally the Latter End of October when they Husk their Indian Corn, for it has ben a Quere Often Started as Wether there is not more Bastards got in New England a Husking Time then in Old England in the Nutting Season. But to return to their Administration of Justice; the most Remarkable Case Is that of the Plymouth Collony where they Hung one Phenias Prat a useless Bedrid weaver in the Room of a Teaching Cobler who had Kill'd an Indian The Story is at Large in Hudibrass as Follows

Justice gives Sentance many Times
On one man for anothers Crimes
Our Bretheren in New England use
Choise Malafactors to Excuse
And Hang the Guiltless in their Stead
Of whom the Churches have Less Need
As it Lately hapned in a Town
There was a Cobler and but one
Who out of Doctrines Could Cut use
And mend mens Lives as well as Shoes
This Precious Brother having Slain
In Times of Peace an Indian
Not out of Malice but meer Zeal
Because he was an Infidel
The Mighty Totty potty moy
Sent to our Elders an Envoy
Complaining much of breach of Trust
And League held forth by Brother Patch
Inforc'd the Articles in Power
Betwixt both Churches his and our
They required them to render
Into their Hands or hang th Offender
But they having the Case Maturely Weigh'd
And Considering they had no more than him o'th Trade

That Serv'd them in a Double
Capasity to Teach and Cobble
Yet to doe
The Indian Hoganmogan Justice too
In his Stead did
Hang an Old Weaver that was bedrid
So Justice while She Whinks on Crimes
Stumble on Inocence Sometimes[263]

This Case hapned about 3 years after their first Landing in these American parts in the year 1623.[264]

By their Charter granted too them by King James the 1st[265] and other Succeeding Princes they have the Previlidge of Enacting Laws for the Better Regullation and Governing their Colloneys but those Laws are to be as near the English as Possible and they are to Appeal to England if Occation

[263] In Hudibras, the last half of this passage reads, more correctly:

"The mighty Tottipottimoy
Sent to our elders an envoy,
Complaining sorely of the breach
Of league, held forth by brother Patch,
Against the articles in force
Between both churches, his and ours;
For which he crav'd the saints to render
Into his hands, or hang th' offender:
But they maturely having weigh'd
They had no more but him o' th' trade,
A man that serv'd them in a double
Capacity, to teach and cobble,
Resolv'd to spare him; yet to do
The Indian Hoghan Moghan too
Impartial justice, in his stead did
Hang an old weaver that was bed-rid:
When wherefore may not you be skipp'd,
And in your room another whipp'd?
For all philosophers, but the sceptic,
Hold whipping may be sympathetic."

—Butler, *Hudibras*, Part II., Canto II., lines 407–440.

[264] Phinehas Pratt died in Charlestown, Massachusetts, April 19, 1680.

[265] The author of the journal is not very accurate in his history. The first charter to the Governor and Company of the Massachusetts Bay in New England was issued by Charles I, March 4, 1628/9.

Require where the Rigor of the Law if often Mittigated. But these Saints or rather Puritans who for an undefiled Conscience and the Love of Pure Christianity first left their Native and Pleasant Land and Encountered all the Dangers of the Tumultuous Ocean in Search of some Uncultivated Land where they might Quietly enjoy their Religious Liberties and Transmit them to Posterity; yet these Saints I say no sooner got into their hands their Charter then they fell to Law Making with great precipitation and Hurry and laid hold on all who Dissented from them, as the Quakers; Annabaptists and Some few Churchmen; whom they Persicuted to Death and Confiscation of Goods; Some they Hung, others they burnt; Some they Whip'd Unmercifully and all this without once giveing them the Previlidge of Appealing to England; Nay so very rigorous where they to the Quakers and Annabaptists that they would not Suffer them to Settle Amongst them but put them into an Open Shallop without any oars Rudder or Tackling and turnd them Adrift to the Whide Ocean.[266] Thus Foreign Popery may prove a Curse But English Popery is Worse. Of these who were Turnd Adrift their Number were 18 where they Landed at a place to which they gave the Name of Providence which together with Rhode Island after they had Purchased it of the Indians they Procured a Charter and form'd themselves into a Government by the Name of the Collony of Rhode Island and Providence Plantations in New England. One thing is Worthy of Remark As that when these Aforesaid 18 Persons Landed in these parts here were Swarms of Indians who never Interupted them but on the other hand very readily assisted them in Planting and raising Corn for their Subsistance till at Length these 18 were Inabled to purchase of the Indians the whole Island for Blankets Hatchets etc. which being Punctually paid the Indians by Order of their Sachem (or King) Drew off the

[266] In the banishment of Roger Williams and Anne Hutchinson, and its treatment of the Quakers, Massachusetts Bay Colony has enough to answer for, without the addition of these untrue details.

Island and never Came on again to molest 'em.[267] And about the year 1657 several Gentlemen on the Island made a Considerable Purchase on the main Called the Petaquamscut Purchase and the same year they Purchased the Island of Canonicut as the smaller Islands had ben Purchased before.

In 1665 Misquamicut was purchased of the Indians and it was Granted a Township by the Name of Westerly 1669; In 1672 Manisses Call'd Block Island was made a Township by the Name of New Shoreham.

In 1674 the Inhabitants at Petaquamscut and Parts adjacent had their Lands Incorporated a Township by the Name of Kingston, and In 1677 the Town of East Green-which was Incorporated; and in 1678 Canonicut Island was Incorporated by the Name of James Town; In 1722 the Lands properly Called Narraganset were Divided into two Townships of No. and So. Kingston; In 1729 the whole Colony was Divided into 3 Counties for the ease of the Inhabitants; And in 1730 the Town of Providence was Divided into the 4 Towns of Providence, Smithfield, Glocester, and Scituate The whole Land being filled with Inhabitants Partly by the Coming over of some Few from other places, but Chiefly by the Natural Increase of the first Settlers.

In the foresaid year 1730 there was by the Kings Order an Exact account taken of the Number of souls in the Collony and they were found to be as in the following table. The Number of Inhabitants in the 2 Towns on Rhode Island vizt. Newport and Pourtsmouth were as above said to be 5458 of which the Town of Newport Contains 4640 of them; who are at this Time Increased to Upwards of 5000 souls At Present there are Above 100 sail of vessells belonging to this Town, besides what belong to the rest of the Collony.

[267] Thus far Mr. John Callender's Historical Discourse from the first Settlement in 1638 to the End of the 1't Century 1739. [Note by the author of the journal, citing John Callender, *An Historical Discourse on the Civil and Religious Affairs of the Colony of Rhode-Island and Providence Plantations in New-England in America. From the First Settlement 1638 to the End of the First Century* (Boston, 1739); reprinted in Rhode Island Historical Society *Collections*, IV, (Providence, 1838); and again at Boston, 1843.]

TOWNS	WHITES	NEGROES	INDIANS
Newport	3843	649	184
Providence	3707	128	81
Portsmouth	643	100	70
Warwick	1028	77	73
Westerly	1620	56	250
North Kingston	1875	165	65
South Kingston	965	333	225
East Greenwich	1149	40	34
James Town	222	80	19
New Shoreham	250	20	20
Total	15302	1648	985

Thus, from Small Beginings great things may be accomplished Esspecially where there is Unanmity in their Counsells; for though they are Divided into many Different Sects and Parties with regard to their Publick Worship they very rarely Ever Wrangle about the Roade to Life to Come, because allmost Every one take a Different Path; which by the by is the right way to prevent their Jostling one another; An Interest in Trade is the Chief Aim they Drive at, for doe but Ask any one of them what Opinion he is of with regard to Religion and he'l tell you he'l sell as Cheap As any body Considering the Present price of Mollasses and the Depreciating their Money; I have my self known Some who have had the Consience to advance above 30 per Cent on a bargin which would have ammounted to upwards of 300£ Sterling because forsouth Mollasses was advanced about 2d. Sterling per Gallon Though it is very much to be Questioned wether he used 6 Gallons in his House the whole year The Depreciating their money is another Grand Topick which they make use of on all Occations where there is a Bargin Depending wether amongst Tradesmen or Handycrafts but for fear they should be overreached by a Foreigner they will be sure to be on the right Side of the Question as their money has fallen within these 2 years about 3 1/2 per Cent they'l advance upon their Goods or Labour above 30 per Cent for fear it should fall still Lower in Short one would Sware they were the Sons of Pawnbrokers Stockjobbers or Jews Since they Overreach by Instinct and Cheat by Constitution.

This Island of Rhode Island is about 14 or 15 miles Long and about 4 or 5 miles Broad and is justly Esteemed the Paradise of New England for the Fruitfullness of the Soil and the Temperateness of the Climate that tho' it be not above 65 miles South of Boston is a Coate warmer in winter and being Surrounded by the Ocean is not so much Affected in Summer with the hot Land Breezes as the Towns on the Continent; here is all the Summer a South or Southwesterly Sea Breeze allmost Every Day which riseth about 10 A M and wonderfully cools the air and by that means renders it more Healthy then those Towns on the Continent as before Observe'd. this pleasantness of Situation, the Conveniency of Trade, the Nature of their Government, the Inconsiderable Imposts usally paid for Foreign Goods, And the Tollaration given to all Sects in Religious matters are Strong Inducements to Strangers to Settle amongst them; and if he has but Money he may find an Oppertunity to Improve it to very great Advantage; And be Caress'd by the Great, Vulgar, and the small; but if by repeated Losses and Misfortunes he should be reduced; they'l be Sure to run over his back to pay their respects to the Next fortune's favourite they see rising in their Hemisphere. In Short; A man who has Money here (no matter how he came by it) he is Every thing, and wanting that he's a meer Nothing let his Conduct be Ever so Ereproachable. Money is here the True fullers Earth for Reputation there is not a Spot or a Stain but it will take out. Therefere

T'have Money is a necessary Task,
From whence t'is got the world will never ask.
He that grows Rich by Scowring of a Sink
Gets Wherewithall to Justifie the Stink[268]

These things being Wisely considered amongst them, they leave no Stone unturn'd to accomplish their Design of gaining Wealth, and as they are Naturally Credilous with-

[268] Unidentified.

all; they freequently apply themselves to those Gentry call'd Conjurers of which here are many who Make a Gainfull Trade of their Credility Though they'l Dispose of Fortunes favours at an Easy rate; The price is 20 Shillings Old Tenor for the which they'l promise you at Least 2000£'s worth of Good Fortune if he finds the Stars to favour his Design and he has made no Blunder in the Calculation; this Last Salvo is freequently put in to Save his reputation for if the Party should in the Course of his affairs prove unsuccessfull Mr. Conju'r will then save his Credit by telling him he had Mistook a Figure in the Calculation.

I by Axident fell into the Company of one of these Gentlemen Conjurers one Evening who was telling of his Neighbor of his Wonderfull Successes in the Course of his Practice, and that he had sent out of the Harbour of New London in the Colony of Conecticut 17 Sail of vessells at the Critical minute prescrib'd by him, and that Every one of them got Safe home and had made prodigeous voyages; with a great many other Wonderfull things he had done during his 20 years Practice in that Study, which Induced me to ask of him some Questions Concerning his Art; As how he could foretell those Events which Exactly fell out according to his predixtions, he told me he did it by the Certain and Infailable Rules of Art; I ask'd him farther what those Rules were, he told me that he got his Bread by it and that he had Taught it to many; I then to sooth his vanity told him that if I Could be once assured there was Certain and Infalible Rules to goe by I would be his Schollar He then run on with a heap of Jargon worse then Ever was Coin'd by Ptolomy, Agripia, Bumbartus or any or all of the Antient Star gazers or Cunjurers Though Conjuring according to Bailey's Deffinition of the word is an Actual dealing with the Devil; and then.

> If the Devil is of their Counsell
> Much may be Done my Noble Donsell
> —*Hudibrass*[269]

[269] "But if the Devil's of your counsel,
Much may be done, my noble donsel;"
—*Hudibras*, Part II., Canto II., lines 571–572.

But to proceed; I told him I did not under Stand all that heap of Stuff, I wanted to be Inform'd how he proceeded with regard to his Calculating Nativities since as he often Insisted that he proceeded by Certain and Infailiable Rules and therefore I had Concieved they were such rules as was made use of in the Course of Practical Astronomy of which I ask'd him if he was vers'd in them he frankly told me no but he could calculate the places of the Planets to a Notch as he Calld it and that he could tell when any of them were in Oposition to or from the Sun when they were in a Trine, or Quartile, or Conjunction; when they Shed their Sweetest Influences and then was the Time to undertake any Business and I should be sure of Succeeding in the affair; he could Calculate when they were in Oposition and when their influences were most Dangerous to man or Beast; in Short if you would but believe him he was the very Epitomy of S'r Sidrophel

> Who knew the Seat of Paradise
> Could tell in what Degree it Lies
> And as he was Disposed could prove it
> Below the Moon or Else above it
>
> —*Hudibrass*[270]

At Length I found I was not like to be one jot the wiser for him; though I verily believe he would have told me somthing had he known any thing himself; till an oppertunity offered it Self to put a final End to the Dispute in hand and Convince me at once of his Ignorance the Case was thus; I rose up to goe out of the Room and saw one of the Planets and one of the most Remarkable as it was then the Evening Star which was then about 20 Degrees high and shone very bright; I Call'd to Mr. Star gazer and asked him what Star that was pointing to the Planet; he answered after A Little pause that it was the great Dog Star Calld Sirus; I told him that he must surely be mistaken and therefore I would have him recollect but he would not but in a Chafe told me he knew the Stars too well to be told by any one I then told

[270] *Hudibras,* Part I., Canto I., lines 173–176.

him he had Sufficiently convinced me that he knew Nothing of the matter for Mr. Star gazer Said I you could not have pitched upon such another Star in our Hemisphere to Display your Ignorance; for don't you know that it is now the Dog days and that the Dog Star is with the Sun and Therefore cannot be seen at all in our Hemisphere nor will not be seen by us for some Weeks; and farther that the Star which you now see and Insisted was the Dog Star is no other then the Planet Venus which is now the Evening Star; 'tis Strange you should not know your most Intimate friends when you see them but still more Strange that you Should Calculate their places in the Heavens and yet Mistake a Planet for a Star of the first Magnitude But I would ask these Star gazing Gentry (had they but wit Enough) this one Question Wether the Stars repell or Decline; If they say they Repell they Speak Little Less then Blaspheamy by Ascribing too much to Nature; Should they Say they Decline then what sure ground have they to goe on, since as Butler says in his Hudibrass

> Ther's but the Twinkling of a Star,
> Between a man of Peace, and War,
> A Fool, a Justice, and a Knave,
> A Huffing Officer, and a Slave,
> A Crafty Lawer, and Pickpocket,
> A Formal Preacher, and a Blockhead,
> As though men from the Stars did Suck
> Old Age Diseases, and Ill Luck
> And Drew with the first air they breath,
> Battle and Murder, Sudden Death;
> Are not these fine Comodities,
> To be Imported from the Skies,
> And Vended here amongst the Rable,
> As Staple goods, and Warrentable;
> Like Money of the Druiads Borrow'd
> In the other world to be Restored.[271]

But let the folly of peoples Enquiring after their futer fortunes appear never so Rediculous and these Conjurers as they call be never so Ignorant they will not want Votaries

[271] *Hudibras*, Part II., Canto III., lines 957–976.

so long as some who have got Money apply to these Cuning men for advise in all their affairs for, say they, dont tell me that it is all a mere Juggle when Every body knows that Mr. such a one and his Partners never send a vessel to sea nor will they Transact any Business of Importance without first applying to the Cuning man to know the Critical minute the vessell is to sail or when they are to undertake their Business; and we find that these men never meet with a Loss at Sea nor by Land but have got good Estates Therefore why may not my fortune be as good as their Could I but know the Critical Minute to make use of it which I may Easily doe 'tis but Riding a few miles to the Cuning man; and as to the Charge it is but 20 Shillings Old Tenor a meere Trifle Considering that for that Sum I secure a vessell and her Cargoe out and home; These Considerations have Induced many Tradesmen as well Machanicks to Trust their fortunes to Sea and if in two or Three voyages they prove Successfull they then Commence Merchants of which Sort the Generality of Newport now Consists.

> Whose knowledge oft with utmost Stretch of Brain,
> No further then this vast Secret can attain,
> Five and four is nine, take two and Seven remain.[272]

But I Shall now Conclude my remarks on New England with the following Prayer of a Godly Bostonian who goes to the Meeting twice a Day and is very well Effected to these Present Governments. Lord thou know'st I have nine Houses in the Town of Boston, and that I have Lately Purchased an Estate in Fee Simple in the Colony of new Hampshire; Lord I beg of the to have an Eye of Compassion on the two Colony's of the Massachusets and Hampshire And as I have a Mortagage in Conecticut I would beg of the to have an Eye of Compassion on that Colony allso; As to the rest of the Colony's thou may'st deal with them as Seemest best unto the; Lord thou hast Said the Days of the Wicked are but Short and I hope thou would'st not forget

[272] Unidentified.

thy Promise having lately Purchased an Estate in Reversion of Mr. A, B; a Profligate young man; Keep my Son Caleb out of Evil Company and Gameing Houses and my Daughter Patience from Carnal Apetites; and Sanctifie O Lord I Beseech the this night unto me by keeping me from Thieves and fier, and make my Servants Honest and Carefull while I they Servant Lay Down in the O Lord;

Amen.[273]

When Heav'n for mans Wicked Deeds
Turn'd Eden to a Scene of Weeds
To Punish Adams Guilt
One place uncursed there yet remain'd
The face of Paradise Retain'd
And there was Boston Built
But Heav'n least the Old Deciever
Satan should once again Endeavour
By his Artifice to undoe man
Out of his Gracious Care from hence
He voted out the Tree of Sence
Nor Left one Tempting Woman[274]

On the 16th of August as was Said before I Arived in Boston and on the 2d of Sept'r I gained a Passage in a sloop for Rhode Island and arived there the 9th.

Wed. 23d. Saw the Ship London Captn. Moodie[275] Launch'd off Mr. David Jones's Ways;[276] her Dimentions as follows; 80 Foot Keel Streight Rabit and 29 F: 8 In Beam Tons 370 49/95 at 18£ 6671£: 4s: 9d. = 667: 2: 5 3/4 Sterling

Thus 29: 8 Beam × 14: 10 1/2 Beam × 80 Length ÷ 95 = 370 49/95

Wed., Oct'r the 14th 1747. Ship'd on Board the Sloop

[273] Unidentified. Possibly the author is improvising.

[274] Unidentified.

[275] At a cost of £38,414 4*s.* 10-3/4 *d.* a ship of 371 or 390 tons, mounting eighteen guns, was built for John Banister, ship-broker, agent for John Radburn of London. Captain Robert Mudie was to command the vessel. H. M. Chapin, *Rhode Island Privateers in King George's War, 1739–1748* (Providence, 1926), p. 203.

[276] David Jones was a shipwright of Newport, Rhode Island. *Ibid.*

Venus Captn. Digby Edwards bound for St. Christophers[277] Rec'd in p't 24£: 7s: 9d.

Sat. 17th. Came to Saile bound as above; Nothing worthy of Note but hard gales of Wind and a Deep Sea runing till we had got to the Southward of the Island of Bermudos[278] and Cape Hatterass.

Mon., November the 9th. At 1/2 P 11 A M Saw a sail to windward bearing Down upon us, we then bore away WSW't wind at East At about 5 P M finding the Chase come up with us and no Human Probability of getting Clear of them (after She had fired 4 Guns in reach of us we brought too when they ordered us to toss out our Boate and goe on Board of them which we did vizt. Mr. Edward Beaks Merchant and Owner, Captn. Digby Edwards Self and one of the Crew; we found her to be a French Privateer from Martinico[279] Call'd the Balona a new Bermudoss Built Sloop Lately Taken be the famous Pallanca; She mounted 10 Cariage Guns of 4 Pounders and 14 Swiffles and about 60 men; Commanded by Captn. Battar a Gentleman of great humanity and well becoming the Geni of the French Nation; Asson as I Came on Board Captn. Battar Enquired of Captain Edwards who I was and was Informed by him (at my request that I was a Passenger; Captn. Battar then assured us that our Chests and Bedding should be safe and that he had given orders that Nothing Should be Taken out of them for though he came to Sea to Seek his Fortune he Did not come to plunder we Judged our selves when first Chased to be about 18 Leags to windward of the Island St. Batholomew[280] and might in all Probability have got into St. Christophers the Next Day;

Tues. 10th. Saw a sail to which we gave Chase and found her to be a French Privateer from Martinico of 6 Cariage Guns Captn. Battar gave us then our Choice Either to rest

[277] St. Christopher, one of the British West Indies.

[278] Bermuda.

[279] Martinique.

[280] St. Bartholomew.

on board of his Sloop and goe with him to Guardulupe[281] or goe on board our Late Sloop Venus which he was then going to send away to Martinico; the former we Luckly Chose; the Sloop Venus was then sent away. Saw the Island Desarda[282] we then Stood to the Northward till Midnight then Tack'd.

Wed. 11th. At 8 A M Bore away for Guardulupe At 3 P M pass'd by Desarda Island Steering SW't at 7 D'o pass'd by the Islands Maragallant[283] and St. Terra.[284]

Thurs. 12th. At 8 A M Landed at the Town of Basstera[285] on the Island Guardulupe where our Generous Foe Caried us to a Good Tavern and treated us in a Polite Manner and at 1 P M he procured us a Pass from the Governer to goe on Board a Schoner Captn. Howel bound for St. Eustatia[286] a Dutch Island; at 3 D'o went on board and saild Adiew my Generous Enemy you are in the Right of it; Since 'tis Certain;

> None knows what fate is for himself Design'd
> The Thoughts of Human Chance should make men kind[287]

NB Bassatera is the Principle Town on the Island Guardulupe its Divided in the Middle by a fine fresh water River which runs Cross the Town into the Bay were the Ships ride; I was Informed there was 12 Sail of Privateers out of this Little Town on their Cruize 4 more I saw in the Harbour and out of Martinico were 30 sail most of them out on their Cruize against the English.

Sat. 14th. At 8 A M Landed on the Island St. Eustatia where Captn. Leolin LLoid Invited me to his House for that as he had bought a fine Sloop and if I chose it should have

[281] Guadeloupe.

[282] Désirade.

[283] Marie Galante.

[284] Iles des Saintes.

[285] Basse Terre.

[286] St. Eustatius.

[287] "None knows what fate is for himself designed;
The thought of human chance should make us kind."
—Dryden, *Almanzor and Almahide, or The Conquest of Granada,* Act I, Scene I, lines 180–181.

the Prefirence to goe with him as his Second which I then Embraced. Here have ben Lately A Terible Huricane which came on the 19th of September past; and put on Shore in this Rhode 54 sail of vessells most of them Laden out of which there Perished upwards of 300 men. In St. Christophers was put on Shore by the Same Huricane 20 sails of vessells Laden for Europe but very few men Lost Except out of one vessell which foundered.

Fri., November the 20th. Wrote Home and to Mrs. Oldham per Captain Purse via Roterdam Wrote Likewise to Captn. Oldham per Captn. Morange via Salem.

Sat. 28th. Captn. Leolin LLoyd told me this Day that he was like to be Disappointed of his Sloop at Least for Some Time for that Captn. Fielding of the Lowstaff Privateer[288] had Taken out of a Sloop belonging to his principle Owner and Freighter the Sum of 25000 pieces of Eight in Specia off the Island Saba[289] and that it was like to put a Stop to his Affair for some Time; So Conclude to goe for St. Kitts the first oppertunity.

Mon. 30th. At Sun Set left Captn. LLoyd and went for St. Kitts in an open Boate.

Tues., Decemb'r the 1st. Arived in White Flag Bay[290] St. Kitts and Walked to Sandy point where I Lodged with Captn. Thos. Chapman Brother in Law to Mr. Edward Beaks who was our Merchant and owner in the Sloop Venus.

Sun. 6th. At Captn. Thomas Chapmans who Treated me in a very Genteel Manner but as there was no Ships as yet arived from Europe and of Consiquence nothing for me to doe; I Informed my Worthy Friend of a Design I then had of going to St. Cruize[291] with Captn. Rich'd Evans he Courtuously answered me that as I had Such a Design he would recommend me to a Gentleman Mr. Robert Henson who had great Interest there and very Largly Concern'd in Shiping;

[288] The privateer *Lowestoft* of Bristol, Captain Fielding, is mentioned by H. M. Chapin, *Rhode Island Privateers in King George's War, 1739–1748*, p. 167.

[289] Saba, one of the Dutch West Indies.

[290] White Flag Bay is located at the northwest corner of the island of St. Christopher.

[291] Santa Cruz or St. Croix, one of the Danish Virgin Islands.

to whom he wrote in my favour, he gave me Some Nessesaries at parting and Charged me that if I did not Succeed at St. Cruize to return to him again where I Should allways meet with a kind Reception; I went on Board with Captn. Evans and saild Directly.

Tues. the 8th. Arived at St. Cruize and Caried my Letters Recommendatory from my Worthy Friend Captn. Chapman to Mr. Robt. Henson who told me he was verry Sorry I had not come a few hours Before for that a Master of one of his Vessells had left him and run away with his Boate and that he had but just then made one of his Mates Master of the Vessell and Could not in Honour goe from it.

Wed., 9th Decemb'r. Mr. Henson this Day gave me a Letter to Mr. Amanuell Aboab Merchant in Bass End;[292] and Likewise an Order to Mr. Abraham Marsh Innholder that in Case I should not Succeed I should Stay with Mr. Marsh at his Expence till some thing Else offered.

Thurs. 10th. Was advised by Mr. Emanuel Aboab that as he was allready Suplied he would recommend me to his Friend Captn. Beeverhood but he like the former was allready Suplied.

Sat. the 12th. Mr. Henson came to Town to whom I told my Intent of going for Tertola[293] one of the Virgins Island so Call'd by S'r Francis Drake in honour of Q'n Elizabeth; Mr. Henson was pleased to give me Letters to Captn. Pursell[294] now Governer of Tertola, Spainish Town[295] and Isles adjacent.

This Island of St. Cruize is one of the Virgin Isles and now belongs to His Majesty of Deanmark who bought it of the King of France about 16 years agoe when France Drew off the first Setlers to People Hispainola;[296] The Soil is very fertle and produces very good Sugar, Cotton, Ginger, etc.; Its very Unhealthy from as I Aprehend its being so Little

[292] Bassin or Christiansted, St. Croix.

[293] Tortola.

[294] Probably John Purcell, who was formally commissioned lieutenant-governor of Tortola, July 31, 1769.

[295] Spanish Town or Virgin Gorda, to the east of Tortola.

[296] Hispaniola or Haiti.

Cultivated and therefore o're run with Trees; here is Some Good Plantations and others Dayly coming on; the English are the Chief Planters who live not very Easy under a Deanish Government who are Annually Imposing Laws upon them in an unknown Tongue and raising their Imposts which will in Time Drive the English to some Other of the Virgin Isles as Tertola, Spainish Town; the Soil of which is Inviting, besides they are there under a British Government most agreeable to an English man. Here I saw the Wood Ants an account of which I had once met with in Dampier but could give but Little Credit to it as Judging it Impossible for those Little Emmits to acculmunate Such a prodigeous Quantity of Earth together Many of which Nests I saw in the form of a Cone whose Bass was 3 foot Diameter and Height 4 foot.

Wed. 16th. This Morn Meet by Axident one Simon Day Late Drum Majore on the Island St. Kitts but now an Inhabitant Here; he was born in Harlstone in Norff his Unkle by the Mothers Side is Rich'd Goldspink he has ben out of Europe many years and Supposes he is forgotten.

Fri. the 25th. Christmass Day nothing worth Note.

Tues. 29th. Took Possession of the Sloop Hanson bound for the Island Antiqua with Mill Timber of which here are great Quantities yearly Exported.

Fri., January the 1st. Newyear was this Day Taken very Ill and unable to help my Self was Caried on Shore to Mr. Abraham Marshes House where Mr. Hanson came to me with a Learned Physician Dr. Boyl He Likewise Ordered Marsh 30 pieces of Eight for my Subsistance with Orders to Draw upon him if more Should be Wanting; Captn. Andrews gave me a Pistole; Captn. La Gross gave me 1/2 a Pistole; Dr. Titley gave me 10 pieces of Eight; Mr. Brooks gave me 10 pieces of Eight; value Sterling as follows

30 pieces of Eight	6:15:0
A Pistole	:17:6
A half D'o	: 8:9
Ten pieces of Eight	2: 5:0
Ten D'o	2: 5:0
	£ 12:11:3

Tues. 12th. Came in Captn. James Duncan of and from Rhode Island; had from him News of Captn. Oldham.

Wed. 20th. Came in Likewise Captn. Shipman from Conecticut late Master of the Sloop Venus which I was Lately Taken Prisoner in and Caried to Guardulupe as mentioned the 11th of November. I was now So far Recovered as to Walk About and Therefore to Oblidge Mr. Abraham Marsh with whom I Lodged I went to Court to Stand for him as a Good Man as they call it It was on a Case of some Negroes who had made an Attempt to get off the Island Of these Good Men there are on all Occations 2 who allways Set next to the Judge or rather the Kings Atorney General The Evidences were Call'd in on boath sides and gave in their Evidences in English after that our Names were Call'd for which was put to the Evidences given on Either Side the Question; and after the Atorney General had wrote 2 Folio's in the Dean's Language which I Concluded was the Minutes of the Case; he Dismist us and the Prisoners at the Bar without Once Asking us one Single Question Concerning the Case in hand, and therefore we came away just as wise as we went; This upon Enquirey I find to be their Constant Method of Proceeding; however I afterwards heard the Negroes were Acquitted.

Tues. 26th. I this Day gain'd with much Difficulty a Passage in the Sloop Eunison Captn. Joseph Austin for Boston.

Thurs., 28th Jan'ry. Wey'd and Came to sail Wind at East, we had no sooner got out of the Harbour when we Espied a sail we Imediately bore away again and came to an anchor within the Reefs and About Musquet Shot of the Fort; The sail we saw proved to be a Scooner from St. Thomas Isle[297] bound into the Harbour.

Fri. 29th. This Morn Came to Sail again Stood to the No'w'd for Tertola wind EBNo.

Sat. 30th. At 9 A M Spoke with the Privateer Snow

[297] St. Thomas, one of the Danish Virgin Islands.

Reprisal Captn. Dunbar[298] of Rhod Island She stood away to the So'w'd to Cut off a Sloop in Sight; at 11 D'o Came to an Anchor in Tertola Rhode off a small Fort.

Mon., Feb'ry 1st. Saw my Old Friend Captn. Richard Evans with whom I went a Passenger to St. Cruize from St. Kitts; he gave me a pair of Striped Trowsers, 2 Gallons of Wine and one of Rum for my sea Store.

The Produce of Tertola Isle is Chiefly Cotton of which here are Vast Quantities of the Best sort here are some few Sugar Plantations and Indico Works and Others are Dayly coming on; This Island as well as the rest of the Virgins was formally the Rendezvous of Pyrates where they usally Careen'd and reffitted but now as they are Tollarably settled and provided with Forts for their Defence they'l be no Longer a Nest for them Gentry.

Thurs., Feb'ry 4th. Captn. Austin went away in a Small Boate to Spainish Town another of the Virgins Isles to Clear out his vessell he finding it Impraticable to Clear out at Tertola as usal; for Since Captn. Pursell has been Governer he has sworn all his Officers not to Clear out any vessell but Such as Compleatly Load here. for Formaly the North American vessells used to Load at St. Thomas's or St. Cruise 2 Deanish Islands then Stand over to Tertola and purchase a Barrell of Sugar and a Little Cotton and by Virtue of them Clear out the whole Cargoe as the Produce of the British Islands which now Captain Pursells Laudable Conduct hath Prevented those abuses.

Fri. 5th. Weigh'd from Tertola and Came to Sail about Noon; At 8 P M the Body of Saint Johns Island[299] bore SSW't Dist per Judgment 6. Leagues Steering NNW't.

Sat. the 6th. Steering NNW't at 2. P M saw 2 sail to windward on our Beam which had been bearing Down upon us unseen for Some Time; which proved to be 2 Spainish

[298] The snow *Reprisal*, Captain William Dunbar, is mentioned by H. M. Chapin, *Rhode Island Privateers in King George's War, 1739–1748*, pp. 184, 185; *Privateering in King George's War, 1739–1748* (Providence, 1928), pp. 123–124, 177.

[299] Saint John, one of the Danish Virgin Islands.

Privateers from Porto Rico, the one a Sloop of 10. Cariage Guns the other a Sloop of 6 D'o which at 4 P M brought us too; they took the Captn. His Boy and the rest of the hands (Except the Mate and Self) and Caried them on board the Largest of the Privateers; but about 8. D'o they brought Captn. Austin and his boy on Board again, then the Spainards made the best of their way with their Prize and us to Porto Rico Leaving the Privateers on their Cruize.

Mon. the 8th of Feb'ry. Made the Land and on it a Large Town which we found to be 8 Leagues to Leeward of Porto Rico.

Tues. 9th. Bore away for Laguire Bay[300] on the NW't End of the Island where we Came too an Anchor within 1/4 of a Mile from the Shore; Here the Rascall of a Prize Captain calld me into the Cabbin and Strip'd me of Every Rag of Cloaths Even my Shirt, he left me nothing on Except a Wigg and a pair of Shoes; nor would he have left me Either of them had the wigg been fashionable but it had neither Bagg nor Tail too it; or he had Ever wore a pair of Shoes in his Life; However at my Earnest Intreaties and the Spainish Fellows Joining with me he did return me an Old raged Surtoot Coate to Cover my Nakedness; Captn. Austin was Call'd Down Next, they made an Adam of him too; As to the Mate he Being very Ill he was reserved for Another Plunder. I was at this time very sickly but could not forbear Laughing at Our unfortunate Circumstances which made Captn. Austin very Angry Espicially when I told him he might Dance in Quirpo[301] like a Case'd Rabit.

Thurs. 11th. Came too us a Sloop Late from Piscatuay Captn. John Snow who had ben Taken by the Same Privateers a Week before us; he was bound for Jamaica; This Day as I was at the fire roasting a Piece of Jirk Beef, the Rascal of a Prise Captain came to me again and Strip'd me of my Coate which he before had gevin me; for he had now Sold it to a person on Shore; but as Captn. Austin had before got his Cloaths by Bullying, I made use of the same Method

[300] Probably Aguadilla Bay.

[301] A variant of "in cuerpo," an obsolete phrase meaning "in a state of undress."

the Spainards on board joyning with me, and the Person who had bought it, not likeing the bargin he return'd to me again once more.

Fri., Feb'ry 12th. The Mate was Now bravely recovered; I heard by Accident the Rascall of a prize Captn. had Sold the Mates Red Coate on Shore and was bringing the person on board to take it away from the Mate; I asked the Person who had gave me the Inteligence Whether he would Accept of the Coate provided I could perswade the Mate to give it him; he answered that he would Accept of it but would Certainly give the Mate it again so Soon as he was out of the Captains Power; which he afterwards performed; I presently perswaded the mate to give the Fellow the Coate when the Captn. came on Board Soon after with his Chapman and finding themselves Baulk'd of their Design it Caused a Laugh Through the whole Company; The Rascall of a Captn. was so Enraged against me, and finding all or most of his own People in my Interest he this Evening put me on board the Piscatuay Sloop.

Sun., Feb'ry 14th. I was now in much better Circumstances as the prize Captain of this Sloop was a man of some Humanity and had been a Prisoner Amongst the English; he gave me an old pair of Trowsers and a Straw hat without a Crown, however it kept the voiolent heate of the Sun from me; He then asked me if I would goe on Shore and recreate my Self, to the which I Complied with Thanks; He then Ordered a young Fellow to Attend on me who Carried me to his Mothers House where She Treated me with a Great Deal of Civillity and at my Coming away Loaded me with a good Cargo of Sweet Oranges, Coco Nutts, Ripe Benanos and Plantains. At Night we came to Sail, in Company with Captain Austins Sloop; bound for the Harbour of Porto Rico.

Mon. 15th. At Night Captn. Austins Sloop bore away for Laguire Bay.

Fri. 19th. Arrived in the Harbour of Porto Rico but too Late to goe on Shore.

Sat. 20th. Landed on the Island Porto Rico and at the Principle Town of that Name; I apply'd my Self to a Clerk of

Don Pedro Latora who was Owner of the Privateers; I asked him in what Manner I was to Subsist he told me that he would give me a Bit per Day or if I Choose it I might goe to work with the rest of the Prisoners and then I Should have 2. Bits per Day and my Provissions found me which Provissions was Old Decay'd Casarder Bread and Salt Beef; the Cast provissions of their Privateers; I let the Clerk to know that about 2. months before I was Master of a Better Sloop then that I was Taken in and Procured my Letters from Messrs. Hanson to Confirm the Same; that as to Working I was So Weak that I Could not nor in Short I would not; He then gave me a Bit for that Time and I parted with him resolving to Apply my Self to his Master.

Sun. 21st. Don Petro Latora Coming Down to the Warfe I apply'd my Self to him, who after hearing my Case allowed me 2 Bitts per Day to Provide my Self with Provissions, he allso Excused me from Labour.

Note A Spainish Bit is in value 6 pence Therfore on 2 Bits I could Subsist very well as I Could buy 4 lb of very good fresh Beef for 1 Bit tho' it is now Lent; and as for vegitables As Ripe Bananas and Plantens Mountain Cabbage I could buy Enough of Either for one Bit as was Sufficient for Ten men; In Short flower Bread was the only thing Dear here As that was a Bit per pound, but however Cassadar Bread was Cheap and in Great Plenty.

Mon., Feb'ry 22d. This morning there was great Noize and Bustell amongst the English Prisoners who Wrought on Board the vessells at the Warf for Don Predro; For that the Said Don hath allowed 4 Dutch Prisoners Each 4 Bits per Day for the Same work which the English did for 2 Bits per Day and therfore the English Prisoners would not Work any Longer unless they were put on a par with the Dutch Prisoners. Don Pedro came Down to the Warf himself and after hearing the Case he Stow'd them up at the Head of the Warff then ply'd his Cane over the Heads and Shoulders of them which So Scear'd them that they fell to Work again without their Wages being Advanced or any farther noize about it.

Tues., 23d Feb'ry. As my Self nor any of the Prisoners were not Confined in a Prison but had the Liberty of Walking any where about Town all Day, and at night we slept on board the vessells at the Warff I made it my Daily Business to Ingratiate my Self into the favour of Father Michael Marine of the Order of Jesuits, which I very Easily did; he was a man of great Learning and a great Lover of the English Nation; though I have Some Reasons to believe by his Pronounsation of the English Tongue that he was in his younger Days in England, if not born there; or in Ireland, He was Linguist to His Excellency the Governer[302] in the English, Dutch and French Tongues and at the Head of the Colledge of Jesuits; I Prevailed on him this Day to prefir my Petition to his Excellency the Governer for my Discharge. Assoon as the Rever'd Father had read my Petition he Ordered me to Call upon him in a Day or two and he would procure me a Passport from His Excellency the Governer; I thankd him and took my Leave of him for the Present.

Fri., 26th Feb'ry. This Morning the Largest of the Privateer Sloops which took me brought into this Port 37 fine Negroes and their Overseer which they had taken Last Sunday night off a Plantation Call'd the Salt pans on the Island St. Kitts they belonged to S'r Ralph Payne; They Plundered the Overseer's House of Every Moveable, they carried his Wife and 4 Young Children down to the Beach and Stripped them of Every Ragg of Cloaths then Left them there bound together but brought away the Overseer and Landed him here with not one Ragg of Covering on Save a Wigg and a pair of Shoes; (my Case Exactly) however the runaway Negroes here from St. Kitts who had formely known him presently brought him a very Good Shirt and a pair of Strip'd Trowsers.

Leap year.

Mon., 29th Feb'ry. This Morning I waited upon my Rever'd Friend Father Michael Marine who gave me a Written Order to His Excellencies Secratary the which I Carried to him to the Pallace when after a few Questions

[302] Colonel Don Juan José Colomo.

asked me, Concerning our Late Vessell and Cargoe; he granted me a passport to Depart from the Island the first Oppertunity that Should present it Self; I then waited upon my Rever'd Friend to return him thanks; the which he received in a very Courteous Manner.

Thurs., March the 3d. This Morning gain'd a Passage in a small Sloop of and for St. Cruize; She had, ben taken by a French Privateer and brought into this Port but acquitted;

There came Away with us Captain Joseph Austin, Captn. Jno. Snow, their 2 Mates, 2 Boys, my Self, the Master of the Sloop, and 3 men more; in all 11 Persons; Don Pedro allow'd us a Parcle of Cassarder or Timber Bread, Some rotton Baccalew or Salt Codfish, A Parcle of Plantens and a Cask of Water, with a Compass; but would not allow us to take any Ballust or Stones from the Shore of which there was Enough though Earnestly Desir'd we left behind us 11 English and 7 Dutch Prisoners who all might have come away with us had the above Captn. asked it of the Governer, but they were in Short a Couple of as sad Scoundrells as Ever Salt water weet.

Remarks on the Island Porto Rica This Island of Porto Rica or St. John's De Port Rico Lieth in the No. Lat'd of 18° 30′ and West Longitude of 64 56 from the Meridian of London. It is one of the finest Islands I Ever Saw, and I verily believe not any one Island in the West Indies is more Capable of Improvement then this; but through the Pride and Sloath of the Inhabitants it is the far greater part of it Still a Wilderness. It abounds in Oranges, Lemons, Citrons, Limes, etc. in Such Plenty that they are not worth the Gathering. There are Prodigeous Quantities of Bananers, Plantens, Coco Nutts, Pine apples, Mountain Cabbage; with a great many other Fruits and Vegitables. There are fine Fresh water Rivers which runs through the Heart of the Island well Stored with all Sorts of Fish. In Short, there is not any thing for the Support of Human Nature but may here be found or Cultivated.

It might in the Hands of the English or Dutch be rendered a Paradise on Earth, but the Present Inhabitants are Mere Devils. There are fine Springs of Excellent Water, and all

Sorts of Materals for Building Either in brick or Stone They have a Noble Port or Harbour for Ships of any Burthen. The Air of this Island is very Pleasant and healthy; Father Michael Marine my very good Friend assured me, he had not known an Epidemical Distemper there for these 30 years past; a thing very rare to be meet with in any of the West Indian Isles. The Soil of this Island is very firtel and might produce Excellent Sugar Canes, Some of which I saw while on Shore at Laguire Bay of an Uncommon Size yet as I have ben Informed they have not one Sugar Plantation Worthy to be so Call'd. The only Town of Note is Porto Rica whose Harbour is very Easy of Axcess, The Town is Sittuated on an Island and is Wall'd in with a Good Wall on which are Ambraziers for a great many Guns, yet they have not above 40. Mounted on all parts, nor can they bring above 12 or 14 to beare upon Shiping at a Time in going into the Harbour. This Town is a Nest of Pirates in Time of Peace; and an Assylum for runaway Negroes from our Islands, and the Deans, and Dutch, where as Soon as they arive and have Serv'd the King of Spain in the Person of the Governer and are made Christians which is Generally in a year they are for Ever after free and their posterity There was no Less then 19 fine Slaves arived here from St. Cruize in the Time I Left that place and the Last year 42 of them run away with a fine Sloop and brought her in here from St. Cruize and others are Daily coming here from our Islands and the Dutch.

Wed., March the 9th. We Left Porto Rica the 3d Past and this Morning we arived at the West End of St. Cruize and Imediately I Set out alone for Bass End the Principle Town Distant 25 miles the which I Wallked and Arived at 2 P M At 4 D'o Gain'd a Passage in a fine Sloop Captn. Johnson for St. Kitts and Saild Imediately but before I went on Board I had the Good Fortune to Meet with Captn. Tunbrall of Tertola who seeing me in a Tettered Condition he Generously gave me a Jacket, a new Shirt and a pair of Trowsers.

Sun. 13th. Early in the Morning arived at Basseterra[303]

[303] Basseterre, St. Christopher.

Commonly Call'd Backstar on the Island St. Kitts; when I saw Several Sail of Ships goe out of the Rhode for Europe but had no Oppertunity to get a Letter on Board any of them; I Caried with me a Letter from the Overseer who was brought away with the Negroes as mentioned the 26 of Feb'ry Directed to his Wife in St. Kitts whom I presently found out and gave her it; I Staid Dinner with her and then Set out for Sandy point where I arived at Night Dist from Bassaterra 14 miles I went to my Old Friend Captn. Thomas Chapman were I was very friendly Entertained.

Sun., March the 20th. Procured a passage for North America Therefore I this Day wrote a Letter home and left it with the Care of Mr. Nicholass Steel to be forwarded the first Vessell Th't Sail'd.

Tues. 22d. I this Day relapsed into a Fever the same I had at St. Cruize.

1748.[303a] *Sat.* 26th. Was this Day bravely recovered again and in hopes of going for America.

Sun. 27th. At 5 P. M Weigh'd and came to Sail from Sandy point Isle St. Kitts in the Sloop Tryall Captn. Benjamin Trueman for New London in the Colony of Conecticut in Comp'y with a Brigg and a Sloop both for New York.

Fri., Aprill the first. At Night parted with the New York Brigenteen.

Fri. 8th. This Evening we parted by Consent of the New York Sloop She Steering more Westerly then we.

Fri. 15th. Sounded and got Ground on the American Coast 50 Fathams Water ouzey Ground; About 4 hours after we Sounded again and found but 20 Fathams fine Sand; Therfore Judge our Selves off Nantucket Shoals; we then Tack'd and Stood to the Southward.

Mon. 18th. At 5 A M Made the Land, the East point of Long Island Calld Montauk for the which we Steerd wind at SSW't At 3 P M Landed at New London in the Colony of Conecticut; at Sun Sett I Cross'd the Ferry over to the Naruganset Shore, and set out on my way for Rhode Island;

[303a] The marginal note "1748" is placed here by the writer because of the old English custom of beginning the Year on Lady Day, March 25.

Lodged at one Captn. Williams Dist from the above Ferry 6 miles, bad roade.

Tues. 19th. Set out Early in the Morning in Company with 6 men who had ben Prisoners at Port Louis[304] on the Island of Hispainola and Sent away when Admiral Knowles took the place;[305] At night we all Lodged at one Captn. Hills Distant from the aforesaid Ferry 30 miles.

Wed. 20th. At 5 A M Set out again; at 1 P M got to the Naraganset Ferry Dist from the above Ferry 45 miles; we Cross'd the Ferry over to the Island Conanicut, then Walk'd one mile Cross the Island to the Conanicut Ferry the which we Cross'd over to Newport Rhode Island; GLORIA DEO. had the pleasure to find Captn. Oldham in perfict health; but the Mortification to find his Ship not in the forwardness I hoped She would have ben in, through the Severity of the Winter past the Workmen Could not Stand to Work.

Sat., 30th Aprill. Was Launched the Ship Apollo, Captn. Lockerman of Liverpool in Lancashire; She is bound they Say for the Coast of Guinia This Day began to Plank the Ship Lydia Captain John Oldham; my Self Drove the first Trennel in Her Bottom

> Our Pasions gone, and reason in her Throne,
> Amaz'd we Se, the Mischiefs we have done;
> After a Tempast, when the winds are laid,
> The Calm Sea Wonders: at the Wrecks it made.[306]

This Day a Cessation of Arms was here Published in Newport Rhode Island; between Great Britaine and France with Spain;[307] and 'Tis Said The powers are Mutally to restore the places Taken During the War is so, what have we got During a Long and Expencive War? not any thing more then The Two Welsh men in the following Tale. . . .[308]

[304] Port Louis, on the southwest peninsula of the island of Haiti.

[305] Rear-Admiral Charles Knowles took Port Louis in March, 1747/8.

[306] Unidentified.

[307] Preliminary articles of peace were signed at Aix-la-Chapelle, April 19, 1748, and a definitive treaty of peace, at the same place, October 7, 1748.

[308] Omitted.

1748. *Mon.* 23d May. Launched the Ship Lydia's Longboate and Riggd her with 2 masts and Scooner Sails.

Sat., 23d July. was Taken very ill in the Lydia's Longboate in Company with Captain Oldham who Carried me on shore at Bullocks neck[309] where I had a Doctor to me.

Sat., 20th August. Captn. Oldham Informd me to my no small Surprise that Messrs. Touchet and Comp'y had protested his Bill which he had Drawn upon them; I fear this affair will Detain us much Longer then we Expected.

Sun. 28th. Saild the Pink Hull Merchant Captn. Fullerton for Hull by whom I wrote home as did Captn. Oldham about his Late protested Bills and their reason for so doing.

Mon. 29th. Went to Mr. Gideon Freeborns[310] on the Isle Prudence to Teach his Sons and others some Branches of the Mathematicks as I can now be of no great Service to Captain Oldham Since his Bills have lately return'd protested by which means an Entire Stop has ben put to the Building of the Ship at Least till the return of Ships the next Spring.

Extracts from the Rever'd Thos. Prince's Thanksgiving Sermon Preach'd in Boston New England November the 27th 1746.[311]

1st. Early in the Spring the French with the utmost Application fitted out at Brest and Rochford the Greatest and most Powerfull Armament against these Northern Colonies that was Ever Sent into No. America having 20 men of war 100 Transports about 8000 well Desciplind Troops with Veteran Officers and Vast Quantities of Provission, Powder, Shot, arms, Cannon, Bombs, and morters Sufficient to take the Strongest place.

2d. That they were all under one Commander of Figure

[309] Bullocks Point, Providence.

[310] At this time Gideon Freeborne was a justice of the inferior court of common pleas.

[311] Thomas Prince, *The Salvation of God in 1746* (Boston, 1746; London, 1747); reprinted as *Extract of a Sermon preach'd at the South Church, in Boston, November 27th, 1746*, . . . (Boston, 1776).

Duke De Anville; a Nobleman of Ability, Skill, and Courage; who came with resolution To Exert himself to his own Honour and to the Glory of his King and Nation or Die in the Cause.

3d. They own'd they had the best plans and most Skill-full Pilotes with them well acquainted with all the Coasts and Harbours of Newfoundland, Cape Briton, Nova Scotia, and New England in Perticular of Louisburgh, Canso, Chebucta, Anapoliss; Casco Bay and Boston etc.

4th. They Came with very Exciting Motives both of Resentment, Policy and Necessity; of resentment, for our Saving Anapoliss and Disappointing the French Invation there in 44 and for our Taking Louisburgh, Distroying there Fishery, Blocking up the Bay of St. Laurence and Taking their great Men of War and the East India and South Sea Ships in the year 45.

Of Policy, to recover their Lost Fortified City and Harbour of Louisburgh, their Lost Oppertunity by their Privateers thence to Sieze our Vessells; their Lost Fort and Harbour of Annapoliss, their Lost Terratory of Nova Scotia, and their Lost Reputation both in Europe and America Espicially amongst the Indian Savages; and Lastly, of Necessity; to Save their Canada, with all their Settlements and Trade in North America.

At Length they got out of Brest and Saild to Rochford; on June the 11th they Saild from this Last Port and pass'd by Admiral Martins Squad'n unobserved; And after their getting Clear of the Coast of France they bore so far to the Southward wherby they not only went from their Straighter Course but likewise into a more Rarified Air and Calmer Latitudes which further serv'd to Lengthen Their Voyage to 90 Days from Rochfort; that it was the 9th of September before the forwardest of them Arived in Chebuta That by the means above God was pleased to Visit them with a mortal Sickness that they owned 1300 died at sea and the rest Extreamly Weakned and Dispirited.

And by Terible Storms they were so Dispersed in the midst

of the Ocean that by August the 30th they had Left but 12 Ships of the Line and 41 Others besides 5 Prizes they hapned to meet with.[312]

On September the 2d at about Noon when they came near the Shoals of the Isle of Sables the most Dangerous place in all their Passage and had but 3 Days sail to Chebucta; God was pleased to raise against them Such a Violent Storm of wind which held all that Day and night[313] Wherin one of their Transports was put on Shore and Lost on the Shoals; 4 Ships of the Line and another Transport were Seen in great Distress and never heard on after and the rest of the Fleet had like to have run on the Shoals in that Terible night.

About the Middle of September Eight Ship of the Line and about 40 others arive in Chebucta the Port of their Rendezvous on the SE Shore of Nova Scotia one of the finest Harbours On the Globe; in which the British Nation had Utterly Neglected for a Course of 30 years from the Peace of Utrecht to Settle one Inhabitant; and in the very way to Interupt all our Fishery and Even all the Trade from great Britain, Ireland, Newfoundland and Cape Britain to the Colonies on the main and from these to them; There they Water, Wood, refresh, Careen, refit, Thence take our Ships; Strike Surprise and Terrour thro' the Countries round about them.

On September the 12th the Duke De Anvilla arived in Chebucta with his Vice Admiral and 3 more men of War and 5 others as Transports there being but one of the fleet got in but 3 Days before him his Rear Admiral and 10 of the Line and all the rest of the Transports yet missing and finding his few Ships So Shattered, So many men Dead, So many Sickly and no more of his fleet come in, he sunk into Discouragement and September the 15th Died but in Such

[312] NB by a mistake in the Sermon he Says August the 26th but the Gale did not come on till the 28th when my Self and the rest of the Prisoners was Encamp'd in a wood near Bay Vert or Green Bay See August the 28th in the Journal. [Note by the author of the journal.]

[313] See Sept'r the 2d in the Journal when all the Transports which was to Carry us to Canada was put on Shore. [Note by the author of the journal.]

Condition and so much Swell'd it was Generally thought he Poysened himself and was Buried without any Ceremony; upon which their Government fell upon their Counsell of War, their Union was Intirely Broken and their Counsells Divided; upon the Death of the Duke the Vice Admiral Estournell in Consideration of the Deplorable Case they were in proposed to return to France to save the rest of the men but the Counsell of War Opposing and Voting against him he was on September the 19th in the morning found in his Apartment fallen on his Sword and the next morning Died allso; wherby the Chief Command Devolved to Rear Admiral Jonquire who arived a few Days before; who with the Counsell of War Resolved to Attack some English place in these Northern parts before they would think of returning

In the Mean while they Landed their Men to refresh them and yet their Sickness so prevailed that they owned there Died 1130 more at Chebucta before they Left it.

October the 10th. the French Counsell of War at Chebucta being sensible that by Dispersing Storms and Wasting Sickness they are Utterly Disable'd for Attempting Louisburgh, resolve to sail and take Annapoliss; and if they had but Staid but one week Longer they would have had a Season of Suitable Weather for it but a Cruizer of theirs having happily Taken an Express from Governer Shirly to Louisburgh with the London Prints Informing of Admiral Lestocks Expected Coming and the Master of the vessell happily forgetting to Observe his Orders and throw his Paquet overboard, they were Carried into Chabucta and Opened on the 11th Early in the morning in a Counsell of War upon which Surprised in the Utmost Hurry they Pull down all their Tents; burn a Line of Battle Ship with a Snow from Carolina a Vessell from Antigua and Some fishing Scooners and Embark their Soldiers Order 2000 French and Indians to march from Meniss to Annapoliss and October the 13th with about 40 sail, 20 Engineers and 30 Pilots from near Annapoliss they came out to goe round Cape Sable and meet them there.

The next Day they sent 3 or 4 of their Fleet with their

Sick to France the Distemper Still Increasing our Captives Saw them throw their Dead out of most vessells into the Sea for 3 Days together after they left Chebucta, The 15th near the Isle of Sables a Second Time came on a Great and Cold Storm which Scattered them again; Yet the next Day getting once more together and Persevering in their Purpose they Dismissed their Captives who that night left them Laying by and saw them no more.

But the Same Day vizt. October the 16th is kept a Day of General fasting and Prayer throughout the Churches in this Province on this great Emergency and that very night Ensuing the Glorious God Entirely Baffled all their Purposes and put a Total End to their Mischevious Enterprize, he Sent a more furious Storm of wind and rain and Hail then Ever which held till the next Day noon which they could not Stand before which so Dispersed and broke them that they could never get together again and Several Ships so Crazey and Weakly handed that 'tis apprehended by our Dismiss'd Captives who were in the Storm that some were Overset some others foundred and sunk in the Mighty waters; and the remaining Men of war in View so shattered and Discouraged that they Determined for the West Indies and sent their Nova Scotia Pilotes home with Orders to the French and Indians Army who had March'd to Annapoliss to Leave their Enterprize and get away; the Scattered remains it Seems most Likely are gone back to France Abased and Confouded.

1748. *Wed.*, 7th of September. Began to Lay the Ship Lydia's Lower Deck.

Sun., 16th of October. Rec'd a Letter from the Reverend John Norton Dated the 4th he was a Prisoner with me in Canada and was Chaplin of the Massachusetts Fort when Taken by the French and Indians.

Tues., 18th of October. at Mr. Gideon Freeborns House were I was Treated with a great deal of respect and Esteem This Island of Prudence lieth in the Narrhagansett Bay Opposite the North End of Rhode Island and is in Length 7 miles 1/4 it hath on it 7 fine farms whereof that of Mr.

Freeborns where I now reside is the best by far it being in Length 2 1/4 miles and 100 foot of rail fence Divides him from all Neighbours This Farm produceth allmost Every thing for the Support of Human Nature as Hemp and Flax of which they make very good Linnen Wooll and Lamb the best in all the Colony. It produceth all Sorts of Grain; Here are fine Orchards well Stored with fruit Trees, Such as Apples, Pears, Plumbs, Peaches, the Latter they often beate down by Combs to their Hoggs; All sorts of vegitables they have here Exceeding Good as Surpasses Common Belief; to Instance only the Musk and water Mellon which have as fine a flavour as any I Ever Eate in Spain or Italy and of an uncommon Size Some of which I have Seen weigh'd 43 lb but the Generality of them usally weigh 28 or 30 lb. They have Likewise Peas, Beans, of all sorts; Cabbages, Turnips, Potatoes, Beets, Oynions, Radishes, Cod Pepper, and all sorts of Sallads Their Usal Grain which they make use of is the Indian Corn as being best Adapted to the Soil and Cli mate besides which they have Generally 3 Crops in that one; for first they plant the Corn five of which grains they put in a hole which holes are made in Rows and Cross Each other at right angles which when they Hoo the Corn they Carry in a Double Pocket or Bagg a Quantity of Kidney Beans and Pumkin Seeds of which they Throw in 3 of Each and Gather the mould together with their Hoo like our Hop Hills; Thus have they 3 Crops in the Ground at once, that when the Corn comes to Shoot up into Large Stalks the Kidney Beans Lay hold of them with their Claspers and run up with it while the Pumpkins Shoot out their Vines through all the Intermediate Spaces below. The Beans are usally Gathered when they Top the Stalks of the Corn for fodder for their Cattle which Beans they give to their Hoggs or Sell them to the Poor The Pumpkins are not Gathered till about September after the Corn is all in and House'd when they Lay them up in Deep Cellars to prevent the frost coming at them. With these Pumpkins they fat their Cattle in the Same manner as we doe ours with Turnips Either by Tieing them up or giving them abroad, the meat of which when Kill'd is

Exceeding Sweet, and their Cows give a Great Quantity of Exelent Milk; Their Indian Corn they usally Grind which being mixed with about 1/3 part Rye makes very good bread Mr. Freeborn usally planted of this Corn about 20 Acres and about 5 with Rye Every year which Supply'd his Family never Less then 30 besides fatning his Cattle, Hoggs and Fowls.

Here are in the Creeks and Bays round this Farm Vast Quantities of wild fowl in the winter Season Such as Wild Goose; Duck and Mallard; Teal, Widgeon, Smee, and abundance of other Sorts which I never before Saw which are Easily Shot by Stalking too them with an Horse; I have often seen in a Small Bay when it has blown hard Such a Quantity of Wild fowl as have Covered the water for near a furlong Square and Close to the Shore. Here are likewise Vast Quantities of Exelent Fish Such as Bass, which are usally in Length from 18 Inches to 3 Foot with Large Scales but of an Exelent Tast The Tortogue or Black fish in Coulour and Shape much like our Fresh water Tench and not unlike in Tast they usally weigh from 3/4 to 4 lb. The Sheeps head so Call'd from its Teeth and Jaw resembling that Animal is a very Delicious fish, they are very Difficult to Take; with a nett 'Tis Impossible because of their Lying under the Rocks; they usally Angle for them but if you hook 10 'Tis odds if you take one Except you Should Hook them in the Corner of their Mouth otherwise you are Sure to Loose your Hook if they take it in their mouth for their Grinders are a Double Row of hard Knobbs with which they will Grind a Hook to pieces in an Instant; they usally Weigh from 1½ lb. to 6 lb.; The Jaw of one of them I have now by me. They have Rock fish Likewise in great abundance; Mackrell, Horse Mackrell Herring, Ale Wifes; Monhaden; the Latter of which they Export many hundred Barrells to the West Indies.

Besides which this farm (and no other on the Island) has all Sorts of Shell fish Such as Lobsters, Crabbs, Scollops, Muscells, Quahauggs, Clamms, and Oysters the best I Ever Eate and in Such Quantities that a man and Boy at

Low water will take as many as a pair of Oxen can bring home in a Cart and that in Less then an hour's Time the beds not being a furlong from their Door. Here are Likewise Great Quantities of Land Fowl Such as Paterage, Quails, Pidgeons, which fly in large flocks; but the most remarkable and allmost Incrediable is that of the fish Hawk; An Account of which I have ben at Some pains to gather while I resided here near 10 months.

This Fowl is in Coulour and Size much like our Small Eagle and Preys on fish therefore cannot be Eaten, they are birds of Passage and Disappear at the Atumnal Equinox vizt. the 10th of September and very rarely is there any to be seen on the 11th they Build their nests on Large Oaks which are all of them Dead some Say these Birds Pyson them with their Fish they bring to their Nests but I never could [see] any of their nests on a growing Tree; 'Tis very Entertaining to See these Fowls in the month of August filling up their Nests with Sea weed and then Covering them over with Sticks and after that Thatching them Over with Sea weed so very Thick and Strong that it will keep out the weather and preserve their nests till their return at the 10th of March when they fall to work and uncover their nests and prepare them for Laying in their Eggs. At their first Arival here (for they Build no where Else but on this Farm nor no where Else in the Colony that I Could Ever hear of) The Bays and Lakes are frozen and therefore can get no fish in them but they fly to the Falls or Cascades which are allways Open and there they Take great Quantities of Fresh water Fish which may be very Easily taken from them as I have done it Divers Times my self with a Gun and a Little Powder for by fiering off the Gun as they are flying over me with the Fish in their Tallons they will Imediately drop it and make the best of their way for more. They are a very fierce Bird as not Suffering any bird of Prey to come unto the farm if he should he is sure to Die by which means they preserve their fowls from any other birds of Prey On which Account the People on the farm doe not Care that any one Should Destroy them; notwithstanding which I could never find they Increased in their Number.

By means of these Birds they rear up a Prodigeous Quantity of Fowl Such as Geese, Turkeys Peacocks, Ducks and Dunghill Fowls; They have Likewise great Quantities of Hares and Rabits which doe not Burrow in the Ground but Lurk about in the Stone wall fences in and about the Farm; they are Considerabley Less then ours; but very good Eating This Exelent Farm in the year 1742 was at the yearly Rent of 700£ old Tenor value 70£ but now the Present Tenant Mr. Gideon Freeborn pays 1200 Pounds old Tenor value 120£ Sterling, And he has often told me he has made his Rent out of the wooll in Fleece.

Farther remarks on the Colony of Rhode Island etc. in No. America.

The Assembly in this Colony Sat 48 hours on a Quere wether oysters where Fish or vegitables[314] Caried per the former per 4 votes.

FINIS

[314] The session of the general assembly of Rhode Island and Providence Plantations of February 18, 1734/5, passed a law empowering the council of each town to make such laws and orders for the preservation of oysters, in the act called Shell Fish, as seemed necessary. Possibly it is to the passage of this act that our journalist refers. *Rhode Island Records*, IV., 502; *Acts and Laws of His Majesty's Colony of Rhode-Island, and Providence-Plantations* (Newport, 1745), pp. 184–185.

EXTRACT FROM THE JOURNAL OF MAJOR JOHN SMITH, 1756–1757[1]

French Forts where Major John Smith Commander of a Company of Rangers on the frontiers of Virginia, was Prisoner for eleven months, taken with his Party of ten men in a Blockhouse, towards the head of James River on the 25th of June 1756. by Monsieur Belester[2] Com'der of Miamee Fort (about 500 miles from the head of James River) at the head of 205 Indians, and 25 French Canadians, of which Party, Major Smith killed 40 w'ch obliged Captain Belester, to return without penetrating to Wariock, within 60 miles from Williamsburgh where he intended; according to the Information of his Shawanoe Indians his Spies, who passed through the Settlements of Virginia some months before, as Cherokees and our Friends

Fort Miamee	16 Soldiers Regulars	no Guns
Fort St. Joseph	22 Militia for 3 years service	no Guns
Fort Egery	10 D'o	no Guns
Fort at the mouth of St. Joseph's river	15 D'o	no Guns
Fort Detroite	700 mostly Traders and Planters	no Guns
Fort Huron	16 Militia	no Guns
For Presque Isle	100 Soldiers and others	about 6 Swivels
Fort at the Trading house	20 Soldiers	no Guns
Fort Magara[3]	200 Soldiers	40 Guns
Fort Frontenac	220 Soldiers	Number not known

NB. More particular accounts of these Forts Major Smith gives in his Journal.

[1] Public Record Office, London, Chatham Papers, Gifts and Deposits, 8: 95, no. 16; photostat in the Library of Congress. The document is endorsed: "Extract from Major Smiths Journal 1756/7 America no 16 in Mr. Abercrombie's letter of Nov. 16 1757 to Mr. Wood."

[2] Marie François Picoté, Sieur de Bellestre, led a raid into the Carolinas in 1756.

[3] An error for Fort Niagara.

The Indian Nations where Major Smith passed through and resided during his Captivity, all which Nations are ever aided by the French

First The Shawanoes, not quite 300 Gunmen, great Emimys of late to the English.

Miamees or Putts. about 200 may be gained over from the French having been our friends formerly.

Putoataways. in the whole of their Towns about 2000 inclined to come over to the English, for better Trade, could they get off from the French, they took Major Smith, into their Counsel as a sachem, went to their King, danced under the English Colours, taken from Gen'l Braddock, and fired through the French Colours, held Council with Major Smith, agreed with him in a project formed by him for taking Fort Dequesne by their assistance with 1500 of their People. The intimacy between them and the Major being suspected, he was removed, he speaks the Language.

Hottaways about 300 follow their Neighbours to the French.

Twigtwees. about 1400 formerly our friends, they suffered greatly on our account, but are still desireous to be with us ag't the French, if safe for them so to do.

Uttaways. about 350. are under the influence of the Putuattaways, the rest of them, pretty numerous under the French.

Hurons. about 150 go with the Putuattoways.

The whole thus Stated are in number 4700. Gunmen, by gaining the Putuattoways to our Interest, with whom Major Smith lived for some months, we get the whole of these Indians under our influence, and thereby the whole hunting Country, the best in America, from the Ohio, to the river Illonoise,[4] there not being one Great Gun, in any of the French forts in all that Country, to oppose us, in any incursion to be made amongst them, which Major Smith thinks very practicable, more especially in Winter, and early in the Spring, when all the Gunmen, are in their hunt, and *Honey-harvest*,[5] for that Enterprise he thinks 1000 Woods men are

[4] Illinois River.

[5] Marginal note: "The juice of the sweet Maple Tree extracted in the Spring, boiled produces good Sugar."

sufficient, with some Cherokees or Catabas Indians, either may be had, taking with them on their backs, no more than 15 Days provision at their setting out, with their ammunition, trusting to more by hunting, and Provisions to be had from Indian Towns in their way, having no Great River to pass but the Ohio, (which he proposes to cross at the mouth of the Great Conway) till they come to Detroite Fort, the Ohio to be crossed in Bark Canoes, one whereof may be made in three hours by three men, which will carry 10 men and their Luggage, having crossed the Ohio, to fall in with the Shawnesse path, that leads to the Miamee Fort making from the Ohio to this Fort eight Days, at the rate of 20 miles per Day, the Sioto river[6] being only knee deep at most; from Miamee, to Fort Joseph, four Days, from thence to the Putuattoway Town, four Days, burning Fort Egery and an other Small Fort in their way, from Putuattoway to Detroite a very little way, and here are many trading Batteaus for the Trade of Lake Erie, by means whereof they may transport themselves to the Landing place, on the southside of the Lake, from whence goes a near cut to return to the Ohio, through the Shawanoes, or if well assisted, by the Putuattoways, to proceed along the Lake to the river Beauff,[7] where Fort Prisque Isle is, attempt this Fort, or if too strong for being taken by Surprize, or assault, they leave it, and proceed down the river to the Ohio, as Col'l Washington did on his Interview with the Commander of this Fort, on the Commencement of the Ohio war.[8]

Such are the outlines of Major Smiths project to be executed by himself, or any other person acquainted with this way of Warring.

[6] Scioto River.

[7] River Le Bœuf.

[8] Bearing a message from Lieutenant-Governor Robert Dinwiddie of Virginia to Legardeur de Saint-Pierre, commander at Fort Le Bœuf, George Washington was at Fort Le Bœuf, December 11, 1753. "Journal of Mr. Christopher Gist," Massachusetts Historical Society *Collections*, 3rd series, V., 104; George Washington, *Writings*, I. (Washington, 1931), 26.

INTELLIGENCE FROM COLONEL PETER SCHUYLER

Intelligence from Colonel Peter Schuyler of the New Jersey Regiment, taken at Oswego, and now a Prisoner at Quebec: sent by Joseph Morse, who left that place October 4, 1757.[1]

That in the Course of the last Summer there arriv'd at Quebec, through the Straits of Belle Isle,[2] 43 Vessels, of which two were Men of War of 64 guns, and one a frigate of 36 guns; Some of the Merchantmen were very large, carrying from sixteen to twenty six Guns; Their Cargoes consisted chiefly of Brandy and Dry Goods, with some Stores of War, and a small portion of Provisions. The frigate left Quebec on the 21st of August, and the two 64 gun Ships on the 30th of the same Month.

There are in Canada

Two Reg'ts of Regulars, call'd the Colony Troops	1000	7200. Regular Troops
The old Regiments of six Battalions, not full	2700	
Arriv'd the last Summer in the above Ships from France	3500	

Colonel Schuyler is of Opinion, from his own Observation, and from the best Accounts he can collect, that the whole

[1] Public Record Office, London, Chatham Papers, Gifts and Deposits, 8: 95, no. 7; photostat in the Library of Congress. The document is endorsed: "Int Virginia America 1757 No. 7." Peter Schuyler was commissioned a colonel of the New Jersey Blues in 1746. Ten years later he and one-half of his regiment were captured by the French at Oswego and carried first to Montreal and later to Quebec. For an account of him by a fellow-prisoner at Quebec, see *The Dangers and Sufferings of Robert Eastburn, and His Deliverance from Indian Captivity*, reprinted from the original edition of 1758, with introduction and notes by John R. Spears (Cleveland, 1904), pp. 63–64. In October, 1757, Schuyler was released on parole.

The Strait of Belle Isle separates Labrador and Newfoundland.

Number of Troops in Canada, consisting of Regulars, Canadeans, and Indians, do not exceed 24,000.

That Provisions of all kinds are very scarce; The Prisoners and Inhabitants being at an Allowance of four ounces of Bread per Day, and a little salt fish; the Soldiers at 9 ounces of Bread per Day, and Meat only two Days in the week. Colonel Schuyler is of Opinion That the provisions will all be consumed about the end of february. And says if the Mouth of the River be well guarded in time, the Distresses of the Troops and Inhabitants will be greater the next Summer, than it was the last.

That all the Provisions taken at Oswego were sent away, by Niagara, to the Forts upon the Lakes and the River Ohio.

That for above a twelve Month past the french have been assisted by great Numbers of Indians of the six Nations formerly in friendship with us, many of whom were personally known to the prisoners. That about 300 Men of those Tribes were with the french in the action on Lake George, when great part of Schuyler's Regiment, then under the command of Lieut. Col. Parker, was cut off.[3]

That the Indians used the English Prisoners, taken on the Lake George and at Fort William Henry, with great Cruelty, killing and eating several in Sight of the french Troops.

That Col. Schuyler, who had found Means of negotiating his Bills, had purchas'd from the Indians as many prisoners as he could, and afterwards supplied them with cloathing. That in this Service he had expended near seven thousand pounds Sterling.

That about the 25th of Sep'r great preparations were made for an Expedition, as the french said against Nova Scotia; That the Troops destined for that Service were 2000 Regulars, 2400 Canadeans, and 1600 Indians. That on the 4th of October, when Morse the Informant came away, they were

[3] In the summer of 1757 Louis, Marquis de Montcalm, crossed Lake George with about 8000 French and Indians. After a six days' siege, he took Fort William Henry at the southern end of the lake. Colonel John Parker of the New Jersey regiment was one of those who advised the surrender of the fort. S. M. Pargellis, *Lord Loudoun in North America* (New Haven, 1933), pp. 243–250.

all gone down the River St. Lawrance, except General Montcalm and his Guard of 500 Men.

N.B. As Colonel Schuyler has upon many Occasions exerted himself for his Majesty's Service, has a considerable Estate and Influence in North America, and is now well acquainted with the Country he is in, it is to be wished his Liberty could be obtained.

WILLIAM DENNY TO EDWARD BOSCAWEN[1]

Sir, PHILADELPHIA 16th Septem'r 1758

I have the Honour of yours of the 5th of August requesting a Supply of 300 Seamen for the Maning the Eccho Man of War, which you was pleased to offer for the defence of this Coast. I immediately applied to the Assembly, who are now sitting, and on their declining to enable me to furnish the above Supply, I sent a written Message to the House, which is inclosed, with their Answer.[2]

There will be a Regiment Quartered here in the Winter, as We have Barracks lately built for fourteen hundred Men. If you think proper to order one of your Ships on this Station, I will give all the Assistance in my power for a general Press.

I have endeavoured to prevent as much as possible the Exportation of Provisions to Suspected Ports, from whence the Kings Enemies may be furnished; notwithstanding, there is certainly a clandestine Trade carried on, which might be surpressed by a Ship of War. The Provincial Armed Frigate is a bad Sailor, and there are one hundred and sixty Men, Officers included, on board her, which might be turned over to the King's Ship.

Inclosed is the Examination of an English Sailor that came

[1] Public Record Office, London, Chatham Papers, Gifts and Deposits, 8: 96; photostat in the Library of Congress. William Denny was Lieutenant-Governor of Pennsylvania from 1756 to 1759. Admiral Edward Boscawen commanded the fleet that took Louisburg, July 26, 1758.

[2] In a letter dated "Namur, Louisbourg Harbor, the 5th of August, 1758," Boscawen requested Denny to furnish him with 300 recruits to man the fleet, in return for which he offered to send the *Eccho*, a ship of thirty-two guns, to Philadelphia. On September 5 Denny sent Boscawen's request to the assembly, but the house refused to comply with the request. On September 11 the council, and on September 12 the governor asked the house to reconsider its refusal, without result. *Minutes of the Provincial Council of Pennsylvania*, VIII., 163–167, 170; "Papers of the Governors, 1747–1759," *Pennsylvania Archives*, 4th series, II., 940–942.

in a Flag of Truce from New Orleans, with three others, who were examined Separately, and confirmed what he said.

General Forbes in his Letter of the 4th Instant writes me, that he has opened a very good New Road fourteen Miles to the right of General Braddocks, and that his Advanced Post, consisting of Fifteen hundred Men, and a Detachment of Artillery, was within forty Miles of Fort Duquesne.[3]

I have the Pleasure to inform you by the inclosed Gazettee of the Success of Colonel Bradstreet's Expedition against Frontenac.[4]

I am, Sir,
Your most obedient
and most humble servant
WILLIAM DENNY

[3] For the letter of Brigadier-General John Forbes, dated Fort Loudoun, September 9, 1758, see *Minutes of the Provincial Council of Pennsylvania*, VIII., 167–169.

[4] Colonel John Bradstreet took Fort Frontenac or Cataraqui, August 27, 1758.

EXAMINATION OF WILLIAM PERRY

The Examination of William Perry, a Mariner on board the Flag of Truce Captain Viviat, who arrived yesterday from New Orleans, taken this 27th Day of May 1758, before William Allen Esq'r Chief Justice of the Province of Pensilvania.[1]

This Examinant saith, that he sailed from Rhode Island the Twentieth Day of May was Twelve month in the Ship Sea Flower, Captain Thomas Robinson, bound to the Bay of Honduras, and in her Voyage there, on the Thirtieth Day of June last, in Sight of the Havannah, the Sea-Flower was taken by a French Privateer of Eight Guns, Captain Desnaire—That Five French Men were put on board; and in Distress of Weather, being bound to the Mississippi, put into a Spanish Port, called Pansacola, about Thirty Leagues North East of the Mississippi, and from thence sailed to the Mississippi, but out of Sight of Land—That at the Entrance of the Mississippi there is a great Bar near One Hundred Feet in Breadth, on which is no more than Twelve Feet Water—No Rocks, a hard, blue, Clay—That there is a Fort of Six or Eight Guns, where the Pilots reside, at the Entrance into the River, at an Island called La Balise—That when they came to the Bar in the Prize Sloop, there they found the Ship Lancaster, and the Privateer Sloop that took them, lying in the River—That the Privateer left them, and the Ship was lightened of Logwood, in order to enable her to go over the Bar—That the Ship and Sloop Sea-Flower passed the Bar together, and went up to New Orleans, and he was told by the King's Pilot, it was Thirty Four Leagues from

[1] This enclosure is endorsed: "Copy Examination of William Perry, a Mariner, on board Capt. Viviat in the Pauline a French Flag of Truce from New Orleans taken 27th May 1758." Captain Viviat brought a letter from the Governor of Louisiana. *Minutes of the Provincial Council of Pennsylvania*, VIII., 124.

the Bar to New Orleans—That in going up the River he saw Two Forts, nearly opposite to one another, about halfway up, not of much Force, and that they were building a new Battery, or Fort, about Six or Seven Miles above these—That there is no Stone in the Country, but very good Clay.

That at New Orleans there are about Two Hundred Soldiers, but it is unfortified—That there are a few Cannon to fire on a rejoicing Day—That New Orleans is about as big as Bristol, in Rhode Island Government—That he saw Numbers of Indians in Town, fifty or sixty in a Gang, and he was told, that the French, who go out of Town any where into the Country, are frequently scalped—That a Barrel of Flower was sold for Thirty Five Pieces of Eight—That there was there a small Prize Brig Captain Spring of Philadelphia laden with Flower, and that her Flower sold for Thirty Five Pieces of Eight a Barrel—That there arrived from Bourdeaux a Brig of Six Guns, laden chiefly with Wine, and a Snow, a Letter of Marque, of Ten Guns, bound for Cape Francois—That a French Ship of Sixty Hands and Ten Guns of the Warwicks taken by the English, and retaken by a small Privateer came into New Orleans—That three Vessels sailed from New Orleans a few Days before them, a Brig of Fourteen, and Two Wooden, Guns, a Brig of Twelve Guns, and a Schooner of Eight Guns concerted with the Brig of Twelve Guns, and, as they were told, intended for Augustine, and then for this Coast—That they were afraid of being attacked by an Army from South Carolina, and collected their Militia, which he does not believe exceeds Four Hundred—That there was a great Scarcity of Provisions, and Flower, and every other Sort but Rice, of which there is plenty. That a Vessel, with Soldiers from Old France to New Orleans, was taken, and that Sixteen Store Ships, laden with Provisions and Ammunition, were all taken by the English, except one, which arrived there, and this Examinant helped to fit her out.

That in the Jayl, where he was, he saw one Thomas Morris, who told him he was an Indian Trader, and had traded with an Officer belonging to a large Fort that the French had,

Four or Five Hundred Leagues up the Mississippi, near the Mouth of the Carolina River, and went there to demand the Money due to him; but, instead of being paid, he was arrested, put into Confinement and sent to New Orleans.

That he saw William Tipper, a Londoner, a Seaman, who was pressed at Charles Town into the Provincial Forces; that he had deserted, and was found by a Party of Indians in the Woods, near the above Fort, almost starved, and carried by them to New Orleans, and there remained in Jayl, having been a Prisoner about a Year.

This Examinant says, that, in the Month of January a Message was sent to the Governor of New Orleans from their friendly Indians, that if they did not send them a Supply of Cloathing and Ammunition, they would come and destroy them, on which they mustered their Forces, expecting the Indians to come.

That the Goods they get is from Jamaica, in Flags of Truce —That there were Two Flags of Truce, a Brig and a Sloop, from Jamaica, while he was there, laden with Bales of Goods and Flower, and above a hundred Negroes to trade with, with a few Prisoners, and that they took back only Twelve Prisoners, and a Lading of Indigo, Beaver, Deer Skins, Parchment and Logwood. That New Orleans is so bad a Place and so little Employ to be had there, that the French would rather remain in Jayl at Jamaica, than come to New Orleans—That their Days Allowance is a Bitt, for which they can get no more than Three Eggs.

William Perry

Sworn before me
Will: Allen

ECONOMIC SERVITUDES

ELIZABETH SPRIGS TO JOHN SPRIGS[1]

To Mr. John Sprigs White Smith in White Cross Street near Cripple Gate London

Honred Father MARYLAND Sept'r 22'd 1756.

My being for ever banished from your sight, will I hope pardon the Boldness I now take of troubling you with these, my long silence has been purely owing to my undutifullness to you, and well knowing I had offended in the highest Degree, put a tie to my tongue and pen, for fear I should be extinct from your good Graces and add a further Trouble to you, but too well knowing your care and tenderness for me so long as I retaind my Duty to you, induced me once again to endeavour if possible, to kindle up that flame again. O Dear Father, belive what I am going to relate the words of truth and sincerity, and Ballance my former bad Conduct [to] my sufferings here, and then I am sure you'll pitty your Destres-s [ed] Daughter, What we unfortunat English People suffer here is beyond the probibility of you in England to Conceive, let it suffice that I one of the unhappy Number, am toiling almost Day and Night, and very often in the Horses druggery, with only this comfort that you Bitch you do not halfe enough, and then tied up and whipp'd to that Degree that you'd not serve an Annimal, scarce any thing but Indian Corn and Salt to eat and that even begrudged nay many Neagroes are better used, almost naked no shoes nor stockings to wear, and the comfort after slaving dureing Masters pleasure, what rest we can get is to rap ourselves up in a Blanket and ly upon the Ground, this is the deplorable Condition your poor Betty endures, and now I beg if you have any Bowels of Compassion left show it by sending me

[1] Public Record Office, London, High Court of Admiralty, 30: 258, no. 106; photostat in the Library of Congress.

some Relief, Cothing is the principal thing wanting, which if you should condiscend to, may easely send them to me by any of the ships bound to Baltimore Town Patapsco River Maryland, and give me leave to conclude in Duty to you and Uncles and Aunts, and Respect to all Friends

Honred Father
Your undutifull and Disobedient Child
ELIZABETH SPRIGS

Please to direct for me
at Mr. Rich'd Crosses to
be left at Mr. Luxes[2] Merc't
in Baltimore Town Patapsco River
Maryland

[2] On members of the Lux family of Baltimore, see A. L. Sioussat, *Old Baltimore* (New York, 1931), pp. 44, 91.

THOMAS SAUNDERS TO THEADOSIA SAUNDERS[1]

For Mrs. Theadosia Saunders at the sign of the Acorn in little Wild Street near linclons inn fields London These per Capt. Jones.

Octob'r the 9 1756.

Hon'rd Mother

These with my kind love and duty to you hoepeing these fue lines will find you in good health as i and my family is at present thanck god for it my wife and son gives their kind loves and duty to you your Grandson is goeing on of four years old since the soeventh day of last august we have lost one. dear mother i rec'd the Cask of Brases and pewter Books and sundrys wich you sent me by Wm Dallam Junior and i humbly thanck you for them But it is not in my power at present for to make you a return for i have like a great many other prodigall sons gone thorugh a great deal of trouble but by the assistance of god through his all mighty grace it apeiares to be all most over for now the heat of youth is past all my Care is in Virtue and honesty and for my ofspring thats Come and to Come i thanck god he inpires me with a spirit of industry and ever has done so since i left you i bought an irich Convict servant Named Owen desmond from Cork Just as i was married he soon after Rob'd me of the Chief of my Cloaths and also my Wifes and run a way and i never heard of him since his first Cost was twenty pounds and at the same time lost a mare Cost me Eight pounds thes losses seem to hurt me at first but thanck god i rubd through them and saved my land wich was of more value than all but was obliged to mortgage it But it is Just Cleer i have 160 Acrer of good land wich i bougt before i was married my wife is but young about 22 years old now and seems pregnat

[1] Public Record Office, London, High Court of Admiralty, 30: 258, no. 143; photostat in the Library of Congress.

Enough soe you need not fear Grand Chilldren Enough from that one branch you seem'd to mention some thinge about Religion i beg you give your self noe trouble about that for my Chief Care is that also i desire youl Consider that your Growing older daly and not to hurt y'r self for me that has been like the prodigall son but i thanck god it has not hurt me much since it Enlivenes my mind to devine grace it is very troublesome times or Else you might Expect to see me soon for i am afraid of being prest aboard of a kings ship and then maybe i might not giet a shoar redyly[2] pray give my kind love and service to all friends and relations in generall my son is named after my father John so no more at present from your most loving and affectionate son till death

THO'S SAUNDERS[3]

PS pray derect for Thos Saunders Joyner at the head of Bush river Maryland. i had not oppertunity to write by Wm. Dallam for they gott loaded in pertuexent river[4] above 100 miles of but you may send by him an answer if you please or by Capt Meleglin or any Capt thats Coming to patapseco river[5] and i shall recvie it safe home ever you in trusted to pack those goods they did not pack them safe Considering what rouges sailors is

[2] "Seamen feared impressment for the royal navy, and for that reason hesitated to ship on a merchant vessel where they would be in particular danger." D. M. Clark, *British Opinion and the American Revolution* (New Haven, 1930), p. 97.

[3] In 1776 the names of Thomas, Joseph, William, and Elizabeth Saunders occur in a list of the inhabitants of Bush River Lower Hundred, Maryland. In 1778 Thomas Saunders, farmer, and William Saunders took the oath of fidelity in Harford County, Maryland. G. M. Brumbaugh, *Maryland Records*, II. (Baltimore, 1928), 134, 233.

[4] Patuxent River.

[5] Patapsco River.

THOMAS LLOYD TO EDMOND HECTOR[1]

To Mr. Edmond Hector, Surgeon In Birmingham, Warwickshire England

AUGUSTA COURT HOUSE Octob'r 10 1756 (Frontiers of Virginia)

Hon'ble Sir

This Day I Rec'd a Letter from my Wife bearing date April 21st 1755. and w'd have s'd Answ'r Immediately but fear'd Mr. Freeman w'd be gone therefore I humbly hope you'l Excuse me for this Freedom knowing y'r Character and that I might have greater dependance of its coming to You than to her. Hon'd Sir You must know that I am an Indented Serv't have 2 yrs ½ of my Time to come from 3d of Nov'r next to give a Description of my Servitude is Impossible so as to Expect you w'd Credit it. But will give You an Acc't of one Years Employ. I was Surgeon to 300 Men who went out against the Shauneeb Indians Town[2] but we had 500 Miles to go and having a bad Pilate out of 200 Horses we broug't in but 4 or 5 the chief of the Rest we were forc'd to Eat being all like to Perish Several Times since I have been upon Scouts I have fasted 3 or 4 Days

[1] Public Record Office, London, High Court of Admiralty, 30: 258, no. 229; photostat in the Library of Congress.

[2] On December 15, 1755, Lieutenant-Governor Robert Dinwiddie of Virginia instructed Captain William Preston of Staunton, Virginia, to take part in an expedition under Colonel Andrew Lewis against the Shawnee towns to the west of the Ohio River. This was the most pretentious undertaking of Virginia in 1756. By 29 George II, c. 35, an "Act for the better recruiting His Majesty's Forces on the Continent of North America," the enlistment of indentured servants upon compensating their masters was permitted, but Lloyd seems to have been serving in the forces of Virginia with his masters. Virginia Historical Society, *The Official Records of Robert Dinwiddie, Lieutenant-Governor of the Colony of Virginia, 1751–1758* (2 vols., Richmond, 1883–1884), I., xii; Wisconsin Historical Society, *The Preston and Virginia Papers of the Draper Collection of Manuscripts* (Madison, 1915), pp. 9, 10; S. M. Pargellis, *Lord Loudoun in North America* (New Haven, 1933), pp. 116–120.

together as for Beding and Cloathing I am so [u]sd to it now if I get a Blanket I am satisfy'd, the French Ind's have killd our Men and Inhab's all round the Camp and they are [so] much of the Nature of a Wolf that if we dont come on them while at there Prey its needless They'l lye in Ambush and Fire on us before we are Sensible. My first Mast. Colo. Patton[3] was killd and 12 Men close by our Camp we foll'd them 200 Miles but to know purpose Our County is reduc'd to one half of the Inhabitants there is 150 Miles Leng: 300 or 400 in Curcumference laid Waste most of them Killd and the rest fled w'th Difficulty Its in this Wastepts we Range but as Yet w'th little Success having not Killd above 10 of our Enemy and they have killd some Hundreds of our People. The Hand of God seems to Cooperate with the Heath'n perhaps as a Scourge for our Sins. Pensylvania is likewise sorely Handled.

My Wife writes to me to s'd some Money but I cannot having not had 5s. this Year and half I humbly beg you'l do y'r Endeav'rs to get my Friends to contribute to the Value of £20 Sterl'g for me and Commission Mr. Wm. Freeman to pay it to me who will have freqt. Opportunity of sending it to me from Philadelphia.

You need not be Scrupulous on my former Follies for I am sensibly Fam'd. The Gentle'n above can give you an Acc't of my Pst Character I expect he'll be in Birmingham before this. Your Civility to my Wife is a Mark of y'r good Character (w'ch never can be Extinguishd) I Hope You'l do y'r utmost for me per Mr. Freeman and Assure Y'rself I shall always be ready to Acknowledge it. From Sir

Y'r most Ob't and Hble Serv't

THOMAS LLOYD

P.S. Please to Remember my Duty to my Mother Love to Bro'rs and Sisters and Hble Service to Mrs. Hector and 2 Mas'r Careless.

[3] Colonel James Patton received a grant of 120,000 acres of land in Augusta County, which he settled with "redemptioners" brought from Ireland. After serving as high sheriff and lieutenant of the county, he was murdered by the Indians in 1755.

N.B. Sir I wish youd send me a Case of Launces and a common Case of Pocket Instrum'ts: if my Mother will pay for them, by Mr. Freeman.

Whether you send the Money or know or the Launces and Instrument Case (I Beleive you may get them for 18s. plain and a Bistoury.[4] I Beg you'l doit if you can If not be pleasd to Honour me w'th a Letter from You. and it will be great Consolation to my Distressd Heart

THOMAS LLOYD[5]

If they dont send money to purchase my Time if I get the above it will be great Satisfaction and Advantage to me the are so Dear here. I cou'd raise as much Money as w'd pay that but have no Opportunity of send'g it y'r Honour

[4] A small, slender, surgical knife.

[5] Thomas Lloyd seems to have continued to practice medicine in Augusta County, Virginia. See L. Chalkley, *Chronicles of the Scotch-Irish Settlement in Virginia* (3 vols., Washington, 1912–1913), *passim.*

THOMAS LLOYD TO MOLLY LLOYD[1]

Dear Molly

I hope You'l forgive me not Writing at this Time to You, thinking this above may be of more use to us, Assure yourself, altho you charge me w'th Expressions w'ch I ev'r deny and please God I live to return My Behav'r and Actions I hope will Confirm it Falsitude

From D'r Molly
Y'rs Affectionately
THOS. LLLOYD

Excuse Scrawl and Stile the Gent'n waiting to take it to the Land'g Augusta Court House were I now am being 200 Miles from it.

Please to Direct to me as foll's

To
Doctor Thomas Lloyd Living at
Capt. Willm. Prestons
Augusta Court House
Virginia.

N.B. Ever 2 or 3 months I can get a Line from or to Mr. Freeman. Pedlears from here being ev'r now and then in Philadelphia.

[1] Enclosed in the letter to Edmond Hector.

RICHARD TUGGEY, JR., TO RICHARD TUGGEY, SR.[1]

To Mr. Tuggey at Low Tewting in Surrey[2]

ANOPLIS November the 2 1756

Honerd Father and mother

I take this opertinewtey of riting to you to Lett you know that i am in maryland and a footman to the Honrable Colnall Taskur[3] and i am in a Good Place and i am much surprisd i never Receved a letter from you I have sent 2 too you I Live as well as aney one Can but to be so Long fron hering or seeing from you i think you are Ded I shall be Glad to heer from you but as i have sent 2 Letters to you and never Receved an Answer i Expect you are Ded I live Ass well as aney one Can in the world I am marrad since i Com heer and I hope to be in England in a bout 12 mounths and shall bring my wife with me and Pray send to me som knives som buckls and Butins and Aney thing you think Proper for i Can make Good money heer I have i all a bout two hundred pound in money since i hive been heer Pray send me a Letter by the first ship Com'g to maryland and Drict it to mr Teogget att the Honrable Collnl. Taskers in Anoplis i Maryland Pray Give my Love to All my frinds in England

[1] Public Record Office, London, High Court of Admiralty, 30: 258, no. 90; photostat in the Library of Congress.

[2] Richard Tuggey, Sr., of the parish of Tooting Graveney in Surrey, apparently could not write and signed his name with a mark. Although at various times he served as overseer of the poor, surveyor of the highways, and churchwarden of his parish, and in November, 1729, contributed 1*s.* to the poor rate, he seems often to have lived in want. In 1753 he was proceeded against for failing to pay his rates. In the same year the overseers of the poor paid him 2*s.* 6*d.* In 1757 they paid 10*s.* 6*d.* to a woman to sit up with the sick and helpless Mr. Tuggey, and for coals and necessaries for him for a period of two weeks. W. E. Morden, *The History of Tooting-Graveney* (London, 1897), *passim.*

[3] Colonel Benjamin Tasker, Jr., was a member of the council and naval officer at Annapolis. A. L. Sioussat, *Old Baltimore* (New York, 1931), p. 54.

as knows me my Love to my sister and broth' Ann and James and i wish them helth and hapyness and my most sacret Dewtey to my father and mothar and All my frind frinds
P S
I have marrad as sweat a gall a Ever was Born shee Is as trew to me as the verelle Sun an i [s]hall bring hur to England will me plees God i Live Pray send me a Letter to me by the firs Ship a Coms for i Long to heer from you Pray Excuse the bad riting to you for you knou i am a bad coller your Dewtful Sun

RICHARD TUGGEYY

DANIEL STURGES TO SUSANNAH ANDREWS[1]

To Mrs. Susannah Andrews To be left at S'r Arthur Haslerigs to Nosly-Hall[2] near Ilson[3] in Leicester Shire

VIRGINIA June 11th 1756

Hon'd Aunt—

Recd yours in October Last as also your present. accept of my humble Acknowledgement w'ch is all the return I am able to make as I believe you expect. Mr. Earlom dispos'd of it w'th ½ a Guinea he aded himself very much to my advantage and has always and in all things been my perticular friend. I hope God will reward both you kindnesses...

You desired me to informd you in all I cou'd concerning my Bussiness and the Country I live in. the best of w'ch that I can give please to receive as followeth... my bussiness is Merchandizing, I am Storekeeper for Mr. Hump'y Bell[4] under his Factor, Stores here are much like Shops in London only w'th this difference, the Shops sells but one Kind or Specie of Wares, (Viz't Haberdashers sells Haberdashry Grocers Grocery etc.) and Stores all Kinds as Haberdashry, Grocery, Cutlary, Ironware, India Goods, Silks, Linnens, Woollens etc. these Commodities we sell to Planters, and receive in return Tobacco; a Weed of very little service to mankind as to it's Use yet as it is the promoter of a great Trade is of infinite advantage to Great Britain when I am out of my Time w'ch will be 10th August next ensueing I shall be employ'd in the same Service at ab't 25 or 30£ per Annum w'ch together w'th the oppertunity I have of improveing it and some perquisites I have besides may afford me a sufficiency to live on.

[1] Public Record Office, London, High Court of Admiralty, 30: 258, no. 276; photostat in the Library of Congress.

[2] Noseley Hall was the seat of the Hesilrige or Hazlerigg family.

[3] Illston-on-the-Hill is nine miles southeast of Leicester.

[4] In 1763 John Bell of Crutched-friars, London, perhaps a son of Humphrey Bell, was listed as a Virginia merchant. *The Universal Director* (London, 1763).

Virginia is a large Fruitfull and indifferently Pleasant Country, and considering it's infancey is very populous there being upwards of two hundred thousand white inhabitants Game Viz't Deer Hares Wild Turkeys Geese Ducks Partridges Pheasants etc. are Plentifull in some places, and most there is some . . . the Land produces all sorts of European Grain and Fruits as well as Indian Corn (w'ch last is the most common.) in abundance considering the quantity of Ground there is tended w'th it, the little Manure and the time people bestow on it. for you must know the Virginians betow not ½ their time on Grain for they Tend all their Rich natural Ground, and that w'ch is made rich by manure, in Tobacco. Peaches and Apples we have abundance of. so plenty as to feed Hoggs w'th 'em, other sorts are very plenty tho' not so plenty as those I have mention'd. the peoole neither so Industrous nor so religious as the English, they are fond of pageantry and Grandure, most lives above themselves; Great [Game] sters, the Family I am in are people of Good morals to whom I owe not a little for [my edu]cation.

If ever my Circumstances shall be so favourable as to afford me enough to spare to pay my Passage to England and my expences there believe shall take a Trip to my native country, w'ch I have I have a great desire of seeing again. when you may be sure I shall go to pay my Acknowledgments to all whom I am under any obligation either by Gratitude or Duty.

I have lamented your loss tho now am not so much concern'd since I find you and your Children are so well provided for, Agurs[5] wish if we consider rightly is the happiest state, for that State of Life w'ch will make us forget our maker must be most Misserable.

I Thank you for your advise, and hope God will enable me to follow it. am Glad to hear her Ladyship[6] is well I pray God she may continue so. it was her Ladyships commands that I should write to her once a Year but as you

[5] Proverbs 30: 7–9.

[6] In June, 1725, Sir Arthur Hesilrige married Hannah Sturges, to whom Daniel Sturges may have been related. J. Nichols, *The History and Antiquities of the County of Leicester*, II., part II. (London, 1798), 749, 756.

live so near (and suppose you'l show her this) think it is needless. . . . I have now nothing more to add but that I am by Gods Grace in good health in w'ch I hope It will find you and all my Relations; and that I give my Duty to her Ladyship and yourself my Love to all my Cousins especially Cousin Fanny and desire to be remember'd to all Friends And remain

Your Dutyfull Nephew
and Humble Servant
DANIEL STURGES

P: S pray excuse the inacuracies of this being wrote in hast—

To
M'rs. Susanna Andrews
to be left at S'r Arthur Hasilriggs
at Nosly Hall
Leicester Shire

VIRGINIA Nov'r 4th 1756

Madam

Not having an oppertunity of sending the inclosed till this present I opened it to see what I had wrote—since I wrote that I am become my own Man. I live still at the same Place and in the same bussiness. I have 25£ per Year my Board etc. and may expect to be advanced if I am not oblig'd to the Wars, as we are Apprehensive all the Young Men in this Collony will be in the Spring.[7] could communicate some news concerning it but supposing you don't concern yourself w'th such Affairs. do conclude w'th subscribing myself

Your dutifull Godson and Nephew
DANIEL STURGES

[7] The session of the Virginia legislature of September 20, 1756, passed "An Act for raising recruits for His Majesty's service; and for other purposes therein mentioned." By this act £8,000 was appropriated to be used for enlisting men in the Royal American Regiment, for paying the masters of enlisted servants, and for transporting those enlisted to New York, etc. The session of April 14, 1757, passed "An Act for granting an aid to His Majesty for the better protection of this colony, and for other purposes therein mentioned." This act authorized the drafting of soldiers. W. W. Hening, *Statutes at Large*, VII., 61–63, 69–87.

DANIEL STURGES TO WILLIAM EARLOM[1]

To Mr. William Earlom in Cowlane near West-smithfield London To be left at Mr. Humphry Bell's

VIRGINIA Nov'r 4th 1756

Sir

This oppertunity I take to inform you that I am out of my Time and am still living at the same place. I have 25£ a Year Wages w'ch w'th the oppertunities I have of improving it may afford me a sufficiencey to live on. M: Bell's Trade is but small now but when he leaves off and his Factor sets up for himself I may expect more. tho I am afraid Trade and all things else (but War) will be knock'd on the head the French make such advances and our Forces are so unsuccessfull that we are apprehensive we must all be oblig'd to take the Field in the Spring especially the young Men. . . . I suppose you have heard e'er this gets to your hands, of Oswego's being taken,[2] w'ch was the most important fortification on our Frontiers. It was surrender'd up as cowardly or Treacherously, as St. Philips Castle[3] was brave and honourable. . . . there was but five Men and the Commandant killd when it was surrenderd. . . . the next letter I send may probably be dated from our Camp. . . . having but Just heard of this oppertunity to write to you I cou'd not get Time to write to my Father Your Showing this to him I presume may do as well and as I intend to write soon

[1] Public Record Office, London, High Court of Admiralty, 30: 258, no. 276; photostat in the Library of Congress.

[2] Louis, Marquis de Montcalm, in command of the French forces in Canada, took Oswego, August 14, 1756.

[3] For an account of the surrender of St. Philip's Castle and the loss of the island of Minorca by the British in 1756, for which Admiral John Byng was court-martialed and shot, see Brian Tunstall, *Admiral Byng and the Loss of Minorca* (London, 1928).

hope the neglect may be excused especially as I am obligd to Answer a Letter of my Aunt Andrew's.

If you have any Thing deposited in your hands for me by any of my Friends, please to remit it in Books. . . . my propper compliments to all my Friends . . . I remain

Your dutifull Nephew
DANIEL STURGES

PS pray excuse haste—

MARCHES

THE JOURNAL OF CHARLOTTE BROWN, MATRON OF THE GENERAL HOSPITAL WITH THE ENGLISH FORCES IN AMERICA, 1754–1756[1]

On Sunday November 17th my Brother and self a Man Servant and Maid; embark'd on Board the Ship London Capt. Browne,[2] Laden with Stores for the Hospital.

Nov'r the 24. We arrived at Gravesend; provided Stores for our Voyage to Cork: took in Mr. Cherrington and Mr. Bass; got under Sail. 12 Mess'd in the Cabbin.

Dece'r the 5. At 4 in the Morning made Mizen Head[3] and we all expected to have been lost. I being Mr. Cherringtons Banker, he came to my state room and said; Mrs. Browne get up, and if you please put my Purse in your Pockett; But remember Lady you are not dressing for Court. I dress'd myself immediately and came on Deck and found my Brother tying two Planks together for us to set upon, but at last we happily got clear.

Dece'r the 9. At 4 in the After-noon we came to Anchor at Cove[4] 12 Miles from Cork.

[1] Original formerly in the possession of S. A. Courtauld, London; photostat in the Library of Congress. After the loss of Fort Necessity to the French, the British government sent Major-General Edward Braddock with the 44th and 48th Regiments commanded by Sir Peter Halkett and Colonel Thomas Dunbar to America. Impatient because of delays, Major-General Braddock and Admiral Keppel sailed from the Downs, December 24, 1754, and arrived at Hampton Roads, February 20, 1755. Taking up his residence in the Carlyle mansion in Alexandria, Virginia, Braddock commissioned George Washington as aide and called a convention of the governors of the colonies. Braddock and the colonial governors met in the Blue Room of the Carlyle mansion, April 14, 1755, and planned the subjugation of Fort Duquesne, Fort Niagara, Fort Frontenac, and Crown Point. Meanwhile, thirteen transports, three ordnance ships, and two convoys, to carry the 44th and 48th Regiments to America, assembled off the southwest coast of Ireland. With the expedition was Charlotte Brown, matron of the general hospital, for which Parliament had appropriated £1779 *7s. 6d.*

[2] The *London*, Captain Brown, was one of the transports.

[3] On the southwest coast of Ireland.

[4] Robert's Cove.

Dece'r the 10. All the Gentlemen went to Cork, myself and Servant went on Shore and dined, and was happy at a good fire; which we had not been at, all the Passage.

Dece'r the 13. All the Gentlemen returned from Cork, my Brother had Letters from London, all was well.

Dece'r the 15. Being Sunday Mr. Cherrington and Mr. Bass had a Squall on Deck, Mr. Bass had severall times given hints of Miss Davis a friendly fair of Mr. Cherringtons, he insisted on his explaining himself, which Mr. Bass did, but not in the Lady's favour many Ill natured Truths were said, Mr. Bass was forbid coming into the Cabbin, but he told him that he had as much right as himself; so he kept his footing; but Mr. Cherrington not being able to bear the Insolence of the little fellow, mov'd of to Cork.

Dece'r the 26. I went on Shore to Cove with my Brother and some of the Gentlemen we went to the best House in the Place we play'd a Game of Quadrille and then went to dancing till 12 and on going to the Boat Mr. Couch was molested by a fellow who knock'd him down a Riot insued at which numbers of the Cove Ladys interposed, but to no Purpose Mr. Couch gave them severall Blessing which all the rest joyn'd in, and it ended at 3 in the Morning with the spoiling of a new suit of Cloaths and breaking of 2 Guns.

Dece'r the 27. At a 11 in the Morning having nothing to eat the Gentlemen went to Market, and return'd at 12 at Night, but forgot what they went for so brought nothing.

Dece'r the 30. Went into my new Cabbin Mrs. Barbut an Officers[5] Lady came on Board and took the next to mine.

Dece'r the 31. M[y] Brother self and Maid went to Cork which is a disagreable dirty Place, we stay'd 3 Days my Brother was very ill and had fitts, return'd on Board with Mrs. Barbut.

Jan'y the 12, 1755. Being Sunday a great Squall on Deck between Mr. Cherrington and Capt. Browne, it began about the loss of some water gruel, and ended with the great favour I had reced to have my Cabbin in the Steerage.

Jan'y the 13. A Signal was made for sailing came on Board

[5] Lieutenant Theodore Barbut of the 48th Regiment.

the Director and at 4 in the after noon set sail with 16 Transports the Nightingale Man of War and the Sea Horse Commodore,[6] I this Day began to work a pair of Catgut Ruffles.

Jan'y the 14. A Fresh Gale of 7 Nots all the Passengers casting up their Accounts Capt. Browne very ill with gravely Disorder or something worse Mrs. Barbut close under Cape Rugg.

Jan'y the 15. All Hands call'd on Deck the Snow Concord had like to have been on board of us but we happily got clear Mrs. Barbut in Bed but has some thougths of getting up in a Day or two Mr. Barbut assisting her.

Jan'y the 16. On going into the Hold of the Ship a sad discovery was made 30 Gallons of Brandy run out that was for our sea Store all the Sailors lamenting that all the Megrins was out no more Grog to be had poor Pompy the Negroe allmost turn'd white on the thoughts of it but Mr. Lash the Mate said it was all run to Hell but they should have good Grog the next time that they pump'd the Ship.

Jan'y the 17. Lost Company of 2 of the Fleet, a fresh gale of 6 knots Capt. Browne and Mr. Couch made their first Appearance they both look'd on the lying in Order.

Jan'y the 18. Lost sight of all the Fleet Mrs. Barbut up and at work very bad Weather.

Jan'y the 20. At 6 in the Morning all Hands call'd on Deck and we were much suppriz'd with the Sight of Land on the Coast of Portingal[7] wore the Ship and got clear.

Jan'y the 21. We lost a Sheep and Mr. Cherrington 2 Pigs and 8 Turkys and 6 Ducks there was a great Dispute with Mr. Cherrington and my Brother Mr. Cherrington said it was not clear to him why so many of his should die and not one of ours.

Jan'y the 23. At 10 in the Morning Mr. Barbut got up and went to washing his Wife willing to follow his example heaved out at 12 but was extreamly Ill at rising so soon.

Jan'y the 25. A great Squall on Deck, with Mr. Lash the Mate and Mr. Black the Clerk of the Hospitall about the

[6] The *Nightingale* and the *Seahorse* were the convoys.

[7] Portugal.

tapping of some Beer Mr. Lash order'd it to be tap'd Mr. Black forbid it at which Mr. Lash in a great Rage told him that it was as thick as Hell and he should never tast it, that it was but the other Day that he carried a knot on his Back but now he was so much on his Hisy Prizy there was no speaking to him, the Day ended with a Dispute in the Cabbin with Mr. Cherrington and Mr. Couch.

Jan'y the 26. Being Sunday Mr. Willsford the Clerk of the Hospital read Prayers we saw a Sail a fair Wind.

Jan'y the 27. Saw a Sail to the East, a fair Wind Mrs. Barbut up and making a sea Pye being the first she ever made.

Jan'y the 28. A Calm Sea saw a Turtle set a Dog after it but lost it a getting it up the Ships side, Mr. Couch in the Cabbin deep in the Horrors, and will neither eat, drink or speak and is at a loss to tell whether he is alive or dead.

Jan'y the 29. A fair Wind saw a piece of gulf Weed Mr. Barbut up and a mending of Stockings, his Wife fast Asleep.

Feb'y the 2. A Great Squall on Deck of Wind and Rain the Reason of it was as the Men say; because Mrs. Barbut heav'd out so soon being up before 11.

Feb'y the 3. Being Sunday[8] had Prayers saw 9 of the Fleet a flying Fish came on Board it was 2 foot from one tip of the Wing to the other and 20 Inches long; we eat it for Dinner it eat like a young Sturgeon.

Feb'y the 4. A Calm lost sight of all the Fleet, Mr. Cherringtons sheep brought forth a fine Lamb.

Feb'y the 6. Received an Invitation from the Director[9] to dine with him had for Dinner a Ham 3 Fowls and a Pudding but the Weather was so bad the Director went to bed Mrs. Barbut very ill and did the same.

Feb'y the 8. A Fresh Gale went 10 knots one of the Sailors wash'd overboard but happily sav'd himself by catching hold of a Rope going down the side of a Ship.

[8] The lady is in error. February 2 was Sunday, and February 3, Monday.

[9] James Napier, master surgeon of the hospitals in Flanders during the preceding war, was appointed director and chief surgeon of the general hospital with the English forces in America. S. M. Pargellis, *Lord Loudoun in North America* (New Haven, 1933), p. 325.

Feb'y the 10. Being Sunday[10] had Prayers a fair Wind as hot as in June in England.

Feb'y the 14. Mrs. Barbut up but not able to work, Mr. Black came to see us in our Lower Regions stay'd so long and drank so much Grog, that he was at a loss how to go to Bed, he was invisible all the next Day.

Feb'y the 17. Sunday[11] had Prayers Mrs. Barbut up but not able to go to Prayers not being dress'd, we had a present of a Q'r of Pork from the Cabbin Mess.

Feb'y the 20. A Fair Wind but very Hot Capt. Browne at Breakfast on Tea and Cheshire Cheese his Equipage a Stone Jar a tin Pot a Pewter Basin a Can one saucer and an old rusty Cannister.

Feb'y the 21. Mr. Shirly the 2'd Mate made Bed being the first Time this Passage I fear we shall have a Bad Wind.

Feb'y the 22. Mrs. Barbut up by 8 this Morning but the Sailors desired her to tumble in again or else they should have a bad Wind. Saw a large Grampus.

Feb'y the 23. Sunday my Brother read Prayers Mr. Willsford being ill Very Hot Weather.

Feb'y the 24. I this Day finished my Catgut Ruffles. Mrs. Barbut 4 Hours making a Cake bak'd it 6 in a rusty Pudding Pan it eat like a Pancake.

Feb'y the 25. Mr. Cherrington learnt Mrs. Barbut to read and construe Greek in an Hour. A very bad Wind in the Lattitude of 30.

Feb'y the 27. Mrs. Barbuts Birth Day, had the Captains Mess to dine with us on a Ham, a Turky and Fowls and for Drink French Wine and Bristol Beer.

Feb'y the 28. Killed a Pig and very busy making Black Puddings. Mr. Barbut a fishing and brought up with his Line a Portugal Man of War. Spoke with a Sloop from Gorgia it had been out two Days was bound for St. Kits.

March the 2. Sunday but had no Prayers till After-Noon our Parson being indispos'd by drinking too much Grog the Night before.

[10] The author is again in error. February 9 was Sunday, and February 10, Monday.

[11] Another error. February 16 was Sunday, and February 17, Monday.

March the 3. Mr. Cherrington came down into our lower Regions and say'd he would do himself the Honour to treat me with a Dish of Turky Coffee stay'd to Supper on Black Puddings all of us in great Fears about Cape Hattoras[12] till 12 at Night and then was clear of it.

March the 4. All in great Spiritts spoke with the terrible Bomb one of our Fleet;[13] all was well on Board, Saw two Penquins got the Anchors ready to Cast and a two o'Clock in the Afternoon cast the first Lead and found Ground.

March the 5. All of us on the Flats again. A cruel Storm at N.W. drove us of soundings within 12 Hours sail of the Cape of Virginia.

March the 6. The Storm abated. saw one of the Fleet. Mr. Lash at breakfast on salt Junk and Tea.

March the 8th. Cast the Lead and found Ground.

March the 9. At Break of Day made the Land. the Wind not in our Favour. had Prayers. and at 4 in the Afternoon the Wind came about. 7 of our Fleet in sight.

March the 10. At 4 in the Afternoon made Cape Henery[14] a fair Wind and at 7 cast Anchor in Hamton Road. all in great Spirits. 4 Officers came on Board. drank out 15 Bottles of Port all in the Cabbin drunk (but Mr. Cherrington) to be free of Hamton.[15]

March the 11. The Captain went on board the Commodore, and recieved his Orders to sail up the River Potomack[16] in 28 Hours My Brother and self went on shore to Hamton in the Pilots Boat. gave 7s. 6d. for rowing 2 Miles went to the Kings Arms and Breakfasted. walk'd till Dinner. A very agreable Place and all the Houses extreemly neat had for Dinner a Ham and Turky, a Breast of Veal and Oysters to drink, Madeira Wine, Punch and Cyder stay'd till 4 in the Afternoon and then went on Board.

March the 12. Very Busy writing to England a Ship being

[12] Cape Hatteras.

[13] The *Terrible* was one of the transports.

[14] Cape Henry, Virginia.

[15] Hampton Roads.

[16] Potomac River.

ready to sail. came Orders from the Commodore for us to sail.

March the 13. At 7 in the Morning we set sail for Potomack. a fair Wind left Mr. Cherrington and Mr. Black behind.

March the 14. Came a N.W. Wind lay'd too at the Island of Dangers extreem cold.

March the 16. At 6 in the Morning weigh'd Anchor and set sail a fair Wind and at 5 cast Anchor.

March the 17. At 5 in the Morning weigh'd Anchor and set sail with a fair Wind and at 11 at Night came in sight of the Point a Pilot came on Board the Captain sent his Boat on Shore with Mr. and Mrs. Barbut cast Anchor.

March the 18. Extreem cold with Snow a bad Wind our Boat went on Shore a shooting and returned at Night and brought me from an unknown Lady a Present of 12 Eggs, 12 Limes, some fine Gingerbread and some Greens which were very acceptable.

March the 19. At 6 in the Morning weigh'd Anchor and set Sail with a fair Wind and at 12 cast Anchor the Boat went on Shore returned at Night and brought me some fine Fish.

March the 20. At 8 in the Morning weigh'd Anchor and set Sail; A pleasant Day. pass'd by several Plantations. Mr. Tuton came on board from the Terrible Bomb staid and dined, at 7 at Night cast Anchor in Sandy Point.[17]

March the 21. At 7 in the Morning weigh'd Anchor and set Sail but the Wind not being in our Favour we were obliged to tack about and at 11 the Ship run a Ground they hoisted out their long Boat and Yawl and tow'd her of and at 12 got clear and cast Anchor, and at 2 in the Morning weigh'd Anchor and set Sail with a fair Wind and at 11 cast Anchor in Bellhaven harbour.[18]

March the 22. Went on Shore to Bellhaven with Mr. Bass. Extremely hot but as Agreable a Place as could be expected it being inhabited but 4 Years; went with Mr. Lake to every

[17] At the entrance to Belmont harbor, Fairfax County.

[18] Belhaven was the first name of the settlement which in 1749 received the name of Alexandria. For a time both names seem to have been used.

House in the Place to get a Lodging and at last was Obliged to take a Room but little larger than to hold my Bed and not so much as a Chair in it. Went on Board at Night.

March the 23. Sunday was hurried on Shore with all my Baggage to my Lodging. My Brother took one the next Door. I now think myself very happy that I am at Liberty once more, having been a Prisoner in that wooden World call'd the London 4 Month and 4 Days. I have sail'd since I left England 3 Thousand Leagues.

Daily Occurrances at Bellhaven

March the 26. My Brother went to his Lodgings at a dutch Mans. 5 of the Doctors being at a Loss where to go, came to board with us staid 3 Weeks and then were order'd to Will's Creek.[19]

April the 22. All the Troops march'd to Will's Creek left behind 1 Officer and 40 Men, my Brother and self in care of the Sick having 50 Ill.

April the 29. Words cannot express my Joy received a Letter from England being the first since I left them; my dear Children and all were well it was dated the 4 of February. My Mind much more at ease.

May the 3. Major Carlile's Lady[20] came to see me but I was at a loss to seat her not having a Chair in the House, she sent home for 3.

May the 4. This Day was oblig'd to quit our grand Parlour the Man of the House being at a loss for a Room for the Soldiers to drink Cyder and dance Jiggs in.

May the 5. Removed into our first Floor it consisted of a Bed Chamber and Dining Room not over large. The Furniture was 3 Chairs, a Table, a Case to hold Liquor and a Tea Chest.

May the 6. This Unhappy Day 2 Years depriv'd me of my dear Husband and ever since to this Day my Life has been one continual Scene of Anxiety and Care.

[19] Wills Creek flows south into the Potomac River at Cumberland.

[20] Sarah (Fairfax) Carlyle, the wife of Major John Carlyle, at whose home in Alexandria Major-General Braddock had lived.

May the 21. Extremely Hot, discharg'd my Servant Betty, having found of mine in he[r] Box a pair of Ruffles a pair of Stockings and an Apron.

May the 21. Mr. Wood gave my Brother and self an Invitation to go to see his Daughter, it was 4 Miles up the River set of at 4 and came to her House at 6 but to great Disappointment she was out but her Mother receiv'd us with a friendly wellcome we stay'd till 8 and then with great difficulty got into our Boat it being a Shore and when we had got half way home our Cockswain run us a Ground and we were some Hours before we could get clear at 11 we got home. But I was much fatigued with my Journey.

May the 24. 5 Waggons came in we wait for 4 more Mr. Napper sent us 2 Markeys[21] very busy in getting ready to march.

May the 25. Most of this Day spent in making a Tilt for my Waggon which is to be my Bed Chamber on my March to Wills's Creek.

May the 26. My new Servant came sent a Letter to England by the Man of War Capt. Deggs bound for Hampton.

May the 27. Went with Capt. Johnson's Lady[22] to Mr. Roshars in Maryland, we were receiv'd with great Politeness. the neatest House I have seen since I left England, and furnish'd in Taste. we stay'd till Night.

May the 28. Capt. Wests Lady[23] came to see me and found me very busy packing up, spent the Evening at Capt. Johnson's much intreated to stay all Night, but did not.

May the 29. Received a Card from Mrs. Salkeldat with her Comp'ts and desired my Company to her Husbands Funeral at 2.[24] he has been dead a Month it is the Custom of this Place to bury their Relations in their Gardens.

May the 30. Extreem hot very busy making Bread and Ginger Bread and boiling Hams for our March; had Company to dine with us in our Anti Chamber which is as hot as

[21] A marquee is a large tent.

[22] The wife of George Johnston, one of the first trustees of Alexandria.

[23] At this time there were several individuals by the name of West in Alexandria.

[24] Henry Salkeld, a landowner at Alexandria, died in 1755.

a Bagnio,[25] we are to march on Sunday for Will's Creek if Mr. Falkner our commanding Officer does not get in his upper Rooms and forget it.

May the 31. Spent this Day in packing up and loading my Waggon and fixing my Tilt sup'd at Capt. Johnsons and lay'd at Mr. Moxly's but had no sleep not having layn'd on a Bed since I left England.

Remarks on a March from Bellhaven in Virginia to Wills's Creek.

June the 1. At 4 in the Morning I was call'd up by Mrs. Johnson who came to take her leave of me and at 6 we March'd for Wills's Creek with one Officer, my Brother, self and Servant, 2 Nurses, 2 Cooks and 40 Men to guard us. 12 Waggons with the sick, Lame, and Blind, my Waggon in the Rear. my Equipage 3 Horses and a Mare good in Spirit but poor in Flesh which I mention'd to Mr. Gore (my Coachman) who told me that if they were right fat they would faint by the Way my Brother came padding on his Horse in the Rear but as my Friend Gore observ'd there was no fear of his fainting by the Way being very poor in Flesh we had March'd 3 Miles when my Coachman was for taking a better Road but the Sentrys forbid it; but he said it was very hard if the Other Waggons drove to the Old Boy he must follow them we halted at 3 and din'd on a Piece of salt Pork and Water to Drink and at 6 we came to the old Court House[26] 17 Miles from Bellhaven laid in a Room with but 3 Beds in it.

June the 2. At Break of Day the Drum beat I was extreemly sleepy but got up and as soon as our Officer had eat 6 Eggs and drank a dram or two and some Punch we march'd; but my Waggon being in the Rear the Day before my Coachman insisted that it was not right that Madam Browne should be behind and if they did not give way they should feel the soft End of his Whip, he gain'd his Point and got in Front. The Roads are so Bad that I am almost disjointed, at 12 we halted at Mr. Colemans pitch'd our Markeys and dined on salt Gammon nothing better to be had.

[25] A bathing house, especially one with vapor baths and appliances for sweating.
[26] Probably Fairfax, Virginia.

June the 3. At 3 in the Morning was awak'd by the Drum but was so stiff That I Was at a loss to tell whether I had any Limbs I breakfasted in my Waggon and then set of in front at which all the rest were very much inrag'd but to no Purpose for my Coachman told them that he had but one Officer to Obey and she was in his Waggon and it was not right that she should be blinded with Dust My Brother the Day before left his Cloak behind so sent his Man back for it on his Horse and march'd on Foot and on the Road met with Mr. Adams a Parson who left his Horse and padded with them on foot we halted at Mr. Minors we order'd some Fowls for Dinner but not one to be had so was obliged to set down to our old Dish Gammon and Greens the Officer and the Parson replenish'd their Bowl so often that they began to be very Joyous untill their Servant told them that their Horses were lost at which the Parson was much inrag'd and pop'd out an Oath but Mr. Falkner said never mind your Horse Doctor but have you a Sermon ready for next Sunday. I being the Doctors country Woman he made me many Comp'ts and told me he should be very happy if he could be better accquainted with me but hop'd when I came that way again I would do him the Honour to spend some Time at his House I chatted till 11 and then took my leave and left them a full Bowl before them.

June the 4. At break of Day my Coachman came and tap'd at my Chamber Door and said Madam all is ready and it is right early I went to my Waggon and we moved on Left Mr. Falkner behind in Pursuit of his Horse march'd 14 Miles and halted at an old sage Quakers with silver Locks, his Wife on my coming in accosted me in the following manner. Welcome Friend set down thou seem's full Bulky to travel but thou are young and that will enable thee we were once so ourselves but we have been married 44 Years and may say we have lived to see the Days that we have no Pleasure therein; we had recourse to our old Dish Gammon nothing else to be had, but they said they had some Liquor they call'd Whisky which was made of Peaches My Friend Thompson being a Preacher when the Soldiers came in as the Spirit mov'd him held forth to them and told them the great Virtue of Temperance they all stared at him like Pigs but had not a Word to say in their Justification.

June the 5. My Lodgings not being very clean I had so many close Companions call'd Ticks that depriv'd me of my Nights Rest but I indulg'd till 7 we halted this Day, all the Nurses Baking Bread and Boiling Beef for to March to Morrow, a fine Regale 2 Chicken with Milk and Water to Drink which my friend Thompson said was fine temperate Liquor; several things lost out of my Waggon amongst the rest they took 2 of my Hams which My Coachmam said was an Abomination to him and if he could find out who took them he would make them remember taking the next.

June the 6. Took my leave of my Friend Thompson who bid me farewell A great Gust of Thunder and Lightning and Rain so that we were allmost drown'd. Extreem bad Roads we pass'd over the Blue Ridge which was one continual Mountain for 3 Miles forg'd through 2 Rivers at 1 we halted at Mr. Keys a fine Plantation had for Dinner 2 Chicken. The Soldiers desired my Brother to advance them some Whisky for they told him he had better kill them at once than to let them dye by Inches for without they could not live he complied with their Request and it soon began to operate they all went to dancing and bid Defiance to the French my Friend Gore began to shake a Leg I ask'd him if it was consistant as a Member of his Society to dance he told me that he was not at all united with them and that there were some of this People who call'd themselves Quakers and stood up for their Church but had no more Religion in them than his Mare I then told him I should set him down as a Ranter.

June the 7. Having no Room to lodge in I lay'd in the Chimney so wanted no calling in the Morning having no Sleep all Night at 4 we began to March left Mr. Falkner behind who did not choose to March with an empty Stomach. Great Gusts of Rain My Waggon and every thing in it Wet and all the Sick allmost drown'd at 4 we halted at my Friend Laidlers who bid me wellcome but had no Whisky which was the Soldiers first Enquiry for they were still in the Opinion that they could not live without it we now live high had for Dinner a Q'r of Lamb and a Pye to drink my Friend Thomsoms temperate Liquor Spring Water I spent the Evening very agreable Mr. Falkner favour'd me with severall Tunes on his Flute chatted till 10 and then retired.

June the 8. I slept but poorly laying on a deal Feather Bed having had no Sleep for 2 Nights did not hear the Drum we march'd at 4 at 9 we halted at my Friend Bellingers[27] who bid me wellcome My Brother set of for Winchester 8 off but Mr. Falkner said he would do himself the Pleasure of staying with me, we spent the Day very agreably had for Dinner some Veal and Greens to Drink frensh Wine and for Supper Milk Punch.

June the 9. Lay'd on some Planks halted all this Day the Nurses busy baking Bread and boiling Beef and Washing Mr. Falkner went a Shooting return'd and brought me some Squirrills dress'd them for Dinner My Brother return'd from Winchester there same with him Mr. Savage an Officer and Thirteen Recruits and a Waggon with a Nurse and four sick Men one at the Point of Death.

June the 10. Up before the Sun and march'd till 12 extreem hot and very bad Roads I was obliged to walk we halted at 7 at my Friend Rogers who had nothing for us to eat Mr. Falkner and Mr. Savage went a Shooting and brought me some Pidgeons had them for Supper which made us a fine Regale to drink Milk and Water at 10 I went to bed in my Waggon but lay'd extreemly cold Mr. Falkner order'd a Centinel to be at my Waggon all Night so that no one should molest me.

June the 11. The Drum beat and awaked me but I was at a loss for some time to tell where I was My Coachman put the Horses to the Waggon and march'd on and desired me not to disturb myself the Roads were so bad that the poor Horses were not able to Keep on their Legs which I observ'd to my Coachman who said they were right tough and good

[27] Harry Gordon, an engineer of the 48th Regiment, who passed over this route a short time before Charlotte Brown, mentions a Widow Barringers, five miles from Winchester. A. B. Hulbert, *Braddock's Road* (Cleveland, 1903), p. 87.

and that every one was not to be taken by their Looks and as to Black and Brown they were as good as ever stretch'd a Chain we left one of the Nurses and a sick man behind he not being able to march any further 2 of the Waggons broke down, halted till they were mended, I walked till my [feet] were blister'd we came to a Place call'd Spring Mountain and there we encampt'd we drank Tea and supt on the Stump of an old Tree we had nothing to eat but salt Pork to drink humble Grog we chatted till 11 and were very merry and then retired to our respective Waggons.

June the 12. At 2 in the Morning the Drum beat but I could have wish'd it to have stay'd a few Hours longer being very sleepy we march'd but there is no describing the badness of the Roads I walked as far as I was Able the poor Horses no longer regard the Smack of the Whip or beat of the Drum and as to Black she could go no further 2 of the Waggons broke down. at 10 we came to the River and waited 6 Hours before we could ferry over at 8 at Night we halted at a Rattle snake Colonels nam'd Crisop[28] had for Supper some Lamb to drink some very bad Wine which was but 5d. a Quart I could get no Bed so went to My Waggon.

June the 13. At 3 we march'd but I was so ill I could not hold up my Head 3 of the Waggons broke down down at 4 in the After-Noon Mr. Bass came to meet us and gave me some Letters from England and at 6 we came to to Fort Cumberland[29] the most desolate Place I ever saw went to

[28] For brief accounts of Thomas Cresap and his son Michael, see the *Dictionary of American Biography*. In his journal, Harry Gordon says: "May 8th: Ferried over the River into Maryland; and March'd to Mr. Jacksons, 8 Miles from Mr. Cox's where we found a Maryland Company encamp'd in a fine Situation on the Banks of the Potomack; with clear'd ground about it; there lives Colonel Cressop, a Rattle Snake, Colonel, and a D—d Rascal; calls himself a Frontierman, being nearest the Ohio; he had a Summons some time since from the French to retire from his Settlement; which they claimed as their property, but he refused it like a man of Spirit; . . . " A. B. Hulbert, *Braddock's Road*, pp. 88–89.

[29] In his journal, Harry Gordon says: "May 11th: Fort Cumberland, is Situated within 200 Yards of Wills Creek on a Hill 400 Yards from the Potomack, it's greatest length from East to West is 200 Yards, and breadth 40 it is built with Loggs drove into the Ground: and 12 feet above it Embrazures are cut for 12 Guns which are 4. Pounders, though 10 are only Mounted with loopholes for small Arms." *Ibid.*, p. 90.

Mr. Cherrington who reciev'd me kindly drank Tea and then went to the Governor[30] to apply for Quarters I was put into a Hole that I could see day light through every Log and 1 port Hole for a Window which was as good a Room as any in the Fort.

Daily Occurrances at Fort Cumberland

June the 14. I was taken very ill with a Fever and other Disorders which continued 10 Days and was not able to get out of my Bed.

July the 1. My Brother was taken ill with a Fever and Flux and Fits my Maid taken ill with a Fever.

July the 4. All greatly alarm'd with the Indians scalping several Familys within 10 Miles of us one poor Boy brought in with his Scalp of he liv'd 4 Days. Several Familys left their Homes and came to the Fort for Protection.

July the 7. My Brother extreemly ill he was blister'd. Several who call'd themselves friendly Indians came to the Fort but the Gates were order'd to be shut they stay'd 4 Hours and then went to the Camp and we had not a drop of Water there being no Well in the Fort.

July the 8. My Brother still the same and maid very ill and I can get no Nurse so that I am very much fatigued.

July the 11. My Brother much better all of us greatly alarm'd a Boy came from the Camp and said the General was kill'd 4 Miles from the French Fort[31] and that allmost all S'r Peter Hackets Regiment is cut of by a Party of French and Indians who were behind Trees[32] Dunbars Regiment was in the rear so that they lost but few Men[33] it is not pos-

[30] Colonel James Innes was governor at Fort Cumberland. The general hospital advanced no farther.

[31] The engagement on the Monongahela had taken place on July 9, 1755, but Braddock did not die of his wounds until July 13, 1755. George Washington mentions "the affrighted Waggoners, who ran off without taking leave." George Washington, *Writings*, I. (Washington, 1931), 148.

[32] Sir Peter Halkett, commander of the 44th Regiment, was killed on the field of battle.

[33] At the time of the battle, Colonel Thomas Dunbar, commander of the 48th Regiment, was stationed seven miles beyond the Great Meadows.

sible to describe the Distraction of the poor Women for their Husbands. I pack'd up my Things to send for we expected the Indians every Hour my Brother desired me to leave the Fort but I am resolv'd not to go but share my Fate with him.

July the 12. My Brother better no news from the Camp so we hope that it is not true what the Boy said.

July the 13. I am in great Distress my Brother told me if he was not better he could not live but a few Days he submitted to have Mr. Tuton one of the Dr. to attend him he gave him 2 Draughts which had a supprizing effect and I hope that he is better. An Officer is come from the Camp and confirms all what the Boy said.

July the 14. I set up with my Brother and was much suppriz'd in the Night he was so convuls'd I thought he was dying he dose'd and I hope that he is better.

July the 15. My Brother much Better 2 Off'r came from the Camp wounded and several Waggons with the Sick and some at the Point of Death.

July the 17. Oh! how shall I express my Distraction this unhappy Day at 2 in the After Noon deprived me of my dear Brother in whom I have lost my kind Guardian and Protector and am now left a friendless Exile from all that is dear to me.

July the 19. I am in so much Grief I can think of nothing Mr. Cherrington was so kind as to order my Brother's funeral.

July the 20. I was taken very ill with a Fever and flux which I have had 6 Weeks.

July the 22. Very Ill and in the greatest Pain. I wrote the unhappy News to my Brother and sent to England by a Packet which was going.

July the 25. Very Bad my Disord still increasing I can get no Nurse my Servant is gone to her Husband to the Camp.

August the 1. I have got a Nurse but a very bad one. I can neither Eat drink or Sleep my Mind being allways on my Brother.

August the 12. My Fever a little better got up but could not set, I was so faint.

August the 15. A little better but can get nothing that I can eat for here is nothing to be had but Beef.

August the 16. Much better the Director says we must march very soon to Fredericks Town in Maryland[34] which is 150 Miles God only knows how I shall get there. My Brother having made me promise him on his Death Bed not to travel in a Carriage as he said it would soon kill me.

August the 17. I went out of my Room supported by 2 the Day is fix'd we are to march the 20 and I am resolv'd not to stay behind if I am able to set on a Horse which I have not been on this 16 Years.

August the 18. Very busy packing up for my March which increas'd my Disorder very much Mr. Cherrington is gone so that I shall not be so happy as to go in his Party He is the only one I can call my Friend. I can get no Horse so fear I must be left behind.

August the 20. I happily met with a Horse I bought it and set of with my Nurse walking by my Side, all the Gentlemen were gone before. I was so weak I could hardly set I met with Mr. Adair[35] who seeing me alone was so kind as to send his Servant with me we had march'd 6 Miles and my Horse did not chuse to go any further but laid down with me on his Back a Servant of the Generals seeing me in Distress got down and set me on his Horse and march'd with me we halted till 3 and I was so weak that I was supported by 2 into the House all the Beds were taken up by the Officers before I came so I was obliged to lay on the Ground on an old Hammock. I had no Sleep.

August the 21. I was extreemly ill but was oblig'd to march my Horse threw me going down a Hill but happily got no Hurt.

August the 22. I was a little better I had march'd 4 Miles and we came to the River Potomack in forging of which my Horse threw me I must have been lost had not one of the

[34] Frederick, Maryland.

[35] A member of the staff of the general hospital.

men with one Arm came to my Assistance I rode in my wet Cloaths 6 Miles and then came to a House but could get no bed so laid on the Ground on some Indian Corn I could get no Sleep.

August the 23. Very Ill but was obliged to march having a Pain in my Limbs we halted at 6 I laid on my old Lodging the Ground.

August the 24. We halted I was very busy mending my Saddle which I was at a loss to do very Ill I could get nothing I could eat or Drink.

August the 26. I was up with Sun but was so ill I could not march fast I halted at 3 in the Afternoon but could get no Bed.

August the 27. Extreemly ill and could not march but at 11 I was a little better and march'd and at 5 in the Afternoon, I halted in extreem Pain.

August the 28. I halted all Day very ill but could get no place to lay on but the Ground and stay'd all Day.

August the 29. I was extreemly [ill] apply'd to the Doctor who gave a Bottle to take every 2 Hours, in great Distress I lost my way in the Woods for 2 Hours and expected to be scalp'd every minute but coming to several Roads I let my Horse go which way he chose and he carried me to a House where was Mr. Cherrington who had heard I was coming and had provided a good Bed for me which is the first I have had since I left the Fort.

August the 30. I was very ill and not able to march with the rest Mr. Anderson was so kind as to leave his Servant to attend me we march'd at 10 and at 6 arriv'd at Frederick's Town in Maryland Mr. Bass came to meet me he had taken a Lodging for me at the Widow De Butts I was very much fatigued having march'd since I left the Fort 150 Miles and was very ill with a Fever and Flux.

Daily Occurrances at Frederick's Town

Mr. Couch came to see me and gave me a Dose which reliev'd me very much but am not able to get out of my Bed.

September the 1. I am a little better but so weak I cannot walk and can eat nothing.

Sep'r the 6. Much better my Disorder begins to abate but can get no Sleep.

Sep'r the 10. Better every Day and begin to walk out to see the Town which is a very Pleasant Place most of the People are Dutch.

Sep'r the 15. Recēd the Comp't of all the English Ladies in the Town who came to see all at once and gave me an Invitation to their Houses which I excepted and was reciev'd with great Politeness.

Sep'r the 20. I had an Invitation to go to a Ball which was compos'd of Romans, Jews, and Hereticks who in this Town flock together The Ladys danced without Stays or Hoops and it ended with a Jig from each Lady.

Sep'r the 25. I receiv'd an Invitation to go out of Town I went to a farm House and was receiv'd with a friendly well-come I had for Breakfast a fine Dish of Fish and a Pig I stayd 2 Days and the Good Man and his Wife waited on me home.

Sep'r the 30. Parson Miller and his Lady came to see and invited me to his House 6 Miles out of Town.

October the 1. The Director is arrived from Philadelphia but no Letters from England we are to march as soon as the sick come from Fort Cumberland.

Oct'r the 5. All the Sick are come from Fort Cumberland but they were obliged to leave some of the Baggage behind being alarm'd by the Indians.[36]

Oct'r the 7. An Express is arriv'd from near Fort Cumberland with an Account that the Indians have scalp'd 5 Families and that they are in the greatest Distress having Bread but for 3 Days and cannot go out for more.

Oct'r the 8. An Express is arriv'd from Fort Cumberland with an Account that the Indians are near them and beg some Assistance.

[36] The Maryland *Gazette* of October 9, 1755, carried an account of Indian depredations near Colonel Cresap's, Frazier's plantation, Patterson's Creek, and Stoddert's Fort. To meet the situation, Governor Sharpe of Maryland called out the provincial militia, October 18. J. T. Scharf, *History of Maryland* (3 vols., Baltimore, 1879), I., 470–471.

Oct'r the 9. Very busy packing up to go to Philadelphia having but 2 Days notice.

Oct'r the 10. 5 Waggons with sick are marched for Philadelphia Mr. Cherrington desired me not to go with them but to favour him with my Company.

Oct'r the 11. Took my Leave of Fredericks Town and went 6 miles on my Road to Philadelphia where I shall stay till Mr. Cherrington comes for me.

Remarks on a March to Philadelphia

Oct'r the 12. At 1 Mr. Cherrington called on me we staid and dined and set of at 3 Mr. Cherrington in his Chaise full without side and within behind 2 Portmanteaus in the Box Tea, Coffee, Sugar, Cake, Butter Bread and Rum etc. on one side a Blunderbus on the other 2 Pistols and a Gun himself in the Centre his Wifes Dressing Box under his Feet The Horses not quite of a Colour 1 being White the other Black not more than 15 Years each myself on a good Pad my Saddle older than any thing but its Fashion my Dress an old Bonnet and riding Coat which were old Campaigners Mr. Cherrington boled on and I by his side and his man Tim Kept up the Rear at 6 at Night we came to Mr. Trucks we supt and desired to have 2 Beds but the Mistress of the house said she presumed we were Man and Wife and that one would do Mr. Cherr'n said it was true I was his Wife but it was very seldom that he was favoured with part of my Bed she said she was sorry for it and at last Complied I was favour'd with a Bed of Down and Mr. Cherr'n with one of Straw.

Oct'r the 13. At Break of Day Mr. Cherr'n call'd his man Tim to get all Things in order, it rain'd and he desired me to do him the Honour to take a place in his Chaise which I accepted we set of and drove away till we came to Blind Michaels and then breakfasted staid 2 Hours and set of there came on a Gust of Thunder and Lightning (several Tree were blown down) which we escaped at 7 we put up. we supt and chatted till 10 and then retired.

Oct'r the 14. As usual Mr. Cherr'n was up with the Sun

and as soon as Tim had put all Things in order in the Chaise which was allways 3 Hours Work we set of and drove away till we came to a River which we ferried over and were 3 Hours in the Rain we came to a House but could get nothing to eat nor no Lodging we went on and came to Dutch Farmers who took Pity on us it being very dark they gave us for Supper Milk Butter Honey and Apples but I wishd for something more solid having eaten but little all Day we chatted till 10 and then Retired. I was favour'd with 2 Bed one a Top and the other at Botton which is the Dutch Custom but as for Sheets they beg'd to be excused I was extreemly fatigued the Roads being very Bad.

Oct'r the 15. I had but little Sleep being as hot as if I was in a Bagnio I indulg'd till 8 and then was call'd to Breakfast and as soon as Tim had dried our Cloaths we march'd till we came to Lancaster which is a large Pleasant Town we to the Crown where we found all the Waggons with the Sick which were all as well as could be expected we dined on Rump Steaks and Fish and in the Afternoon severall of the Town Ladies came to see me and invited me to their Houses.

Oct'r the 16. I halted till 12 and then rode till 7 and we came to an Inn and supt but Mr. Cherr'n and I not being of the same Opinion as to my Sex in general we had many Disputes several ill natured Truths were said on both Sides it ended with my telling him that he did nothing but to say and unsay and that he was so unaccountable a Riddle I knew not what to make of him he made me a low Bow and said he was much obliged to me and retired.

Oct'r the 17. At Break of Day I was awak'd with Mr. Cherr'n revenging our Quarill on poor Tim but he soon ran out of his reach we met with reserve, at 7 we set of I on my Pad and Mr. Cherr'n in his Chaise we had march'd 6 miles and my Mare threw me broke the Saddle and wrung herself and would go no furthur so was oblig'd to walk but Mr. Cherr'n being uneasy at my staying behind beg'd at me to come into the Chaise which I submitted to and he had drove half a Mile but on going down a Hill he oversett the Chaise but we receiv'd no hurt on which he told me he had the

Honour of overturning me we halted at 7 at an Inn and on taking the Things out of the Chaise we missed a pair of Saddle Bags with mine and Mr. Cherr'n Linnen in them we sent Tim to the Place where we overturn'd but to no Purpose he return'd and said there was not a Mothers Son that he met but he ask'd but could hear nothing of them.

Oct'r the 18. Mr. Cherr'n up with the Sun and sent Tim in pursuit of the Bags we Breakfasted and then set of we dined at 1 and at 7 we ferried over and came to Philadelphia which is London in Miniature we put up at the Indian King[37] the People of the House star'd at me and some said I was Mr. Cherr'n Wife and others his Miss but he soon convinced them that I was neither and then they treated me with much more Respect.

Daily Occurrances at Philadelphia

I sent a Letter to England by a Ship that was ready to sail Tim is return'd and after riding 46 Miles found the Bags I went to the Hospital and the Director order'd me a Room in which I had my Bed fix'd and it was furnish'd with 1 Chair a Block and a stand for a Table a Ship is arrived from England but no Letters for me.

Oct'r the 24. The Director order'd me to market every Day for the Sick 7 of the Town Ladies came to see me but I was at a great Loss to seat them they sent home for Chairs and as to my Tea Equipage it was composed of Stone Delf and China An Express is arriv'd from Lancaster with an Account that the Indians are scalping all before them.[38]

November the 8. Mr. Cherr'n came and paid me his first Visit he came at 4 and staid till 11 I told him that it was very impolite for him to make his first Visit so long. An Express is arrived with an Account that the Indians have burnt a Town within 30 Miles of us and that they would soon be

[37] This inn stood in High Street near Third Street.

[38] At the call of Lieutenant-Governor Morris, the assembly of Pennsylvania convened, November 3, 1755, to deal with the Indian invasion. *Minutes of the Provincial Council of Pennsylvania*, VI., 670; *Pennsylvania Archives*, 4th series, II., 515–517.

here which News had no Effect on the Quakers for they still say they will not take up Arms. The Assembly met but to no purpose for they will not do any thing to defend themselves.

Nov'r the 17. I was awaked at 4 this Morning by a Shock of an Earth quake it continued 5 Minutes the next House was split which alarm'd me very much. Miss Franklin[39] and several other Ladies came to see me and I was very much confused by Mr. Blacks coming very much elevated he told them he must pay them the Scotch Compliment and kiss all round he said they were all very handsome and walked of.

Nov'r the 27. Mrs. Franklin sent her Chaise for me and I was reciev'd with great politeness. I return'd at Night and she did me the favour to drive me home herself. An Express is arrived with an Account that the Indians have scalped 30 Families 30 Miles from this Place a Ship is arrived from England but no Letters for me which makes me very uneasy.

Nov'r the 28. I went with some Ladies to the Fair[40] which was composed of Dutch Pedlers and at Night I went to see them dance My old Shipmate Mrs. Barbut came to see me but she was so full of Engagements she could not afford me an Hour of her Company she was dressed like a Butterfly which put me in mind of June instead of November.

December the 1. I went to Church[41] and to my great Surprize saw Mr. Cherr'n there, I recieved a Letter from England and had the agreable News that my Brother was married and a Prospect of his being happy.

Decem'r the 16. I went to the state House to see 2 men and a Boy that were brought into Town Dead, scalped by the Indians it was the dismallest Sight I ever saw. Sent a Letter to England to my Brother with a set of Bills for £20 Mr. Cherr'n presented me a Tippet and Muf.

January the 1, 1756. I sent a Letter to England by one

[39] Deborah Franklin, the wife of Benjamin Franklin.

[40] At Philadelphia a three-day fair was held in the market place in May and November.

[41] The author probably means November 30. December 1, 1755, fell upon Monday. She doubtless attended Christ Church.

of the Nurses, receiv'd one from England dated Aug't the 29 all were Well.

Jan'y the 24. Mrs. Franklin came to see me the Director is return'd from New York and says we are to march in a few Days.

Jan'y the 25. Went to Church to hear a regimental Sermon preach'd by Mr. Jinnings, dined at Mr. Franklins and drank Tea at Dr. Loyds.

February the 1. I Went to wait on Mrs. Spering an Officers Lady I had seen at Bellhaven.

Feb'y the 12. Went with Mrs. Franklin to the Academy[42] and was agreably entertain'd by hearing the Boys speak. dined at Mr. Smiths[43] and then went to see the State House which is a large compact Building.

Feb'y the 13. Very busy packing up having received Orders to march to New York.

Feb'y the 14. Took Leave of all my Friends and laid at the Indian King.

Remarks on a March to New York

Feb'y the 15. Took Leave of Mrs. Franklin who was so kind as to give me Letters to New York she waited on me to the Boat with Mr. Cherr'n and at 10 I set sail for New York with Mr. Cherr'n Boy Tom to attend me at 2 we came to Burlinton[44] I laid at the Blue Anchor Mr. Shaw's.

Feb'y the 16. I and my Man Tom were up with the Sun and set of in the Stage Waggon we halted at Cranbury and chang'd Horses and then set of. our Company was compos'd of Indians Dutch and English at 1 in the morning we came to Amboy[45] but I could get no Bed so set up all Night.

Feb'y the 17. At Break of Day I ferried over and breakfasted and at 11 set sail for New York but the Wind not

[42] Through the efforts of Benjamin Franklin, an academy was established at Philadelphia in 1750. Three years later it was designated a college, and in 1779, a university. Today it exists as the University of Pennsylvania.

[43] Probably Dr. William Smith, first provost of the college at Philadelphia.

[44] Burlington, New Jersey.

[45] South Amboy, across the river from Perth Amboy, New Jersey.

being in our Favour we laid on the Water all Night it was extream cold at 7 in the Morning we came to New York it is an Island and a large pleasant City. but no Wa[ter] to be had but what you buy.

Daily Occurrances at New York

I Delivered the Letters Mrs. Franklin gave me to Dr. Bard[46] and was kindly received staid and dined and then went to see the Hospital which was in a large House in the Dock I fixed myself in a Room but was at a loss for Furniture not having one thing in the House all our things being on Board a Sloop coming from Philadelphia.

Feb'y the 18. Went to my Landlord and he was so kind as to lend me a Bedstead 4 Chairs and a Table had my Room clean'd and furnish'd and now think myself happy in having a Place I can call my own.

Feb'y the 22. Went to the Dutch Church[47] to hear the Organs and then to the English Church[48] which is the handsomest I have seen since I left England drank Tea at Dr. Bards and was introduced to several Ladies.

Feb'y the 25. Mr. Cherr'n is arrived from Phil'a sent a Letter to England by the Packet.

March the 1. Several of the Town Ladies came to see and gave me Invitations to their Houses.

March the 15. Receiv'd a Account that the Sloop in which is all my Baggage is cast away coming from Phil'a I am now reduced to one Gown Mr. Cherr'n is so good as to go to the Sloop to see if he can save any of my Things.

March the 20. Mr. Cherr'n is return'd and am agreably supprized with a sight of all my Things but very wet with the salt Water.

[46] For a brief account of Dr. John Bard, at this time one of the few reputable physicians of New York City see the *Dictionary of American Biography.*

[47] At this time New York had the "Old Dutch Church" on Garden Street, between William and Broad Streets, and the "New Dutch Church" on Nassau Street. G. P. Disosway, *The Earliest Churches of New York and Its Vicinity* (New York, 1865), pp. 22–24.

[48] Trinity Church, of which Henry Barclay was rector and Dr. Samuel Johnson assistant minister. *Ibid.*, pp. 63–79; H. and C. Schneider, eds., *Samuel Johnson, President of King's College, His Career and Writings* (4 vols., New York, 1929), I., 172.

March the 28. I this Day applied to Mr. Napper for my Tent for I hear we are to march to Albany soon.

March the 31. Very busy packing up to go to Albany.

April the 7. Took Leave of all my Friends in New York Dr. Bard was so kind as to give me Letters of Recommendation to his Friends in Albany.

April the 8. Went on Board the Sloop Delancee bound for Albany set sail with a Fair Wind Mr. Cherr'n commanding Officer on board who gave me the best Cabbin in the Sloop.

April the 10. At 11 in the Morning the Wind being against us the Gentlemen went on Shore and the Sloop run on Ground a 4 the Tide throwed her of and we set sail we were soon inclosed with Rocks which was the most romantick Scene I ever saw being at a loss to tell the Mountains from the Clouds.

April the 12. At 3 in the Afternoon we cast Anchor at Albany all the Gentlemen went on Shore but could get no Lodging the Town being full of Officers so returned at Night.

April the 13. Went on Shore with Mr. Cherr'n who was so kind as to take me a Room Went out to see the Town which is inhabited by the Dutch saw several Indians who were adorned with Beads in their Noses and Ears and black Blankets being in mourning for their Friend who were kill'd in the last Campaign.

April the 16. Went to the Fort to deliver a Letter from Dr. Bard at New York to Col'n Marshall[49] and was receiv'd with great politeness but the Dutch had a very bad Opinion of me saying I could not be good to come so far without a Husband.

April the 26. Receiv'd an Invitation to dine at Col'n Marshalls Miss Miller an old Accquaintance of mine at Louisburg[50] came to see me she told me that the Dutch said I was Gen'l Braddocks Miss but she had convinced them that I was not for that her Father had known me Maid, Wife and Widow and that nobody could say any thing bad of me.

[49] Colonel Hubert Marshall commanded the fort at Albany.

[50] The author writes as though she had been at Louisburg on Cape Breton Island, captured by the English in 1745 but handed back to the French in 1748.

April the 28. Several of the Dutch Ladies came to see me and gave me Invitations to their Houses.

May the 6. This Day arrived Genr. Shirly[51] the Parson[52] and his Wife came to see me.

May the 20. Received an Invitation to go to Green Bush[53] was kindly receiv'd staid till Night.

May the 25. News came from Oswaga[54] that L't Blare and 40 Men were killed by the Indians.[55]

May the 28. 6 Men were Hanged for Desertion.

June the 1. Captain Rogers[56] came from Lake George with a french Prisoner and 1 Scalp.

June the 11. All the Town alarmed 2 Men taken by the Indians not half a Mile of.

June the 12. A Girl taken by the Indians just out of Town All the Fort Ladies came to see me.

June the 14. I Receiv'd an Invitation to go a Mile out of Town with Col'n Glasiar[57] and Miss Miller but were obliged to have a Guard with us for fear of the Indians, we went to see a Dutch Officers Lady and were kindly received we drank Tea and then had a fine Regale with Sweetmeats Strawberries Butter and Cheese which is the dutch Custom we returned at Night in Safety.

[51] In a letter to Secretary of State Henry Fox, May 6, 1756, William Shirley announced his arrival at Albany. William Shirley, *Correspondence* (2 vols., New York, 1912), II., 433–438.

[52] At this time John Ogilvie, a graduate of Yale College in 1748, was chaplain of the fort at Albany and missionary to the Mohawk Indians. F. B. Dexter, *Biographical Sketches of the Graduates of Yale College* (6 vols., New York, 1885–1912), II., 174–177.

[53] Greenbush or East Albany.

[54] Oswego, New York. At Alexandria Braddock and the colonial governors had determined to strengthen this post.

[55] Lieutenant William Blair of the 51st Regiment, a young man of eighteen or nineteen, and another soldier were killed at Oswego, May 17, 1756. E. B. O'Callaghan, *Documentary History of the State of New-York* (4 vols., Albany, 1849–1851), I., 477; S. M. Pargellis, *Lord Loudoun in North America* (New Haven, 1933), p. 156.

[56] Robert Rogers, commissioned captain of a company of rangers by Shirley, March 24, 1756. *Ibid.*, pp. 98, 302, 303, 349.

[57] Beamsley Glazier was a lieutenant in the 60th Regiment and colonel of the New York troops. *Ibid.*, p. 311 n. and index.

June 16. Two Men were hang'd for Desertion.

July 1. This Day arrived two Rigements of Colonel Otaways[58] and Abercromy's[59] from England.

July 5. Went out of Town with Col. Fitch[60] Col. Whiting[61] and Col. Glasier and six dutch Ladies on a Party of Pleasure.

July 7. Extreamly Hot three Men dropp'd down dead as they march'd.

July 10. A Man scalp'd by the Indians on the other Side of the Water.

July 14. Seven hundred english Forces marched for Crown Point commanded by General Winslow.[62]

July 16. General Webbs[63] Rigements marched from Albany to the Half Moon.[64]

July 17. I recēd an Invitation to go to General Johnson's[65] to see the Indians dance.

July 19. News came that Capt. Rogers had taken eight Prisoners and four scalps.

July 26. This Day War was proclaimed in America.[66]

July 28. My Lord Louden[67] arrived at Albany from Hallifax with his Troops.

August 10. This unhappy Day I recēd an Account of the Death of my dear Child Charlott in whom my Soul was center'd. God only knows what I suffer. when shall I die and be at rest!

August 12. All my Friends come to see me; but at present I have no Comfort in any thing. God give me Patience.

[58] General Charles Otway commanded the 35th Regiment.

[59] Major-General James Abercromby had succeeded Sir Peter Halkett as commander of the 44th Regiment.

[60] Lieutenant-Colonel Eleazer Fitch of the 1st Regiment of Connecticut.

[61] Lieutenant-Colonel Nathan Whiting of the 2nd Regiment of Connecticut.

[62] John Winslow, general of the provincial troops.

[63] Daniel Webb, major-general and colonel of the 48th Regiment.

[64] Halfmoon, a village fifteen miles north of Albany.

[65] Sir William Johnson lived near the Mohawk Castle, almost forty miles northwest of Albany.

[66] The king's proclamation of war against France was read at Albany, July 28, 1756. *New York Colonial Documents*, VII., 122.

[67] John Campbell, fourth Earl of Loudoun.

August 14. My good Friend the Minister came to see me and desired me to reconcile myself to my hard fate.

August 23. This Day came an Express with an Account that Oswago was taken and the commanding Officer Coln. Mursur and all the sick kill'd[68] and all the rest taken Prisoners every one here in the greatest Distress for we expect the French will be at Albany soon.

Oct'r 4. My Lord Louden march'd with all the Troops to Fort Henry[69] and Fort Edward[70] to take a View of the Country.

Oct'r 23. Several People died of the small Pox All the New England men left Albany thro' fear.

Nov'r 20. My Lord Louden return'd from the Forts nothing to be done this Year.

Dec'r 1. Mr. Cherrington left Albany for England in whom I have lost all my Friends in one.

Dec'r 6. Extream cold, and I am reduced to my last Stick of Wood there being none to be bought for Mony.

Dec'r 7. My Lord Louden left Albany for New York.

Jan'y 18, 1757. This is the coldest Day I think that I ever knew.

Jan'y 19. Recēd Orders to remove to the Hospital which was no better than a Shed and it was so excessive cold that my Face and Neck were frost bitten in moving.

Jan. 27. News came from the Lake that Capt. Rogers had ingaged with a Party of French and was much wounded and had lost 20 of his Men but he had taken 7 Prisoners and killed them all and retreated.

Jan'y 28. All the Town alarm'd News came that 700 French were within 30 Miles of us; All the Troops under Arms.

[68] Under Louis, Marquis de Montcalm, the French took Oswego, August 14, 1756. In the engagement Lieutenant-Colonel James F. Mercer of the 51st Regiment, commander of the fort, was killed. E. B. O'Callaghan, *Documentary History of the State of New-York*, I., 488–496.

[69] Fort William Henry, at the southern end of Lake George.

[70] Fort Edward, on the east side of the Hudson River, about fifty miles north of Albany.

Feb'y 1. 70 Sick came from Fort Henry 4 Died by the way with the cold.

March 20. An Express is arrived with an Account from Fort Edward that it was surrounded.

March 21. The Drums beat to Arms, all the Malitia came into Town and marched with all the Troops to the Forts except 40 Men.

March 27. All the Malitia return'd with the agreable News that they had beat off the French.

April 8. Mr. Nappier, Mr. Monrow and Mr. Russell sailed for New York having Orders to go with my Lord Louden Mr. Adair left in Albany and appointed Sub Director to the Hospital in Albany.

May 3. This Day was executed a Man who was taken up for a Spy.

May 7. General Abercromy's Rigement sail'd for New York.

July 13. This Day was kept a Fast by Order of Gen'l Hardy.[71]

July 14. News came that the French had scalp'd and killed 18 of our Men near Lake George.

July 20. An Account came that The French have killed several of our Officers and 200 of our Men in crossing the Lake.

July 30. An Express is arrived from Fort Edward with Orders that the Malitia should be called in; for they expected the French to Attack the Fort very soon.

August 3. The Post is arrived with an Account that the French were within 16 Miles of us; At Fort Henry.

August 4. An Express is Arrived from Gener'l Web at Fort Edward to the commanding Officer who says that Fort Henry is besieged with 1100 French and desires that Expresses may be sent to New York and New England for all the Assistance they can send.

I here End My Journal having so much Business on my Hands that I cannot spare Time to write it.

[71] Sir Charles Hardy, governor of New York.

JOURNEYS

FRANÇOIS DE MONTIGNY, S. J., TO THE COMTE DE PONTCHARTRAIN, 1699[1]

Monseigneur:

The last letter that I did myself the honor to write to you was in the month of May of the present year. I was still with the Islinois,[2] where I remained only five or six days, having a long trip to make, for I proposed to go to the sea, where I learned that monsieur d'Hyberville[3] was to be with some vessels in order to begin a settlement at Fort Maurepas.[4] They were surprised that I had not had news of him, having been so close to the sea, but at the beginning of February, a month before he had come to the mouth of the river, I had left the Taensas[5] to go up to the Islinois, and M. d'Hyberville did not arrive until the beginning of the month of March.

The 4th May I left the Islinois. The Rev. Father

[1] Translation of a copy of a letter in the Bibliothèque Nationale, Paris, Manuscrits Français, Nouvelles Acquisitions, 7485, fols. 121–127; photostat and transcript in the Library of Congress. François de Montigny was one of three priests sent to the western Algonquins by the Séminaire des Missions Étrangères at Quebec in 1698. For letters written by him dated Arkansas, January 2, 1699, and Chicago, April 23, 1699, see J. D. G. Shea, *Early Voyages up and down the Mississippi* (Albany, 1861); *Relation de la Mission du Missisipi du Séminiare de Québec en 1700* (New York, 1861); and *Relation des Affaires du Canada, en 1696* (New York, 1865). Although he is sometimes called François Jolliet de Montigny, Amédée Gosselin, in "M. de Montigny," *Le Bulletin des Recherches Historiques*, June, 1925, pp. 171–176, doubts that he was a "Jolliet de France." Louis Phélypeaux, comte de Pontchartrain, was at this time chancellor of France. In translating this and the following letter, Miss Mary Learned, associate professor of Romance Languages in Wells College, has assisted.

[2] The Illinois were an Algonquian tribe.

[3] Pierre le Moyne, sieur d'Iberville, was a French explorer who made his second voyage to Louisiana in 1699.

[4] Fort Maurepas was erected by Iberville on the Bay of Biloxi in 1699.

[5] The Taensas were located to the north of the Natchez, in the present parish of Tensas, Louisiana.

Binneteau[6] joined us 15 or 20 leagues lower down, and we went together as far as the Tamaroüois.[7] On the way we met some canoes of the Puants,[8] who are almost entirely destroyd, the greater part having perished some years ago in Lake Michigan, bad weather having overtaken them on a great journey that they were making in order to evade the Irocois[9] who pursued them. They had set out to make war on the Akansas[10] but were too few in number, and were returning, but being ashamed to appear before the Islinois without having struck a blow, they resolved to appear brave at the expense of two Missouris,[11] whom they triumphantly led as though they had taken them in war. These poor prisoners, whom they forced to sing their song of death, which is a custom which all the savages have, told us that they had been taken only by treason, and that having demanded passage from these men who had always been their friends to go with them in their canoes to the Islinois, after several days of good treatment they had been seized and bound. So Father Binneteau and I urged the Puants to unbind these prisoners, whom we led back to their village, very joyful at such a fortunate encounter, for they ran the risk of being burned before arriving among the Islinois, to whom they were rather near. And we prevented a war which this nation was about to start between several nations who would have taken sides for their allies, some on one side, some on the other.

The 14th May we arrived among the Tamaroüais, where we found Monsieur de Saint Cosme[12] occupied in completing his church. After it was finished we planted a cross with as much solemnity as possible. All the savages were present,

[6] Julien Binneteau, Jesuit, died in Illinois, December 24, 1699.

[7] The Tamaroas were an Illinois tribe on the Mississippi River, not far from the mouth of the Missouri.

[8] The Puants or Winnebagoes were a Siouan tribe.

[9] The Iroquois.

[10] The Arkansas were a Siouan tribe.

[11] The Missouri were also a Siouan tribe.

[12] Jean François Buisson de St. Cosme was a Canadian priest sent to the western Algonquins by the Séminaire des Missions Étrangères at Quebec in 1698.

and expressed great desire for instruction, and to become Christians, and brought their little children in order to have them baptized.

The 22. of the same month I departed from the Tamaroüais; and as far as the Rivière Ouabache,[13] which is 80 leagues distant, I met only a canoe of savages on its way to a lead mine which is about fifteen hundred leagues from the Tamaroüais, where there is a salt-works, and where ordinarily there are numerous wild oxen. Ten leagues below the Ouabache, in rounding a point, we suddenly discovered cabins, the savages in them perceiving us at the same time that we saw them. We were too near to evade them, and, therefore, adopted the policy of going directly to them. Without debarking, however, we asked them who they were, persuading ourselves that they might be Irocois, and perhaps we were not wrong, for they often come into the Rivière Ouabache, which they call the Ohio, one of the arms of which comes from towards the Sonnontoüans.[14] Be that as it may, they immediately recognized us for French. They said to us in Irocois (for we were speaking this language to them) that they were Mahinguans, whom we name elsewhere Loups or Abenakis[15] when they live towards the Chikachas.[16] Without our asking, they assured us that they were not Irocois. Preferring to take their word for it rather than to go to see, we told them that we did not wish to debark, although they urged us to, but that they could come to us in safety in one of their canoes. Straightway three of their men detached themselves and came to us without arms in an elm canoe. One of these three men spoke English and another Irocois. They said to us that they were a war party who were making these elm canoes in order to go to attack a neighboring nation toward the west that they pointed out to us without naming. We conjectured that they were going

[13] The Ohio River.

[14] The Sonnontouans or Senecas.

[15] The Mahingans were an Algonquian tribe.

[16] The Chicasas were a Maskoki tribe.

either to the Meschiganca[17] or to the Akansas. They also said to us that they were only sixteen men and a woman, and that they had some Chaoüannons[18] with them, that they were of those Machingans who had lived at the fort which Monsieur de Lasalle[19] had had built in the river of the Islinois, that they were very sorry to have left the French in order to treat with the English, that they would soon return to the French, and that they would quit the English. And as we demanded of them news of an attack that the Miamis[20] admitted to have recently made on the Irocois whom they encountered toward the Ouabache, they said to us that it was not at all on the Irocois that the blow had been struck, but that it was on themselves, and that the Miamis had indeed beaten them. We gave them some vituals of which they had need. As we left them they said to us that their canoes were almost finished and that they would join us in an hour or two. As we had no need of their escort, and as we did not know how many of them there were, for they would not have scrupled against disguising the truth from us, and since we were persuaded that if they had discovered us first and surprised us by night, they would have shown us no quarter, we continued our route without awaiting them, and aided by the high waters and the rapid current, for in the spring the waters of the Micissipi rise forty and fifty feet higher than they do the balance of the year, we arrived in a very few days among the Akansas.

The Akansas did not constitute a village but were scattered because they had learned that the Chikachas, with whom they have been at war for a long time, were coming to destroy them. It is only in the last few years that the Akansas have begun to fear them, for formerly they always had the advantage over this nation, but since the Chikachas

[17] The Metchigamea, Mitchigameas, or Metchigamikoué lived near the mouth of the Arkansas River.

[18] The Chaouanons or Shawnees were an Algonquian tribe.

[19] René Robert Cavelier, sieur de La Salle, the famous French explorer who reached the mouth of the Mississippi River in 1682.

[20] The Miamis were an Algonquian tribe.

have obtained firearms from the English, these, who have only arrows, would not dare to meet them.

The 4th June we arrived at the mission of Monsieur d'Avion[21] to the Tonicas.[22] He had returned only a few days before from a voyage that he had made to the Chikachas. The reason for this voyage was an Englishman who lives among them, who, having learned that the French were established among the Tonicas, came there with some horses to see him. Monsieur Davion took advantage of this opportunity to go with him to negotiate peace between that nation and all those down here, and at the same time to commence to speak of God to that nation where a missionary had never been, and to baptize dying infants. This voyage had all the success that he had foreseen. There he baptized three infants who were about to die, and persuaded that nation to make no more war on the nations where we are established. They appeared to like the French very much, and a little while ago they came to see us in our missions. There are nine villages which occupy about six leagues of country. All together there are three hundred fifty cabins. They are eighty leagues distant from the Tonicas, fifty of which can be made by water by the river of the Tonicas. On the road one finds the Sabougeas and the Saxoumans,[23] who are on the borders of the same river, who constitute only a little village of about seventy cabins, and eight leagues higher up one finds the Ouitapa, who constitute a rather small village.

Two Englishmen from Carolina who live with them cause the Chikachas to make war on other nations. They send them to war in all directions in order to make as many slaves as they can, whom they afterwards buy from them and resell to the English, who send them to Barbados and to other places. They bring merchandise to these savages

[21] Antoine Davion was a priest sent to the western Algonquins by the Séminaire des Missions Étrangères at Quebec in 1698.

[22] The Tonicas were a southern tribe.

[23] The Saxoumans were located forty leagues above the Tonicas, and on their river.

with much trouble, for there are about a hundred and fifty leagues to cover. Seven days are necessary for a boat to come to the Chaoüanons, whose river goes to Carolina and to the sea, and from the Chaoüanons they are obliged to march by land for twenty days and to have their merchandise carried by the savages over very difficult mountainous country.

Having passed the feast of Pentecost with the Tonicas, Monsieur Davion and I and all our Frenchmen left them the eighth of June to go to find Monsieur d'Hyberville, who, they said, was at the mouth of the Micissipi. The next day we arrived among the Taensas, who during my absence had taken care to build my house. I visited all of the cabins in order to see the sick and to baptize children. Two Taensas and a Chaoüanon who lives with them wished to participate in the journey that we were about to make and joined themselves to us.

The 12. we arrived among the Natchez[24] or as others call them the Chalaouelles, who are about twenty leagues from the Taensas. Having learned of our arrival, the chief of this nation immediately came to the edge of the water where we were. He was accompanied by about two hundred men all with bows and arrows. He had no women or children with him because he did not know whether we came in peace or war. At that time they were having war with almost all the nations of the Mississipi, and it was some risk to pass by there at this time. Nevertheless, we met with no displeasure from them. On the contrary, they received us with much joy, and although they were at war with the Taensas, out of consideration for us, they gave a very good reception to those who were with us. We made the chief understand that the black robes such as we were were not men of war, that on the contrary we exhorted all the world to peace, that they would understand this clearly one day when I knew their language, which is the same as that of the Taensas, and then, after having made them a little present, we separated from one another very content.

[24] The Natchez were a Maskoki tribe.

The 14: we arrived among the Oumats, who are twenty leagues below the Natchez. There we found a letter from Monsieur d'Hyberville, who said that he had come as far as this village with two shallops and two bark canoes, and that he was returning in his ships in order to build a fort on the seacoast. This is a village of about a hundred cabins. Their language is the same as that of the Chikachas and of the Kinipissas[25] and of several other nations, being one of the most extended of these countries. Like the Taensas and the Natchez, they have a temple. They also have some chiefs, but principally a woman appears as the most important person there. We were very well received and they spoke much of Monsieur d'Hyberville and of other Frenchmen who were with him. They showed us the presents which had been made to them. Among other things they admired a cannon-ball of about fourteen pounds, and they understood very well that that would have quite another effect than their arrows.

The 15: having set out to visit the Kinipissas, we encountered some few canoes of savages in which there were two little French boys of fourteen or fifteen years of age whom Monsieur d'Hyberville was sending, [the one] to the Kinipissas, and the other to the Oumats, in order to learn their languages. They informed us more at length concerning all things, and among other things, that Monsieur d'Hyberville had departed the 22: March to return to France; that having gone only as far as the Oumats, they had not known that we were with the Taensas, although they are only forty leagues away; that a fort had been constructed on the seacoast thirty leagues to the east of the mouth of the Micissipi. We took one of these two French boys with us to aid us in finding the fort and continued our journey.

The 17: we arrived among the Kinipissas. There are a hundred cabins including the Bajogoula[26] and the Mogoulacha[27] who are joined to them, all of whom constitute only a

[25] The Acolapissas, Kolapissas, or Quinipissas were a Cha'hta (Choctaw) tribe, located north of New Orleans.

[26] The Bayogoulas were a Cha'hta tribe.

[27] The Mougoulaches were also a Cha'hta tribe.

single village. It is against these Kinipissas that Monsieur de La Salle fought and even killed several of their men in the voyage that he made to the sea by way of the Micissipi. We saw a great cross that the Rev. Father Stanislas, Recollet,[28] had planted there. He had come into this country at other times with Monsieur de La Salle and had returned to France with M. Cavelier[29] from the bay St. Louis[30] through Canada. These latter also told us many good things concerning the French. They were the first whom Monsieur d'Hyberville had seen, for some Bajogoula were hunting in the vicinity where Fort Maurepas is now located, and discovering their fire, Monsieur d'Hyberville was carried there, and learned from them that the Micissipi, by them called the Malbanchia, was not far off, and that they lived on the banks of that river.

The 19: we parted from the Kinipissas, and the 22. arrived at the sea, 60: leagues distant. We did not perceive that we were there until we saw the open sea because the tide is without sufficient force to repell the current of the Micissipi and the river carries its water far into the sea. We thought that upon leaving the Micissipi we had only to follow the seacoast in order to arrive at the fort, and we had been given to understand that we would find much beautiful country and streams of fresh water from place to place. But during the ten days that it took to travel from the mouth of the river to Fort Maurepas we found quite the contrary. It was necessary for us to round a great point which pushed far into the sea, and then to pass a great many islands and bays which render this sea very easy for canoes by breaking the waves of the sea, and which made it possible to keep in sight of land, but which render this vicinity very difficult and even impossible for great ships.

I shall not take time to tell you, Monseigneur, all that we

[28] The Recollects were the reformed fathers of St. Francis.

[29] Jean Cavelier, Sulpitian, a brother of La Salle.

[30] La Salle established Fort St. Louis on the Garcitas River, somewhat up from the bay. H. E. Bolton, "The Location of La Salle's Colony on the Gulf of Mexico," in *Mississippi Valley Historical Review*, II., 165–181.

had to suffer during this time. The heat was very great, we lacked fresh water, we had only Indian corn flour for food, which we did not dare to eat without water for fear of becoming even more thirsty, we had no relief from gadflies by day and mosquitoes or gnats by night. Finally, the greater part of our men could stand the thirst which overcame them no longer, and drank the water, only a little less salt than the sea, although not even that could be found regularly, and which we so bad that they almost all fell ill with a bloody flux. Those who were least ill had more need to be conducted than to conduct the others. Finally, the second of July, the day of the visitation of the Most Holy Virgin, having implored her aid, she assisted us in finding and arriving safely at the fort. Although they saw our French flag, the men of the fort could not persuade themselves that there were Frenchmen in this country. Seeing our two canoes coming at full sail because we had a very favorable wind, they persuaded themselves that it was the Spaniards, and thought of firing the cannon at us. Nevertheless, Mons'r de Bienville[31] came to recognize us and saw clearly that we were neither in a state nor of a mind to do anything against them.

Fort Maurepas is on an elevation and in a very beautiful setting. Built of only stakes and stone on stone, it is, nevertheless, quite regular, and quite difficult to take without cannon, especially as there are a great many cannon at the fort. But there is this drawback. The water of the wells that they have dug there is not good, and in order to find better, you have to go quite far by boat.

We found M. de Sauvolle,[32] ensign of the vessel, in command, who had for officers Monsieur de Bienville, the two Mess'rs Le Vasseur of Canada, one of whom was major of the fort, and M'r Guyon, who had gone to the islands to get provisions, there being only enough for a very short time in the fort. There was also the chaplain from the vessel of

[31] Jean Baptiste le Moyne, sieur de Bienville, a brother of Iberville.

[32] Sauvole de Villantray, a French officer, was a lieutenant under Iberville and in command at Fort Maurepas.

Monsieur Descalette, who had remained there in order to care for spiritual needs, and about fifty men, some of them Canadians, some of them soldiers, and some of them filibusters from Saint Domingo.

We learned there that upon the rumor that had been current in France that we were coming to settle the Micissipi, the Spaniards had forestalled us, and that they had come to settle upon a very beautiful and deep river which they called Pensacola, which is only twenty-two leagues from Fort Maurepas. One could very easily have taken possession of this place and driven the Spaniards out, who are in no condition to withstand three warships, but Messieurs d'Hyberville, d'Escalette, and de Chateau Moran who commanded these vessels did not judge it proper to commence a war, and having gone there, they contented themselves with demanding the water of which they had need, which the Spaniards gave them. There was in this fort four Cordeliers,[33] some of whom passed their time in instructing the savages, and the others in guiding the Spaniards of the fort.

We learned also that the French whom Mons'r de la Salle had left at the bay of St. Louis were all dead, and that they had all been killed by the savages with the exception of one or two young boys who had been taken by the Spaniards and sent by them to Old Spain, but the vessel upon which they were passengers had been taken by the French and sent to France, and from France they had passed to Canada, and that they reported that the Spaniards had taken possession of the bay of Saint Louis but had finally abandoned it.

We left Fort Maurepas after having spent ten days there, during which time the officers overlooked nothing which might contribute to restore us from the fatigue of our voyage. They even added some presents for the chiefs of our missions from those that the crown had sent to the savages. Our men were not perfectly recovered from their illness, and we still had much to suffer. It is true that we had obtained a savage for a guide at the fort, and he con-

[33] The Cordeliers were a Franciscan order.

ducted us by a short[er] and easi[er] road, but the sickness and the number of ill steadily increased, and we had the misfortune to lose the two Taensas who had accompanied us, one of whom died on the portage from the Kinipissas, and the other, among the Oumats. I had been absent some days when the first died, having gone ahead in order to send some food from the village of the Kinipassas to our sick, and since there was no interpreter there at the time, he died without baptism. The second was more fortunate, for having been instructed concerning our mysteries, he died after receiving holy baptism, which he had even told us that he desired before leaving the Taensas. The death of these two men was the more grievous to us because there was every reason for fearing that the savages might accuse us of murdering them. The Chaouanon who had come to the fort with us, and who lived with the Taensas, did not dare to come with us, it being a serious matter (he said) for strangers to carry such news, so he remained with the Oumats. There our sick sojourned for some time, and by taking a bit of rest, recovered. There were two little children who were very ill. One of them was baptized by Monsieur Davion. It was impossible for him to approach the second, however, for the mother of this little child had not yet accustomed herself to seeing habits so long and so black. When she saw Monsieur Davion approach from one direction, she would flee in the other. Finally, Brother Allexandre, hospitalier of Montreal, who had accompanied us on this voyage, and who had edified us by his good conduct and especially by his charity toward the sick over the entire route, having gone to her, baptized it without any difficulty, the mother having no fear of him.

With the Oumats there were several canoes of Natchez, who were on the point of leaving when we arrived there. I took this opportunity to go with them, and after having been with the Taensa at his death, I left with a Frenchman to betake myself to the Natchez. The individuals of this nation spared nothing to testify the joy they had at my arrival. I profited from their good disposition to engage them to do the things which I desired of them. I told them that I planned to pass one part of the year with them, and the other, with the Taensas; that in order to do that, it was necessary that they make peace with them, with the Tonicas, and with the other nations; that it was not necessary that they form a barrier on the Micissipi, and that they ought to permit the French and the savages who wanted to sail there to pass freely. I made known to them also that my occupation was to serve, and to make known to others the great master of life and some other truths of our religion. They listened to what I said to them with enjoyment. They gave evidence of great pleasure that I wished to come to them, and although the Taensas had killed a man only a very few days before, they implored me to say to them that they wished to make war on them no longer, and that before eight days had passed they would conclude peace with them. They also implored me to make known to the Tonicas and to other nations that they no longer wished to make war, but that they wished henceforth to live at peace with them. I passed some days in visiting the cabins. This nation is the most numerous of those that are on the banks of the Micissipi. There are ten or twelve villages, but that which makes it difficult for the missionary is the fact that they are widely scattered either in hamlets or in habitations. They occupy seven or eight leagues of country. Their country is beautiful. They are on the banks which are never flooded. There are almost three hundred cabins, and often in each cabin there are two and three families.

The 17: of the month of August, Monsieur Davion having arrived from the Oumats with our Frenchmen who had remained there, we left the Natchez to return to the Taensas, where we arrived after a three days' march. Before arriving there we had a very extraordinary adventure. A sword fish, which are very large in this country, suddenly threw itself from the water and landed in our canoe, either by chance or because it was pursued by a crocodile or some other great fish. We were very much surprised and even embarrassed, for it almost seriously wounded one of our men, but fortunately we promptly threw a blanket over it, into which it plunged its teeth. Another adventure almost like that had already happened to us at sea. One of our men fired on a porpoise, which with several others was following [our boat]. Feeling itself struck, this animal came with fine fury upon our canoe, which we all thought it would tear to pieces, a bark canoe not being strong enough to resist it, but it contented itself with making the water fly in all directions and thoroughly wetting us, after which it took two or three turns around the canoe and went its way, scraping our canoe with such swiftness, that with the exception of birds, I do not know of any animal on earth that could have caught up with it.

When they learned of our arrival among the Taensas, the chief first sent the most considerable men of the village with the pipe of peace. That is a ceremony which they observe when they wish to testify to a stranger the joy that they have at his arrival and the peace and union that they desire to have with him. When they did not see the two Taensas who had accompanied us, they indeed suspected that something must have happened to them, and in order not to hold them in suspense, I immediately informed them of their deaths. They received this news very well. They agreed that when one drank the water of the sea, it was very harmful for the health, and that they were wrong in not taking better care of themselves when they were thirsty and during their sickness. Thus, only the parents of the deceased mourned them in their usual manner, that is with lamentations which are heard by almost all the village to witness the extreme affection that they had for their defunct relatives and friends.

Afterwards they told us that the Natchez and the Kahapitch, who are nations 30: or 40: leagues distant from the Taensas, had come to see us; and that not having found us, they were soon to come back; that the Mintous, who are now with the Kouroüais at 30: leagues from the Taensas, were also to come; that a chief of the Chikachas had come and had said to them that he no longer wished to make war against them nor against the Tonicas, that a white spirit (for it is thus that the savages of these countries call the French) had come to see them this spring and had said to them that it was not well to kill one another in this way, and that peace was worth more, and that he no longer wished to make war, but wished to talk about Monsieur Davion who had gone to his village in the spring and had persuaded his nation to make peace.

Upon that I said that the Natchez with whom they had warred for a long time would come to conclude peace as soon as possible; that on their behalf they had implored me to carry this word to them; and that for my part I exhorted them to do likewise. There were many of them so inclined, and they did not have much difficulty in agreeing to it.

Three days after my arrival the deputies of the Natchez came to speak of peace. They were given such a reception as they could desire, and afterwards were led in front of the door of the temple, where the chief of the Taensas and the principal men of the nation were assembled. There they went through several ceremonies which it would take very long to describe. The presents that these deputies brought were carried to the temple. They consisted of six robes of muskrat very well made. Afterward peace was concluded. Then the old man who has the chief care of the temple mounted an elevation at the entrance to the temple and there harangued for a long time, sometimes addressing his words to the spirit, and sometimes, to those present, exhorting the two nations to forget the past and henceforth to live in an inviolable peace.

I have not yet been able to discover what this spirit that they revere is, for although they recognize several of them, nevertheless, they consider one the greatest of all. Although the customs and manners of the savages of this country hardly differ from the customs and manners of other savages, yet in regard to their temple and their chief they have manners which for savages appear to be very beautiful.

Strangers never make any considerable present to them that they do not carry it with great respect to the temple, and that they do not thank the spirit by proffering certain words while turning themselves in the direction of the temple, raising their hands toward the sky and then placing them upon their heads, and turning toward the four points of the compass.

When the savages of some other nation arrive, ordinarily they go first to the temple and leave some present before the door there, which they later take care to share with the nation.

Only those who care for the temple enter it. The others believe that they will die if they enter there. There is nothing in these temples except some figures of man and beasts, carved rather rudely, and chests full of bones of the most important chiefs who have died, and they maintain a perpetual fire there.

When some one dies, they say that he goes to a far distant country. That is why, when they see strangers, they often weep, longing for their relatives who are dead. With the dead, they bury their most precious belongings, and all their relatives and friends bring something to place in the grave. They also place little baskets full of grain and other food there, apparently persuading themselves that these articles will be useful in this strange country where they say that they are going.

The Natchez and the Taensas have much more annoying manners, for when their great chief dies, several do themselves the honor of dying with him in order to accompany him into the strange country where he goes. Some offer themselves voluntarily, but when the number of those who offer themselves does not appear sufficient, they carry a present to a family and that family does itself the honor of sending some one to die for the chief. The savages assured us that they killed thirty persons for the last chief of the Natchez who died. One of the Frenchmen who was with us appeared very much surprised at this conduct, and perceiving it, the chief of the Natchez immediately said, what then, if I died, would you not wish to die with me, believing that he was doing him a great honor. But without much hesitation the other assured him that he could die when he wished, but that as far as he was concerned, he had not the least intention of following him.

When the one who presents himself or is sent to death is ready, they light a certain root. When it is consumed, he bows his head and they give him a few blows with a hatchet unless he prefers to be strangled with a rope.

A short time before we arrived for the first time among the Taensas their chief had died and they killed six persons to keep him company.

Although their chief is not absolute, none of them speak of him except with great respect. No woman or child ever lives in his cabin, and only the elders and the most important of the nation enter it. Whether he is there or whether he is not there, in entering and in leaving his cabin they show their respect by their manner. They never speak to the chief and the chief never speakes to them that they do not show their respect in the same way. No one would dare to sit upon his bed, or to use his goblet, or to pass between him and the cabin torch which they light every evening in order to illumine the cabin.

When the time of plowing, sowing, or harvesting has come, all the village assembles. They begin with a great dance. After each has brought his contribution to the repast, they have a big banquet. After the banquet the men and the women all go to the land of the chief, and in a half day, everybody taking a hand in it, his land is plowed, sowed, or harvested. The same thing is done when it is a matter of building a cabin for him or of repairing the temple.

FRANÇOIS DE MONTIGNY, S. J., TO THE COMTE DE PONTCHARTRAIN[1]

From NEWYORK this 17: July 1700:

Monseigneur:

I believe that I ought to let slip no occasion to write to your highness, which is why I am risking this letter by way of New England, where we have been obliged to debark to refresh ourselves, and to provide ourselves with water. I shall write you very briefly, having written you a few months ago by a canoe which Monsieur Le Sueur,[2] who has gone to the Scioux,[3] was supposed to send to Canada.

A very few days after the letter that I had the honor of writing to you last year, I fell ill; and my illness delayed me at Monsieur Davion's mission to the Tonicas the last four months of the year.

I returned to my mission to the Taensas at the beginning of January, where I was very busy because the sickness spread among our savages and a great number of them died. First I baptized the infants who had not yet the use of reason; and later, having perfected myself a little in the language, I also baptized the others who were dying. Among them our great chief approached his end and I baptized him and gave him the name of Michel. I also obtained the promise of the savages that they would not kill any one to accompany him into the other world, for they as well as the Natchez and some other nations have this custom of killing men, women, and children at the death of their great chiefs to accompany them into the other world where they say that they are going, and to render

[1] Translation of a copy of a letter in the Bibliothèque Nationale, Paris, Manuscrits Français, Nouvelles Acquisitions, 7485, fols. 127–131; photostat and transcript in the Library of Congress.

[2] Pierre Charles Le Sueur, a French explorer of the West and South.

[3] A Siouan tribe.

them all the services of which they may have need in this new country. I am also assured that in the vast countries of Mexico, which at present the Spaniards occupy, the savages follow this same custom.

At this same time Monsieur de Tonty,[4] Seigneur of the Islinois, passed by the Taensas with some Frenchmen who came from the Islinois. He was on his way to the fort which the French have at the bay of the Biloxis.

The 14: of March Monsieur d'Hyberville arrived at my mission to the Taensas. He had with him Messieurs de Bienville and de Chasteaugué,[5] his brothers; the Rev. Father Du Ru, Jesuit;[6] MM. Dugué[7] and de Saint Denis;[8] and several Canadians. At this time an accident happened which filled the village with consternation. Lightning struck their temple, which was the most beautiful of those which I have seen. The fire spread everywhere, and it was consumed before they could do anything about it. The extraordinary thing about it all was the ceremonies with which they honored the lightning, which they regard as a great god. Mothers hastily brought little infants still at the breast, and threw them into the flames. Fortunately, we had left some Frenchmen in the village (for at that time we were three leagues from the banks of the Micissipi where Monsieur d'Hyberville had some business), and these Frenchmen prevented them from continuing, or we do not know how many they would have thrown into the flames. Four of them, who fortunately were baptized, were burned to death.[9] After several days with the Taensas, to whom he made very beautiful presents, Monsieur d'Hyberville began the return

[4] Henri de Tonti, commander of Fort St. Louis on the Illinois River.

[5] Louis le Moyne, sieur de Châteauguay, a brother of Iberville.

[6] Paul Du Rue, Jesuit.

[7] Probably Pierre Dugué Boisbriant, a French officer.

[8] Louis Juchereau de St. Denis.

[9] In his relation of a voyage in 1700, Jacques Gravier says that in the preceding year the temple of the Taensas was reduced to ashes by lightning falling upon such combustible materials as the canes with which it was covered. Gravier says that five women threw their children into the flames. R. G. Thwaites, ed., *Jesuit Relations* LXV., 137.

journey to his ships. I took advantage of the opportunity to accompany him as far as the Natchez, where I intended to remain. Although it was not long since I had been there, and I had left the great chief of this village in perfect health, I had learned since my return that he had fallen ill, and as he was very aged, I feared that he would die. I knew that he was very important, and that if he died they would not fail to kill many at his death. In fact he died of this sickness some few days after my arrival. But as I had warned all the important people of the village, upon whom, as far as that goes, this bad custom of killing people was very burdensome, they did not kill any one, and promised me that in the future they would kill no one.[10] I also persuaded them to give up the bad custom that they had of interring with the deceased all that was most previous to him, for not only did they inter his chattels, but all his relatives and friends were obliged to bring the best that they possessed to be interred with him.

The ceremonies at his interment were very long. For six days they did not inter the dead. During this time all the village assembled to weep; the women took no care of their hair, but let it hang loose to mark their grief; they abstained from all games and diversions, ate only certain herbs and deprived themselves of all other food, and remained away from their women.

After the interment of the chief, there were still great ceremonies for the election of another great chief, although ordinarily it is the nephew of the deceased, but the nephew on this sister's side to the exclusion of the nephews on his brothers' side and even of his own sons, [who is chosen].

The last days of the month of March Monsieur Le Sueur on his way to the Scioux arrived among the Natchez in a very fine felucca propelled by sails and oars. He remained there several days, and did not leave until early in holy week after having taken advantage of the opportunity which pre-

[10] Gravier reports that Montigny obtained the promise of the Natchez to put no more people to death at the death of a chief, but that they deceived him. *Ibid.*, p. 143.

sented itself of spending Easter with his people. Having determined to go to France, whither I believed that I ought to journey to promote the affairs of our mission, I left the Natchez at the beginning of the month of May. Several chiefs of the nation accompanied me as far as the forts of the French in order to see our ships, of which they had heard. They had seen some cannon-balls, and greatly admired their weight, but they had never seen cannons and greatly desired to see them.

There was nothing unusual in our voyage as far as the Bajogoula, where we found a young Frenchman who lived there, who told us that five or six days before the chief of this nation had entirely destroyed the Kinipissas nation and the Mogoulachas, all three of which constituted only a single village; that not a single man had escaped, and that they had spared only the women and the children; that that had happened because of the jealousy that the chief of the Bajogoula held against the chief of the Kinipissas and the Mogoulachas because although he and his nation were the latest arrivals in that neighborhood, he always occupied the most honorable place in the assemblies and words were always addressed to him; that before this accident these two nations were already almost entirely destroyed and had only about fifty men able to make war; and that they were killed when they least expected it. We found three of them whom they had scalped still unburied on the banks of the Micissipi.

The 9: of May I arrived at the fort which is on the Micissipi. I found Monsieur Maltot in command in place of Monsieur de Bienville who had gone on a journey to some savage nation. There for several days I awaited Monsieur Davion, who brought with him the chiefs of his nation.

The 19: of May Monsieur Davion and I with our savages arrived at Monsieur d'Hyberville's vessel named *La Renommée*. It is a very beautiful frigate of fifty cannons. Our savages could not sufficiently admire such a great canoe, and were so surprised by our cannon, that I believe that the noise of a single one would have been sufficient to cause all the nations of the Micissipi to flee. We went also to the fort on the bay of Biloxis,[11] of which Monsieur de Sauvole is the commander. We found the Rev. Father Du Ru there, occupied in completing a chapel, the consecration of which was to take place on the day of Pentecost.

After Monsieur d'Hyberville had made several presents to our savages, they began the return journey to their villages, very well satisfied with their journey and the French who had received them so well. Monsieur Davion returned with them to his mission.

The 28: of May we set sail for France. It was already two months since Monsieur de Surgere had set sail on *La Profonde*, which he commanded.

The 10: of June, which was Corpus Christi day, about one o'clock in the afternoon we heard about thirty cannon shots, which the Spaniards of the Island of Cuba were firing in Havanna, a very rich city and a very strong and advantageous port. Apparently the procession was passing by at that time.

The night of the 12: or 13: of the same month we ran a great risk. About eleven o'clock at night we ran aground on the sand and on the rocks. All our sails were set, but by good luck no wind was blowing. We were at the entrance of Bahama Channel, where the currents are extremely rapid, that is to say between the Island of Cuba and the headland of Florida. Fortunately, in less than two hours we got out of this difficult plight by means of our anchors, which the shallop carried far way, drawing the boat after them. Only our rudder was damaged, and that was quickly repaired the next morning, for the body of the ship was very strong and entirely new and was not at all damaged. Since we were on Spanish soil, I believed that Saint Anthony of Padua, whose feast we observed upon this day, and whom the Spaniards have accepted as the patron of navigators, preserved us on this occasion.

We were afterwards a little short of food for the sick, who were beginning to increase in number because of the exces-

[11] The Bay of Biloxi.

sive heat that we had suffered toward the Island of Cuba, where we passed the Tropic of Cancer at the time of greatest heat, both because the sun is directly overhead and because of the reverberation of the heat, which comes on the one hand from the headland of Florida, and on the other hand from the Island of Cuba, and decided to go to get some at the first port. After passing Carolina, Virginia, and Pinsilvanie, we approached Newyork.[12]

We have been here almost three weeks. All our sick have recovered, and only two men have died since we left the Micissipi. Only Monsieur d'Hyberville, who was quite well at sea, was seized with a very bad fever and lumbago about eight or ten days ago. Nevertheless, we hope that it will not be serious.

The city of Newyork is built of brick and very beautiful. There is freedom of religion. The population is composed of Hollanders, English, and French. I do not know which nationality is the most numerous. There is no church but there are two [Protestant] chapels and a Jewish synagogue.

In Pensilvanie they say that there are many Roman Catholics, and that there are Jesuits and Recollets in their robes, but I do not know if that is really true. I have been in York with my long robe and met with only courtesy from everybody. It is indeed true that they stared at me, for I believe that they have never seen secular priests. They spoke to me much concerning Father Bruyas[13] who had come there last autumn with Monsieur de la Valliere.[14] Milord Ballamon,[15] who is governor there, was absent. He was at Boston but they expected him daily.

In the time that we were there five little ships arrived

[12] For accounts of the arrival of Iberville's vessel at New York, see *New York Colonial Documents*, IV., 684, 686.

[13] Jacques Bruyas, Jesuit, sent by Chevalier de Callières, governor of New France, to the Earl of Bellomont in 1699. *Ibid.*, IX., 704, 720.

[14] Sieur de La Vallière was also a member of the mission to Bellomont.

[15] The Earl of Bellomont was commissioned governor of both New York and Massachusetts, June 18, 1697. Lord Cornbury was commissioned to succeed him in New York, November 26, 1701, and Joseph Dudley, in Massachusetts, December 11, 1701.

from England, one in five weeks, the others in six. Hardly any but French families were coming to settle there. They assured me that persecution of the Protestants (as they say) is stronger than ever in France.

The English desire to settle at the Cape of Florida, and there are already several persons associated for this purpose.

The Scotch had settled on the Isle d'Or which is in the gulf of Darien, in that isthmus which is so narrow as you go from the Southern sea to the Northern Sea. That was really making themselves at home in the midst of Spanish territory in Mexico. Therefore, the Spaniards have driven them out of there. Furthermore, that place is very unhealthful. This country has hardly any traffic except in grain which they carry to the islands. They say that Carolina and Virginia are also very unhealthful countries, and that most people go elsewhere to live. Last year the sickness spread into Pinsilvanie, which is a principality where all the Coacres[16] have gathered. It has carried off, as they maintain, more than a third of the population.

We hope to be in France at the end of the month of August, and I hope to return to the Micissipi by the first vessels.

The English and the Spaniards are extremely jealous of our establishment on the Micissipi.

Lat autumn Jean Bar, who is an English captain established in Carolina came into the Micissipi with a vessel of twelve cannons and sailed twenty-five leagues up the river. Monsieur de Bienville met him in a boat, and informed him that the French were established there, and that they even held forts there. In that way he made him withdraw. He came there in order to settle Protestant fugitives from France.

Last February some English boats filled with arms and merchandise came by way of the Ouabache to the Arkansas. I do not know whether they expected to discover us there, but finally they gave several guns to the savages and engaged them to go to war against the Saxoumans in order to enslave

[16] Quakers.

them. The Arkansas did not know how to use firearms, however, and were well beaten, and forced to throw away their guns and flee with no weapons at all, and even lost thirty of their number. The Saxoumans are forty leagues above the Tonicas and on their river.

The Spaniards are no less alarmed by this establishment of the French. In the month of August last they came with three ships, namely, a frigate with 24: pieces of cannon, a barge, and a brigantine. Monsieur de Nola, governor of Pensacola, which is only 22: leagues distant from our fort of Biloxis, was there with his major. There was also a Cordelier father and an Augustine father.

At first they took one of our shallops from us, later returning it to us with their excuses that they had believed it to be an English shallop. Later, having come with their ships, and seeing us very well supplied with two frigates and very well armed with fifty cannon, they said to us that they had come only because they believed that we were English, whom they had orders not to permit to settle. Nevertheless, they left a protest against the settlement. That did not prevent both sides from regaling themselves very well, and courtesies from being exchanged. Unfortunately for them, as they retired they wrecked their frigate on a flat island. The best that they could do was to save themselves and to abandon the vessel. At that, if we had not given them prompt aid, they would all have perished. Before I finish, permit me to pray you . . . .

(*Manuscript incomplete*)

HARRY GORDON'S NOTES ON THE MISSISSIPPI

Notes on the Country along the Mississipi from Cascaskias in the Illinois to New Orleans[1]

The Nature of the Land for near 100 Miles below the Mouth of the Cascaskais River[2] is broken small Ridges, and in Places Rocky, sometimes high from thence to the Ohio, altho the Banks when the River is low, appear of a considerable Height, yet They are certainly overflowed in Times of Flood and the Isthmus, between the Ohio and Mississipi for 8 Leagues upwards from their Confluence; is mostly Mud and full of Ponds and Swamps—

This Nature of Soil seems to continue to the *Mines Au Fer*[3] where for a few 100 Yards the Ground is high—no Height appears from thence to those of Margot,[4] which are on the

[1] British Museum, Haldimand Papers, Additional MSS. 21,686, II, fol. 57; photostat in the Library of Congress. This is an account of territory surveyed by Captain Harry Gordon, chief engineer of the western department of North America, Captain Thomas Hutchins of the 60th or Royal American Regiment, assistant engineer, and Colonel George Croghan, deputy Indian agent. After journeying down the Ohio from Pittsburgh to the Mississippi River, they began the descent of the Mississippi, September 18, 1766, arriving at New Orleans October 14, 1766. Proceeding by way of Mobile and Pensacola, they arrived at Charleston, South Carolina, December 6, 1766. For a map of the Mississippi River in 1765, see Thomas Jefferys, *The American Atlas* (London, 1776). For "Gordon's Journal, May 8, 1766—December 6, 1766," see Illinois State Historical Library *Collections*, XI., 290–311. See also Thomas Hutchins, *A Topographical Description of Virginia, Pennsylvania, Maryland, and North Carolina*, reprinted from the original edition of 1778, edited by F. C. Hicks (Cleveland, 1904); and the same author's *An Historical Narrative and Topographical Description of Louisiana, and West-Florida* (Philadelphia, 1784), reprinted in G. Imlay, *A Topographical Description of the Western Territory of North America* (London, 1797), pp. 388–458.

[2] Kaskaskia River, Illinois.

[3] Mine au Fer or the Iron Mines, on the east side of the Mississippi River, 15 miles to the south of the Ohio River.

[4] The "Écores à Margot" (Margot's Bluffs), Chickasaw Bluffs, where Memphis now stands.

Left in descending; and border, in diff't. Places, along the River, several Miles—The Banks of the River from thence to the Yazous[5] are low, muddy, and most probably overflowed.—here the rising Ground runs but a small Way a few 100 Yds. Hence to the grand Goufre[6] it is low flat Ground along the Banks—This last may be said to be the Beginning of the high Ground of the Natchez[7] altho at 25 Leagues distant from the Fort, there is an Appearance of Stone at the grand Goufre—The Fort of the Natchez is high and pleasantly placed, and affords an extended Prospect of an opened Soil which promises Health and Plenty to its Inhabitants. This is the only Country that seemed worth possessing from the Illinois to New Orleans; and if once inhabited with any Number, will hang, dreaded, over that Town and the Inhabitants near it—A Garrison at Natchez will in Case of Accidents, that may oblige the upper Ports On the Mississipi to be abandoned, receive them in their Retreat—and as an Attack on New Orleans in Time of War, may be conveniently carried on down the Mississipi, the Natchez may serve as a Deposit for the Stores necessary for that Purpose. The Ground along the Banks of the Mississipi, below the Natchez, except at two Places the Roche de Davion[8] and Ecors de Lait[9] is every where Flat and some Seasons overflowed—There are about 100 French Inhabitants at Point Coupee,[10] who raise Tobacco and Corn in Abundance—This Setlement is 30 Leagues below the Natchez and appears prosperous—15 Leagues lower is the Post of Manchac at the Ibberville[11]—The Ditch of the

[5] The Yazoo River.

[6] Grand Gulf at the mouth of Big Black River, 569 miles below the Ohio.

[7] In his journal, Gordon locates this country at 32° 20′ north latitude. Thomas Hutchins says, "the country known by the name of the Natchez, in 31° 40′ north latitude, about 243 computed miles from New Orleans, and 348 from the Balize, following the course of the river." G. Imlay, *A Topographical Description of the Western Territory of North America*, p. 423.

[8] Roche à Davion, 658 miles below the Ohio River.

[9] Les Écores du Lait, 721 miles below the Ohio.

[10] Pointe Coupée, 698 miles below the Ohio.

[11] Iberville River, flowing between Lake Maurepas and the Mississippi River.

Ibberville was 23 Feet above the level of the Water of the Mississipi when we viewed it—[12]However a Road may conveniently be cut, along the Bank of this Ditch to the Ammit,[13] 9 Miles Distance, That will serve as a carrying Place when the Ditch is dry, and by which Oxen may be employed to hale Boats along when there is Water in it—The Impositions of New Orleans, and the Incertainty of that Passage continuing open to Us, are Reasons for endeavouring to open the Communication of the Iberville into the Mississipi; and I am of Opinion the Route then by that Place, may be sooner performed than by N. Orleans, where they have a considerable Way to ascend the Stream of the River between the two Places—The Country from Iberville to New Orleans along the River is all Flat—It begins to be setled 10 Leagues below our Fort—The Plantations towards the Town are considerable where they raise Indigo Tobacco and Rice.

HARRY GORDON.

[12] Thomas Hutchins says, " . . . when I viewed it on the 10th of October 1766, the surface of the water of the Mississippi was then 24 feet below the bed or bottom of the Ibberville." G. Imlay, *A Topographical Description of the Western Territory of North America*, p. 432.

[13] Amité River.

SURVEY OF WEST FLORIDA, 1768[1]

By an Account taken in the Year 66, there were then in the District of Mobile, reckoning from Lake Pontchartrain to the highest Settlements up the Bay and River of Mobile, on both Sides (the Town included) 140 Houses and Plantations, about 300 white Men able to bear Arms, 200 white Women and Children, 240 Negro Men, 120 Negro Women and Children and 8000 Head of Cattle.

I never knew the exact Number of the Inhabitants in the District of Pensacola, but as they were all included in the Town, except a few French Emigrants at Campbell Town, I think they cou'd not, at that Time, exceed the Number of those at Mobile, for there were then scarcely any Plantations in that Part of the Country, and no Cattle, except some Milch Cows, which had been brought from Mobile.

Tho the Soil about Pensacola is, if possible, worse than that about Mobile, yet the former of these Places has many essential Advantages over the latter—it is built upon a dry Sand, and during the Summer Months enjoys the Benefit of the Sea Breezes, the Island of Santa Rosa being too low and narrow to obstruct them. it is therefore tolerably healthy. the Bay is so deep, that a forty Gun Ship can lie at Anchor within a Mile of the Town, and there is always twenty two feet Water upon the Bar, some say four fathoms, which difference may be occasion'd by the Winds and Tide.

Mobile, on the contrary, is situated among Swamps and Marshes, by the Side of a slow River, in which the Tide is very small, not rising above two feet, and that only once in twenty four Hours; thus, there is no Stream of Water to give a Current to the Air, which becomes stagnated and corrupt. its great Distance too from the Coast frequently deprives it of the Sea Breezes during the hot Season, and

[1] Manuscript in the Library of Congress.

even when they do blow, they pass over so many Woods and Marshes, that they come tainted. for all these Reasons it is a most unhealthful Place. it is likewise, in some Respects, as unluckily situated for Commerce, as for Health, there being, only fifteen feet Water upon the Bar, and the Bay soon becoming so shallow, that a Ship of 200 or 300 Tons Burden is oblig'd to anchor three Leagues below the Town.

Notwithstanding these great Disadvantages of Situation, the French were at the Expence of building a regular, but small Brick Fort there, about the Years 18 or 20.[2] they also built another little Fort of Earth at Tombecbé,[3] an Indian Village in the Chactaw Country, about an hundred Leagues higher up the River, but the Distance by Land does not exceed 200 Miles. they had besides a small Post upon the Alibama River,[4] forty Leagues to the eastward of Tombecbé, close to the Country of the Creeks. the French at that Time seem'd to have flatter'd themselves, that they shou'd draw great Riches from Louisiana, of which Province they considerd these Rivers and Forts as a Barrier against the English, the Creek Indians, and even the Spaniards of Florida, with whom they were then at Variance.[5] these Forts were likewise well calculated to prevent the Traders of Carolina and Georgia from carrying on a traffick with the French Indians. they have lost, however, much of their Importance with Respect to us. they are no longer on a Frontier, but in the Heart of our Province. they can be consider'd, at this Time, only as Checks upon the Natives, and even in this Light, small Garrisons at such Places as Tombecbé and Alibama, at so great a Distance from Support, appear rather to be Hostages in the Hands of the Indians, than Restraints upon them; the Expence also of sending Stores and Provisions to them is not inconsiderable.

[2] The French seem to have laid out and fortified Fort Louis de la Mobile as early as 1702. See P. J. Hamilton, *Mobile of the Five Flags* (Mobile, 1913), pp. 42–50.

[3] Fort Tombecbé.

[4] Alabama River.

[5] Trouble between France and Spain ended in 1720.

with Respect to the Spaniards, it is not probable that they will ever pass Lake Pontchartrain, and march through immense Woods to attack a Settlement, from which we only receive a few Deer Skins, and supposing they shou'd be so idle and romantick, these Forts are now improperly situated, for in stead of being cover'd by great Rivers, and difficult of Access, they are on the same Side with the Enemy.

The constructing of Fortifications in that Part of the World, sufficient to resist a Body of troops will be very expensive, but then these Troops, with their Artillery and Provisions, must come by Sea. thus, when the French were in Possession of Mobile, and the Spaniards of Pensacola, tho' such near Neighbours, yet their Attempts upon one another were always made by Sea, during their short War about fifty Years ago.

The whole internal Trade of West Florida consists in Deer Skins, which the Chactaws bring to Mobile on Horses; the annual Value of which, according to the highest Calculation, may amount to 30,000 £; many of them, however, in Spite of all the Precautions taken to prevent it, are carry'd to New Orleans, where the Merchant finds as good a Market as in England, and has a much quicker Return. the Creeks carry their Skins to Carolina and Georgia, they were accustom'd to do so, when the Spaniards were in Possession of Pensacola, and the Trade still remains in the same Channel. as the Indians have Nothing but Skins to give in Exchange for our Commodities, it is our Interest not only to be at Peace with them our Selves, but likewise to prevent, or put an End to, any War, which may arise between their several Tribes, as it interrupts their hunting, and consequently deprives them of the Means of purchasing our Goods. no doubt, our Traders are already sensible of this Effect from the War between the Creeks and Chactaws.[6]

The Lands up the Mobile, at some Distance above the Town, are reported to be good, and grow better the higher

[6] During the summers of 1767 and 1768 the Creeks and Choctaws were at war.

they advance. this River too is navigable for Boats about fifty Leagues. when a Detachment of the 21st Regiment took Possession of the Fort at Tombeebé in July 66, the Boats which carry'd the Provisions, after proceeding about half Way, were stopt by Shoals and oblig'd to return; the Provisions were taken out, and put into others, the flattest that cou'd be procur'd, which with Difficulty arriv'd at the Fort after passing these Shoals the Water deepens again.

The Banks of the Missisippi are extremely fertile, and proper for raising Hemp, Cotton, White Mulberry Trees, and very good Tobacco, but as there is no Tide in this River, the Navigation is difficult and tedious. Boats with twenty Oars and the most expert Rowers, when laden, seldom gain above five Leagues in a Day against the Stream. Ships must either wait for a very fair and strong Wind, sufficient to stem the Current, or else warp up, which is a most laborious and slow Operation, and attended with great Expence. they are besides expos'd, particularly during the Night, to be damaged by the Logs of Timber, which are continually floating down the River. notwithstanding these Difficulties, Ships do sometimes go by the Belise[7] to New Orleans, and after passing a dangerous Bar, are generally a fortnight, or three Weeks, in getting up to the Town, tho' the Distance be only 34 Leagues. there is, however, another Passage to New Orleans by Lake Pontchartrain, and the Bayou of St. John, which all the coasting Vessels and small Craft make Use of, but there is not Water enough for Ships—as it is only about half a League by Land from the West End of the Bayou to the Missisippi, this wou'd be the most convenient Way of sending the Troops, Provisions, and military Stores destined for our Posts upon that River, but the French will not permit it.

From the Difficulties attending the Navigation of the Missisippi, it seems almost impracticable for us ever to establish an advantageous Commerce upon it, especially as our Territory begins only at the Iberville,[8] which is 68

[7] Today Balize is a pilot-village near the mouth of the Mississippi.

[8] Iberville River.

Leagues above the Belise, or Entrance of the River; and as the French and Spaniards are in Possession of the Country on both Sides, for that Space, they will probably throw every Obstacle in our Way. it is even to be feared, that our own Traders will not have publick Spirit enough to pass by New Orleans, where they may have an easy Vent for their Commodities, without the Trouble of re-shipping them, and making a Voyage of 700 Leagues in Search of another Market. I have already mention'd that our People smuggle Deer Skins from Mobile to that Port, when they have an Opportunity, and I much question, whether the Furs of the Ilinois have yet found their Way to England.

The eastern Passage is by the Lakes Pontchartrain and Maurepas, and the Rivers Amite and Iberville. this is by much the shortest way to our Part of the Missisippi, and saves the Labour of contending with a strong Current for 68 Leagues, and yet is never made Use of by us, tho' we have an independent Right to it; our Detachments, and their Provisions always going by the Belise. our Neglect of this Passage proceeds from its being practicable only for Boats during a short Time of the Year. I'm told indeed, that they may get at all Times from Lake Maurepas up the Amite, as far as the Forks, or Junction with the Iberville, which last is improperly call'd a River, as it seems to be merely an over flowing of the Missisippi. it is about ten or twelve Miles long, and is generally from 30 to 40 feet broad, but so narrow in some Places, that a Boat can scarcely make Use of Oars, and has several short Turns, which are very troublesome to Boats of any Length. it was cleared, in the Year 65, of the Logs of Timber, which had choaked it up; but to keep it constantly clear, it wou'd be requisite to cut down the Trees, on both Sides, for some Yards back. when the Missisippi rises, its Channel fills, but its Bed is fourteen feet higher than the Surface of that River at low Water. it was almost dry on the 22d of July 66.

The Missisippi is about half a Mile broad at Fort Bute.[9]

[9] Fort Bute was erected at Manchac in the spring of 1766.

the eastern Bank is high and quite steep. the Western Side opposite to Manchac, which is the Indian Name for the Country about the Iberville, is low and overflow'd every Summer. the River begins to rise towards the End of April, and continues rising till July, when it begins to fall. at the lowest it is about twenty six feet below the east Bank; at the highest it is equal with that Bank, and sometimes overflows it, which renders a Levee of Earth before Fort Bute necessary, otherwise it must be abandond at such Times. I have not heard that the River has risen above its Bank, since the Fort has been built, but the Garrison has been apprehensive of it.

Fort Bute is a Square with half Bastions, built two Years ago by a Detachment of the 21st and 31st Regiments. it has not a Rampart of Earth, but is only palissaded, or picketed, which Kind of Fortification is cheap at the first construction from the great Plenty of Timber, and thought sufficient against Indians, but is attended with a constant Expence, as the Materials soon decay. it is situated about a Quarter of a Mile from the Point Iberville, or Junction of the two Rivers, and an hundred Yards from the Missisippi. it has been placed at this Distance, because the River seems to gain upon the Bank. as it is constructed upon a Plain, and the Bastions are not rais'd, the Guns cannot bear upon the River. the Ground about the Fort is rich, but not marshy. the Water for the Use of the Garrison is taken from the Missisippi, which is very wholesome; tho' a little muddy and shou'd be allow'd to settle. there are Wells for watering Gardens, and such Purposes.

If ever the Commerce of the Missisippi shou'd become considerable, and it shou'd be found most convenient to carry it on by the East Passage, small Vessels must be employ'd from Pensacola, or Mobile, to go through the Lakes, as far as the Mouth of the Amite; the Goods must there be put into Boats, which may proceed up the Amite, and through the Channel of the Iberville, when it is full; but the greatest Part of the Year, they must be landed at the Forks, and carry'd to Fort Bute; in which Case, a strait Road shou'd be cut through the Woods, which wou'd shorten the Distance considerably. the present Path follows the Windings of the Iberville. as the Bank of the Missisippi is high and the Ground falls a little towards the Amite, the Country about the Forks is overflow'd, when the Iberville is full. it will therefore be necessary to raise the Road in some Places. it wou'd, however, be certainly most eligible and advantageous to have, if possible, a constant Communication by Water between Lake Maurepas and the Missisippi. now I'm told, that there is a Part in the Bank of that River, about 300 Yards above Fort Bute, on which the Water strikes with Force, but being turn'd off forms the Point Iberville; by cutting a Canal at this Place, not more than a Mile in Length, to the Iberville, it is probable that the Water wou'd rush into it with such Violence, when at its Hieght, as by Degrees to deepen the Channel, so as to render it navigable for a considerable Part of the Year. perhaps it might in Time change the Course of the River.

All the French Plantations have Levees of Earth before them, which form the Roads and Communications. they extend on the East Side in the Isle of Orleans, within 13 or 14 Leagues of The Iberville, to the Country of the Alibamas and Onmas, two little Indian Tribes. on the West Side they extend within five Leagues of Fort Bute, and are mostly occupied by the Acadians. they begin again above the Fort, at 12 Leagues Distance. it wou'd appear from this, that their Settlements are interrupted for the Space of 17 Leagues, probably by the annual Inundation. their Fort at Pointe coupée is about 14 Leagues distant. some of the Acadians are settled very high up, as far as the Country of the Arcansas. there are likewise several German Families on both Sides of the River. it is, however always to be understood, that they have no Plantations on the East Side, except in the Isle of Orleans.

The Post at the Natchez is 60, or 65 Leagues above Fort Bute. the French had formerly a good Settlement here, but about the Years 27 or 28 their Colony was destroy'd by the

Indians;[10] in Revenge, they afterwards entirely extirpated, or dispersed the Natives, but did not think it adviseable to make a new Settlement since that Time, the Country remained unoccupied by either Indians, or Europeans, till a Detachment of the 21st Regiment took Possession of the old French Fort in the Year 66. it is situated on a rising Ground, three Quarters of a Mile from the Missisippi, and 73 Yards above the Surface of that River at low Water. the adjacent Country is pleasant and fertile, and quite clar'd, particularly to the eastward, tis said, for 30 Miles. however there is Wood enough still remaining to furnish Settlers with Timber for building Houses. the French Village, which was call'd St. Catherine's, was three Miles from the Fort, and had a River of excellent Water running close by it, which rises in the Country of the Chactaws, and falls into the Missisippi. the Village of the Natchez was five Miles from the Fort. the French rais'd here very good Tobacco, which they pretend to say was worth five Livres a Pound. their Plantations of Tobacco are now at Pointe coupée upon the Missisippi, and at Natchitoches a great Way up the River Rouge. the last is the most esteem'd.

a good Boat with twenty Oars takes three Months to go from New Orleans to Fort Chartres in the Country of the Ilinois, computing the Passage at five Leagues a Day, it makes the Distance 450 Leagues I think it can't well be more, (tho' generally reckoned so) from the Difference of Latitude, even allowing that the Windings of the River more than double the Distance. it is however sufficient to render the Commodities of Europe so dear, as to be scarcely saleable.

[10] For accounts of the attack of the Indians on the French at Natchez in 1729, see C. Gayarré, *History of Louisiana* (New Orleans, 1903), I., 396–440; Illinois State Historical Library *Collections*, X., 86–87.

JOURNALS OF SERGEANT WIGHT, 1771

Journal of the Passage of Serj't Wight to the Upper Creek Indian Nation 1771[1]

Tusday 5th Nov'r. Came to Indian Point at ten o Clock at Night.

Wednesday 6th Nov'r. began to March at three in the afternoon Marched ten Miles thro Pine Barren Land and Incamped N.N.E.

Thursday 7th. Uncamped Marched 4 Miles N.E. Came a Cross A Crick Which Runs into Scanby.[2] Marched 6 Miles Came A Cross a large Barren Swamp, then Came to a Creek two Miles Distance Called Little Yellow Water 30 Feet in Breadth and 4 feet in Depth.

Friday 8th. Uncamped Marched 8 Miles Came to a Small Creek that Runs into Yellow Water 20 feet in Breadth 4 feet in Depth, then Mached N E 4 Miles and Came to the Mean Creek of Yellow Watter Breadth About 40 feet and in Depth 16 feet fine Cypress On Each Side of the Said Creek and also Cedar Marched 6 Miles thro Barren Land and encamped N E.

Saturday 9th. Uncamped Marched at two in the Afternoon Marched 5 Miles thro high Land and Swamps and Came to a little Creek that Runs into Yellow Water 4 feet in

[1] British Museum, Haldimand Papers, Additional MSS. 21,686, II, fols. 43–44; photostat in the Library of Congress. The manuscript is endorsed: "Journal of the Passage of Serg: Wight from Pensacola to the Upper Creek Indian Nation and Back to Pensacola." At this time Pensacola was held by the British. For a map of the section, see H. R. Schoolcraft, *Information respecting the History, Condition and Prospects of the Indian Tribes of the United States*, V (Philadelphia, 1855), 252. For the Indian names of the region, see A. S. Gatschet, "Towns and Villages of the Creek Confederacy in the XVIII. and XIX. Centuries," Alabama Historical Society *Publications, Miscellaneous Collections*, I. (Montgomery, 1901), 386–415. The original is not paragraphed by days, as here.

[2] Probably Escambia River, flowing into Escambia Bay.

Breadth 2 feet in Deepth then Marched 3 Miles thro Very high Land Came to a Cedar and Cypers Swamp that Runs Along a large Creek that Runs into Yellow Water 24 feet Broad 4 feet Deep Crossed and encamped on A Very high hill N E.

Sunday 10th. Uncamped at 9 o Clock in the Morning Marched 10 Miles E S E and Came to a large Rune that Runs into Yellow Water 8 feet Broad 2 feet Deep then Marched 2 Miles Came to a Small Run that Went the Sam Way, then Marched 4 Miles Came to a Creek Which Runs into Yellow Water 24 feet Broad 4 feet Deep Barren Land Marched One Mile Encamped E N E

Munday 11th. Uncamped Marched 6 Miles to a Large Run 9 feet Broad 2 feet Deep that Runs into Yellow Water Good Wood about it and Very high Land then Marched 6 Miles and Came to a Small Run then Marched 4 Miles and Came to the Main Yellow Water about 60 feet broad and 16 feet Deep and Encamped E N E All Kinds of Wood about it and Goes A Great way into the Land it Runs into the bay of Yellow Water S S W[8]

Tuesday 12th. Uncamped at 9 o Clock Marched about 8 Miles E N E fine high Land and a Good Woody Country halted about an hour and then Marched about 9 Miles thro barren Land and Encamped N

Wednesday 13th. Uncamped at 7 o Clock Marched 12 Miles at ½ after 11 o Clock Crossed the Main branch of Yellow Water and Came to a Pond 500 Yards Long and Computed it to be Between 30 and 36 feet Broad then Marched 10 Miles and Encamped The Yellow Water has a sandy Bottom all the Way there is No Bridges at all But Logs of Timber put a Cross the Rivers and Runs for a man to Walk Upon to Cross N. E.

Thursday 14th. Uncamped at 8 o Clock Marched thro Barren Land 16 Miles and Encamped by a large Thicket that Runs N:E:

Friday 15th. Uncamped at 8 o Clock and Marched 25

[8] Today Yellow Water or Yellow River flows into Pensacola Bay.

Miles and Came thro a Good Woody Country and Encamped N:

Saturday 16. Uncamped at 8 o Clock Marched 17 Miles and Came to a large Cane Branch and a Small Run Which Runs thro it into Scanby then Marched 4 Miles and Came to the head Branch of Scanby 20 feet Broad and 3 feet Deep and Crossed it twice then Marched 3 Miles and Encamped N E

Sunday 17th. Uncamped at 8 o Clock Marched thro Very high land and Good Wood and Land for Grain 22 Miles Encamped N E

Munday 18th. Uncamped Marched 7 Miles thro high Lands and Plains and Came to the Savannahs Which is about 12 Miles Crossed then Came to a Swamp 2 Miles a Cross and Came to a Creek Called fuexy 18 feet Broad and 2 feet Deep Marched 4 Miles and Came to a Cane Swamp and Crossed a Creek Called Capewayatchie 20 feet Broad and 3 feet Deep, then Marched 5 Miles and Came to a Great Cane Swamp and Crossed a Creek 30 feet Broad 4 feet Deep Called Hulaby then Marched 5 Miles and Came to Tallapusha River[4] Which is about 150 feet a Cross and 4 feet Deep and Came to Mr. Cornells House at Tuckabatchie[5]—Totale from Pensacola to Tuckabatchie is 246 Miles—But the Rivier Tallapusha is from 4 to 10 feet Deep and When in Rainy Weather is Sometimes 40 feet Deep the River is Navigable from Mobile for an 8 Oar Boat for 2 Miles above Mr. Cornells House and the falls is 4 Miles further Tuckabatchie is 4 Miles long and Great Tallisis[6] 2 Miles there is Great and Small Ponds Round Both Towns, Good Level land all about them the Number of Indians in Both Towns is about 120 Besides Women and Children and there is Not one from 8 Years Old of Both Sexes But Can Swim—

[4] Tallapoosa River, a tributary of the Alabama River.

[5] In 1801 Mr. Cornell still lived at Tukabatchi, an Upper Creek town on the western bank of the Tallapoosa River. W. B. Hodgson, *A Sketch of the Creek Country, In 1798 and 1799, by Colonel Benjamin Hawkins, United States Agent for Indian Affairs* (New York, 1848), pp. 29, 31.

[6] Talisi was an Upper Creek town on the eastern bank of the Tallapoosa River.

Dec'r 3d. Marched from Mr. Cornells House at 12 a Clock in the Day Marched 15 Miles Good high and Low Land and Came to Creek that Run to Tallapusha Rivier to the Left Hand Marched 15 Miles further and Came to Little Taless[7] Where the Second Man lives but he Was Not Come Home from Pensacola then Marched 2 Miles and Came to the falls of a Creek 20 feet broad 3 feet Deep that Runs into Coursa Rivier Marched 3 Miles and Came to New Town Due W: to the big Mans house, but he Was Gone a Hunting then Mr. Cornell Sent an Indian off to his Camp the 4th Dec'r: at 5 o Clock in the Morning the Indian Came back at 12 o Clock and Told Mr. Cornell the big Man Was Gone from his Camp, but the Indian left Word that Mr. Cornell Was Waiting for him at New Town—the big Man Came about 7 o Clock that Night to New Town—

Talk With the Big Man or Chief—The first Was that he Spoke Was to Me, that he Was Sorry that Wee Did Not Get the Men we Came about, upon Which I shewed Him My Pass and told him as you Desired Me by the Generals[8] Orders that if any Soldier Should Come up to the Nation Not having a Pass and the Same Seal to take him, that the General Would Reward the Indians for it and if a party of Men Was Sent to the Nation that he and the Rest of the Head Men Would assist them Shewing Such a Pass and Seal to it, if Not to take them and Send them to Pensacola by the Indians, they Will by Rewarded Which the Big Man told Me he Wold and took the Pass and Will Acquaint all the Rest of the Nation be Sides Further the Big Man Sends Word to the General Governor[9] and Captain Stewart,[10] that What he Said about the Lands at Pensacola that he Could do Nothing in it as Yet as the Head Men Was Not Come

[7] Little Talisi was an Upper Creek town on the eastern bank of the Coosa River, two miles above the fork of the river.

[8] Probably General Frederick Haldimand, at this time commander of the southern military district with headquarters at Pensacola.

[9] Elias Durnford was commissioned lieutenant-governor of West Florida, July 31, 1769. Although Peter Chester was commissioned governor, January 25, 1770, Durnford continued to execute the office.

[10] John Stuart, superintendent of Indian affairs in the southern district.

home from hunting but Whole Nation Was to Meet in the Spring and Settle all the affairs of the Nation Further he Sends Word to the General and Governor that Capt. Stewart Must Not leave Pensacola Untill he Comes Down and he Must Not think Long Which Will be as Soon as Possible, With the talk from the Whole Nation Which he hopes Will be agreeable to Both Parties, Further he Says he Was going a hunting this Moon and the Next by that time the Whole Will be at home, the Rivier Coursey at New town is 200 feet broad and 18 feet Deep and is Gravelly bottom and is Navigable from this Place to Mobile for large Craft

Dec'r 5th. Marched from New town E 5 Miles thro Good high and Low Land and then Came by King Wolfes N:E Marched 5 Miles thro Good level Land as any in the World and Came to the Columies town[11] Where there is Good land all Round for Many Miles Marched 20 Miles and Crossed 3 Creeks and Come home to Mr. Cornells house fine Land all the Road

Journal of the Passage of Serj: Wight from the Upper Creek Nation to Pensacola

22d Dec'r 1771. Got Clear of the Creek Nation about 3 o Clock in the afternoon, Crossed the Rivier Tallapusha at the Columie town Which is 250 feet broad Marched 5 Miles Good Land and Encamped S W

Monday 23d. Marched at 8 o Clock and Came 7 Miles and Crossed a Small Creek. Marched 7 Miles and then Crossed Part of the Savannhs and Came to a large Cane Swamp and Crossed a Creek 26 Feet Broad and 2 feet Deep, then Marched 6 Miles thro Part of the Savannahs, and Crossed a Creek 18 feet Broad 3 feet Deep, then Marched 9 Miles thro Good Lands and Wood and Came to a Cane Swamp and Crossed a Creek 14 feet Broad and 2 feet Deep, then Marched 6 Miles and Encamped E:N:E:

Tusday 24th. Marched at 8 o Clock 6 Miles and Came to

[11] Kalumi, an Upper Creek town on the right bank of the Tallapoosa River.

to a Great Cane Swamp, Crossed a Small Creek Marched 24 Miles Good high Lands and Wood all the Days March'd 5 Miles and Encamped at 4 o Clock W:S.W:

Wednesday 25th. Marched at 8 o Clock thro Pine Barren Lands 22 Miles and Encamped at 3 o Clock W:S:W:

Thursday 26th. Marched 6 Miles thro a thicket and Crossed two Small Creeks. Marched 8 Miles thro Pine Barren Land the Waters all to the Right and Came to a Swamp and Crossed the first Creek of Scamby 8 feet broad and one foot Deep Marched 8 Miles Pine barren Land Marched 6 Miles thro a thicket Encamped at 4 o Clock W:S:W:—Rested the 27th the Horses being tired and Wet Weather.

Saturday 28. Marched at 8 o Clock 2 Miles thro a thicket and Crossed a Creek of Scamby 7 feet broad one foot Deep Marched 6 Miles thro Pine Barren Lands and Came to the Departure from Mobile and Pensacola Marched 22 Miles thro Pine Barren Land and Encamped at 3 o Clock S:

Sunday 29th. Marched at 7 o Clock thro Pine Barren Lands 13 Miles and Came to a large Boggy Swamp and Crossed the Main Rivier of Scanby 36 feet Broad 4 feet Deep and Crossed the North Lagoon at the Same time about the Same Breadth and Depth, Marched 7 Miles and Encamped W:S:W:

Monday 30th. Marched at 8 o Clock and Came to a Bogg, and Crossed a Creek 8 feet Broad and 2 feet Deep Marched 3 Milles and Came to a Boggy Swamp and Crossed a Creek 10 feet Broad 2 feet Deep Marched 3 Miles and Came to a boggy Swamp and Crossed a Creek 18 feet Broad and 2 feet Deep, Marched 2 Miles and Came to a boggy Swamp and Crossed a Creek 7 feet broad and 2 feet Deep Marched 8 Miles and Came by a Cedar Swamp on the Right Hand Marched 13 Miles and Crossed two Small Runs Marched one Mile and Crossed a Small Run and Encamp S:W.

Tusday 31st. Marched at 7 o Clock 25 Miles Crossed Several Runs and Came to Pensacola at 2 o Clock in the afternoon The Riviers Creeks and Runs, Were Much Smaller then they Commonly are on a Count that the Season happened to be Dry During the time of Serj't Wight Passing to, and from the Nation

Total from the Nation to Pensacola is 229 Miles
But it is above . . . . 270 D'o

The Way of the Indions house that they Live in at there towns 27 feet long and 15 feet Broad and 12 feet high they Make the frame of Wood they tye Sticks a Cross from one Post to another then they Get Clay and Grass and Mixes up to Geather and Plaisters it a bout Half a foot thick they Cover the Roof With Clapboards and Bark on the top Which Hould out the Rains So that their houses are Seldom Wett Inside—The furnitere they have in their Houses is Brass and tinn Kettles they Make potts and Pans of Clay to put their Wictual in With Cane Sieves to Sift there Corn With When Pounded there Bedsteads Meade of Six forked Sticks put in the Ground So they Put long Sticks from one fork to the other, Covers it Over With Canes tyed Close to Geather. they Spread thier Bear Skins or Deer Skins over the Canes and then their Blankets Which they Wear all Day Servas them at Night and So they liye They Plant Indion Corn Potatoes Beans Pumpkins and Water Melons for thier food they Plant Calabastis to Carey Water from the River they Gather Hickery Nutts Chesnutts and Ground Nutts Which is Part of their food they live on bisides thier Hunting thier Stockes is a few Bullocks and Cows they have a Good Deal of Swine Cocks and Hens Which they kill as they Want they kept Drunk With Rum they fetched from Pensacola for a leven Days But When they Get Sober they Go to a Place they Call the Square in Both towns Which is Tuckabatchie and Great Tallisee to Black Drink that is Made of Cassina and Drink itt Either in the Morning or all Night this Black Drink they Worship at the End of June or July they assemble at Both Squires Every Man and Man Child and Worships the New Corn and Cassina for four Days but Tastis No Salt in that time[12]—the Woman Dos all the Work When the Indi-

[12] "The Ceremony of the Black-Drink" is also described by H. R. Schoolcraft, *Information respecting the History, Condition and Prospects of the Indian Tribes of the United States*, V., 266–267.

ons have any Business to Do it is at this Place they Do it if they have any Prisiners to Put to Death this is the Place of Execution The Nature of the a Indion is as thinxs Some Good and Some Bad and them that is Bad hath Not the Hart till they Get Drunk, they Will Kill Eather father Mother Brothers or Sisters as for the Manners of the Indions they Have None for the Great Men Would think Nothing of Stealing a White Mans Horse and Goods and threation to kill himself to the Bargain, and the Base of it is When they kill a White Man there is No Satisfatesfaction asked for it But Put of from time to time Which they think the White Man is a frear'd of them for they Say So in the Nation for they Expected that When they Ware at Pensacola that Some Would have Dyed for the Samė Deed—

ADDENDUM

AFTER the journal of Mrs. Brown, pp. 169–198, *supra*, had been printed, it was discovered that parts of it, relating to Virginia and Maryland, had been printed in vol. XXXII of the *Virginia Magazine of History*, with useful annotations by Mr. Fairfax Harrison.

As to the expression "A Rattlesnake Colonel" (p. 182) Mr. Albert Matthews has called the attention of the undersigned to two significant passages which explain the expression:

Dr. Alexander Hamilton's *Itinerarium*, p. 94 (July 4, 1744), "Going overboard again at 4 o'clock I killed a snake, which I had almost trod upon as I clambered down the steep. Had it been a rattlesnake I should have been entitled to a colonel's commission, for it is a common saying here that a man has no title to that dignity until he has killed a rattlesnake."

"Mark Pencil," *The White Sulphur Papers* (1839), pp. 46–47, "There is not a tavern keeper, or a stage owner, in all Western Virginia—or a great wood chopper, who has not some military title —General is very high—only the real militia men take that—Colonel predominates—and anyone who kills a rattlesnake is made a major on the spot."

J. F. J.

INDEX